UNDERSTANDING
ATROCITIES

Arts in Action

Jeffrey Keshen, Series Editor

Co-published with Mount Royal University

ISSN 2371-6134 (Print) ISSN 2371-6142 (Online)

This series focuses on illuminating, promoting, or demonstrating the fundamental significance of the Arts, Humanities, and Social Sciences to public well-being and contemporary society – culturally, spiritually, socially, politically, and economically – with the aim of raising awareness of the essential skills, perspectives, and critical understandings of societal issues these disciplines cultivate.

JEFFREY KESHEN, Dean, Faculty of Arts, Mount Royal University

No. 1 · **Understanding Atrocities: Remembering, Representing, and Teaching Genocide** Edited by Scott W. Murray

UNIVERSITY OF CALGARY
Press

UNDERSTANDING ATROCITIES

Remembering, Representing, and Teaching Genocide

Edited by

SCOTT W. MURRAY

Arts in Action Series
ISSN 2371-6134 (Print) ISSN 2371-6142 (Online)

University of Calgary Press
2500 University Drive NW
Calgary, Alberta
Canada T2N 1N4
press.ucalgary.ca

LIBRARY AND ARCHIVES CANADA CATALOGUING IN PUBLICATION

   Understanding atrocities : remembering, representing, and teaching genocide / edited by Scott W. Murray.

(Arts in action ; no. 1)
Includes bibliographical references and index.
Issued in print and electronic formats.
Co-published by: Mount Royal University.
ISBN 978-1-55238-885-3 (softcover).—ISBN 978-1-55238-886-0 (open access PDF).—ISBN 978-1-55238-887-7 (PDF).—ISBN 978-1-55238-888-4 (EPUB).—ISBN 978-1-55238-889-1 (Kindle)

   1. Genocide—Study and teaching. 2. Genocide—Case studies. 3. Atrocities—Study and teaching. 4. Atrocities—Case studies. I. Murray, Scott W. (Scott William), 1962-, editor II. Series: Arts in action (Series) ; 1

HV6322.7.U53 2017   304.6'63071   C2017-900116-7
                                               C2017-900117-5

The University of Calgary Press acknowledges the support of the Government of Alberta through the Alberta Media Fund for our publications. We acknowledge the financial support of the Government of Canada. We acknowledge the financial support of the Canada Council for the Arts for our publishing program.

This book has been published with the help of a grant from the Canadian Federation for the Humanities and Social Sciences, through the Awards to Scholarly Publications Program, using funds provided by the Social Sciences and Humanities Research Council of Canada.

This book has been published with the help of a grant from Mount Royal University Library, through the Mount Royal University Library Open Access Fund.

Alberta Government   Canada   Canada Council for the Arts / Conseil des Arts du Canada   MOUNT ROYAL UNIVERSITY 1910

Copyediting by Ryan Perks
Cover image Colourbox #14352381
Cover design, page design, and typesetting by Melina Cusano

For D. A.

Contents

List of Figures

Acknowledgements

The papers in this volume derive from a conference held at Mount Royal University in Calgary in February 2014. The conference was made possible by funding from the Office of the Provost and Vice President Academic, the Faculty of Arts, and the Department of Humanities at Mount Royal University, as well as the Students' Association of Mount Royal University, the Calgary Jewish Federation, the History Education Network (THEN/ HiER), and Citizenship and Immigration Canada. I would like to thank my co-convener, Tristan Smyth, for bringing me into this important project, as well as all of the conference participants, session chairs, conference organizers and volunteers who made "Understanding Atrocities" a success. For their particular contributions to the conference and to this volume, I especially thank Joe Anderson, Jennifer Pettit, Liam Haggarty, Jeff Keshen, Renae Watchman, Sabina Trimble, Glen Ryland, Natalie Meisner, Sharon Smulders, Penny Stratton, and Pat Proudfoot. I am also grateful to the Faculty of Arts at MRU and the University of Calgary Press for initiating the MRU Arts in Action Series, of which this is the first volume.

Abbreviations

AANDC	Aboriginal Affairs and Northern Development Canada
ARBiH	Army of Bosnia and Herzegovina (Armija Republike Bosne i Hercegovina)
ATAA	Assembly of Turkish American Associations
Bošniak	Bosnian Muslim
CMHC	Canadian Mortgage and Housing Corporation
CMHR	Canadian Museum for Human Rights
CRC	Civil Rights Congress (United States)
CTC	Council of Turkish Canadians
DRIP	Declaration of the Rights of Indigenous People
DutchBat	Dutch United Nations Peacekeeping Battalion
FBiH	Federation of Bosnia and Herzegovina
FTCA	Federation of Turkish Canadian Associations
IAGS	International Association of Genocide Scholars
ICEP	International Crimes Evidence Project
ICJ	International Court of Justice
ICMP	International Commission on Missing Persons
ICTY	International Criminal Tribunal for the former Yugoslavia
INOGS	International Network of Genocide Scholars
IRS	Indian Residential School (Canada)
ISIS	Islamic State of Iraq and Syria
JNA	Yugoslav People's Army
LLRC	Lessons Learnt and Reconciliation Commission
LTTE	Liberation Tigers of Tamil Eelam

NAACP	National Association for the Advancement of Colored People
OHR	Office of the High Representative in BiH
RPF	Rwandan Patriotic Front
RS	Republika Srpska
SLFP	Sri Lanka Freedom Party
TRC	Truth and Reconciliation Commission of Canada
TUF	Tamil United Front
TULF	Tamil United Liberation Front
USHMM	United States Holocaust Memorial Museum
UT	Young Turks
VRS	Bosnian Serb Army (Vojska Republike Srpske)

Introduction

Scott W. Murray

This collection has its origins in a modest, multidisciplinary conference—"Understanding Atrocities: Remembering, Representing and
Teaching Genocide"—held at Mount Royal University in Calgary, Alberta,
in February 2014. The conference brought together leading experts, emerging and established scholars in the field of genocide studies, as well as
undergraduate and graduate students, secondary school teachers, community members, and policy-makers in order to share new scholarship
and new teaching perspectives on the global, transhistorical problem of
genocide. Inspired by the goal of creating a forum bridging scholarly and
community-based efforts to understand genocide, the conference aimed
to augment the important specialized contributions of academic scholarship with insights and perspectives from teachers, non-profit groups interested in peace and conflict studies, members of Indigenous communities,
and other interested members of civil society. Concerned with the auto-
matic—and often, therefore, unexamined—identification of genocide with
atrocity, our aim was the investigation of how this historical relationship
frames and complicates possibilities for the understanding and prevention
of genocide.

A key feature of the scholarly study of genocide has been a steady
broadening of perspectives, beginning with efforts to look beyond the uni-
versality of the Holocaust as *the* genocide. When the journal *Holocaust and
Genocide Studies* was established in 1986, its commitment to carrying out a
scholarly, multidisciplinary examination of the Holocaust included a willingness to consider the subject of other genocides, but it explicitly excluded

the publication of "memoirs, literary, dramatic or musical efforts."[1] Over a decade later the *Journal of Genocide Research* (*JGR*) continued to supplement what were once primarily historical studies of genocide worldwide with other social science perspectives, while leaving room for contributions to a "Poet's Corner" and an "Art Gallery" (although it has since reverted back to being primarily a historical journal).[2] Today the subject is studied from every possible disciplinary perspective in the social sciences and humanities, and it includes genocides that have occurred throughout history and across the globe. The breadth of the contributions to this volume reflects this remarkable evolution in our thinking about genocide, while also affirming its status as an essentially "contested concept."

One challenge we face today, therefore, is to find ways of making this immense, complex, ever-expanding body of scholarship accessible to non-academic audiences, a need stemming from growing pressure to educate people about genocide, primarily with an eye to prevention. It was with this aim in mind that the International Association of Genocide Scholars (IAGS) and the International Institute for Genocide and Human Rights Studies (IIGHRS) teamed up in 2006 to create *Genocide Studies and Prevention* (*GSP*), which, in promoting the development of "new ideas on the prevention of genocidal death-making," aimed to "go beyond safe, approved, and established paradigms of scholarship and science," and was "open to the unusual, the daring, and the courageous."[3] Similarly, the didactic promise of emerging scholarship on genocide and its power therefore to shape policy-making was a key theme at a 2012 symposium revealingly entitled "Imagine the Unimaginable: Ending Genocide in the 21st Century," held at the United States Holocaust Memorial Museum (USHMM) in cooperation (also revealingly) with the US Council on Foreign Relations and CNN.[4] At this same symposium, polling revealed by the USHMM showed that two-thirds of Americans believe that education is key to genocide prevention, while also displaying what historian Timothy Snyder identified as a lamentable lack of historical awareness about almost all other instances of mass atrocity other than the Holocaust.[5]

The conflict in Darfur, Sudan, which raged most devastatingly between 2004 and 2010, was vital in stimulating this new activist interest in genocide more broadly, which in turn helped precipitate the growing distinction between what Jens Meierhenrich has described as the predominant "vocational imperatives" at work in genocide studies today—advocacy and scholarship.[6] The former, which animated the work of such early scholars in the field as Israel Charny and Gregory Stanton, regards the academic study of genocidal violence in such places as Cambodia, Rwanda, the former Yugoslavia, and Sudan as sterile unless it gives practical, policy-focused application to the Holocaust-inspired slogan "never again." Consequently, the IAGS, in addition to organizing conferences and publishing *GSP*, has passed a series of resolutions since 2005 condemning the conduct of such states as Syria, Iran, Turkey, and Zimbabwe, while also calling for military intervention in Darfur.[7] According to Dirk Moses, this movement toward awakening the "consciousness of the scholarly community," as well as the winding down of divisive debates over the uniqueness of the Holocaust, have opened up a discursive space "for a non-sectarian, non-competitive, and non-hierarchical analysis of modern genocide."[8] Nevertheless, the IAGS's controversial advocacy concerning Darfur, which belonged to what some described as an ill-informed humanitarian effort that damaged efforts to find local solutions to the crisis,[9] highlights concerns over what Meierhenrich called the "continued prevalence of moralism in the study of genocide studies."[10] This in turn has helped to strengthen, therefore, the position of the second of genocide studies' vocational imperatives—i.e., scholarship. Manifested in the labours of Jürgen Zimmerer, Donald Bloxham, Dan Stone, Ben Kiernan, and Alexander Hinton, among others—and expressed organizationally through the formation in 2005 of the International Network of Genocide Scholars (INOGS), which publishes the research-focused *JGR*—this emphasis on scholarship over advocacy has, according to Meierhenrich, placed genocide studies on a more solid theoretical and empirical footing, and represents a "maturation" of the field.[11]

Far from achieving anything like a consensus, genocide studies scholars continue to spar over the raison d'être of the field—and *pace* Moses's prediction of accord, *GSP* was relaunched in 2014 as *Genocide Studies International* (*GSI*) in order to address renewed concerns that the latest scholarship on genocide studies has been similarly unsuccessful in influencing policy-making in order to aid with prevention. Echoing the lament of Gabriel Schoenfeld almost twenty years ago regarding the "academicization" of Holocaust history, the editors of *GSI* now argued that "esoteric discussions of abstractions using vocabulary that turns off the public" are emblematic of a "genocide industry" that, through a combination of disciplinary navel-gazing and a stubborn resistance to seeing the enormous complexity of genocidal phenomena, consistently fails to transform scholarly rhetoric into "concrete, effective policy."[12] And so it goes.

In a limited but sincere effort to transcend these debates and divisions within the field of genocide studies, the organizers of the "Understanding Atrocities" conference aimed to raise public awareness, stimulate new kinds of teaching and learning on the subject, and, if possible, positively affect public policy by selecting a universally held assumption about genocide—namely, that it is an atrocity—as the centre of gravity for wide-ranging discussions about the nature and consequences of this "ongoing scourge."[13] Deliberately broad in scope and intellectual ambition, the conference asked participants to consider such questions as: Why is genocide carried out with such viciousness and cruelty? How, if at all, does the demonization of perpetrators of atrocity prevent us from confronting the complicity of others, or of ourselves? What are the limits of the law, of history, of literature, and of education in understanding and representing genocidal atrocity? What are the challenges we face in teaching and learning about extreme events such as these, and how does the language we use contribute to or impair what can be taught and learned about genocide? Dan Stone, in asking whether it can even be said that a discipline of genocide studies exists, argued that scholars in this field, rather than engaging solely in comparative studies of genocide, "must attempt to develop general, empirically informed, theoretical statements about genocide as such—what it is, when it happens, who supports it, and so on."[14] The routine identification of genocide with atrocity surely constitutes just such a statement—and so our concern, therefore, is with the *effects* of this identification on contemporary understandings of genocide, as both a phenomenon and an experience.

One example of these effects that will be familiar to anyone who has taught Holocaust history is how deeply students are affected by the subject matter of such courses, and how often this generates a strong, largely unreflective sympathy for arguments regarding the Holocaust's uniqueness. Because no other mass atrocity in history has been so thoroughly investigated and made visible to the public in every media imaginable, it is very difficult getting students to problematize even basic historiographical claims like uniqueness, even though doing so is necessarily preliminary to understanding the astonishing complexity of the Holocaust as a historical phenomenon. Confronted—indeed, battered—by their encounters with the Holocaust via popular culture, students become resistant to perspectives they believe might diminish the rhetorical power of the Holocaust story to teach us such lessons as "never again," the "triumph of the human spirit," and "all it takes for evil to triumph is for good men to do nothing"—discursive strategies whose commemorative function also, unfortunately, complicates the scholarly project.[15]

The power of the language of atrocity, therefore, to frame debates and proscribe judgments on phenomena such as genocide is considerable. Consider an episode from nineteenth-century European history in which "atrocitarian" language raised concerns among contemporaries about the effects such rhetoric had on the public's ability to judge properly either the events themselves or their government's response to those events. At issue was the April 1876 uprising of Bulgarian nationalists against the Ottoman Empire—a revolt put down brutally by Ottoman forces, who destroyed whole villages and killed upwards of ten thousand people in a short five-week period. Unsurprisingly, the Ottomans' conduct generated strong reactions from people throughout Europe—prompting, for example, British Liberal Party leader William Gladstone to write a best-selling pamphlet entitled the *Bulgarian Horrors and the Question of the East*, in which he exclaimed:

> There is not a criminal in a European gaol, there is not a cannibal in the South Sea Islands, whose indignation would not rise and overboil at the recital of that which has been done, which has too late been examined, but which remains unavenged; which has left behind all the foul and all the fierce passions that produced it, and which may again spring up, in another murderous harvest, from the soil soaked and reeking with blood, and in the air tainted with every imaginable deed of crime and shame.[16]

The British prime minister at the time, Benjamin Disraeli, condemned Gladstone's use of such rhetoric on the grounds that it seriously complicated his government's efforts to respond to the broader European crisis arising from the slow demise of the Ottoman Empire.[17] "The first and cardinal point, at the present moment," Disraeli wrote to Sir Strafford Northcote, the chancellor of the exchequer, "is that no member of the Government should countenance the idea that we are hysterically 'modifying' our policy, in consequence of the excited state of the public mind. If such an idea gets about, we shall become contemptible."[18] The ascription of the label "genocidal" to the group known variously as ISIS, ISIL, the Islamic State, and Daesh almost immediately after it began committing atrocities against prisoners in 2014, and the overwrought response of some Western states to the domestic threats this group poses, is a contemporary example of the same phenomenon.[19]

The need to distinguish, therefore, between genocide and atrocity seems clear, and is preliminary to Amarnath Amarasingam and Christopher Powell's application, in their contribution to this volume, of the concept of "proto-genocide" to the current situation in Sri Lanka. Amarasingam and Powell, extending the scholarship of Zygmunt Bauman, Ben Kiernan, Mark Levene, and Richard Rubenstein, among others, are concerned with genocide as a systemic feature of the modern sovereign state.[20] Their notion of proto-genocide, drawing on both Gregory Stanton's model of the ten stages of genocide, and Tony Barta's argument that genocide must be understood with reference to *"relations* of destruction" rather than policies and intentions, conceives of genocide as a distinctively modern phenomenon connected with the success of the nation-state.[21] Consequently, the steady growth of Sinhala nationalism since the end of the Sri Lankan Civil War in 2009, and the concomitant suppression, socially, culturally, and economically, of Tamils' collective identity, may be prefatory to a more coherent program of cultural extermination and therefore of genocide. The widespread atrocities committed by the Sri Lankan government against the Tamil minority, and the ongoing exclusion of Tamils from what Helen Fein terms "the universe of obligation," indicates that some, but not yet all, of the conditions under which genocide will likely occur currently exist in Sri Lanka—a situation that merits attention from the international community.[22]

Further evidence of the proto-genocidal threat existing in Sri Lanka is that government's conduct in the Lessons Learnt and Reconciliation Commission (LLRC), which operated in northern Sri Lanka between 2009 and 2011. Dismissed by Amnesty International as a "dangerous charade," and criticized by, among others, the Canadian government and the European Union for its lack of accountability and balance in apportioning blame for the atrocities of the civil war, the LLRC nevertheless participated in the construction of what Alexander Hinton has called a "transitional justice imaginary" in which "violent pasts are delimited and narrowed, erasing historical complexities and suggesting an essentialized notion of regressive being."[23] According to Laura Beth Cohen, whose chapter examines the Srebrenica-Potočari Memorial Center and Cemetery to the Victims of the 1995 Genocide, transitional justice mechanisms may collide with the ways in which, at sites of atrocity, local memory persists and intrudes upon the present. Scholars such as Hinton, Roger Duthie, and Priscilla Hayner all argue for the importance of transitional justice initiatives, which nevertheless function uneasily alongside efforts to commemorate sites of atrocity—parallel processes which, as Judy Barsalou and Victoria Baxter have shown, remain highly politicized because they occur in changing frames of time relative to the events being commemorated.[24] Thus, as Cohen demonstrates, atrocities like the Srebrenica genocide, when mediated by transitional justice mechanisms, may become anchored in a persistent, ongoing present that prevents the construction of what Hinton describes as teleological historical narratives that frame the atrocities in terms of pre- and post-conflict states.[25] In other words, genocide-as-atrocity elides both the broader historical frame to which the genocide belongs and the ongoing effects of the violence in post-conflict societies, such that time itself becomes "uncanny," allowing the traumatic legacy of the genocide to persist.

Consider, by way of contrast, the situation in Canada, where the first paragraph of the 2015 report of the Truth and Reconciliation Commission of Canada (TRC) identifies the "cultural genocide" of Indigenous peoples as both a goal and an outcome of Canada's residential school system, among other instruments of settler colonialism in North America. The TRC report, in asserting that "reconciliation must become a way of life," unambiguously identifies the effects of Canada's genocidal legacy on both Aboriginal and non-Aboriginal peoples, and situates the atrocities of the residential school system within an explicit historical framework intended to resist evasion and forgetfulness.[26] Moreover, the transitional justice imaginary performed in the report of Canada's TRC depicts reconciliation as "an ongoing individual and collective process," rather than simply a short-term, interim mechanism for Canada's transition to an idealized post-conflict future.[27] Unsurprisingly, however, the TRC's conclusions also revived a long-running debate over the nature of genocide—namely, whether it requires the physical extermination of a people or can subsist solely in the destruction of a group's social and/or cultural existence.[28] This same topic is examined further here by Adam Muller, who reassesses the impact of settler colonialism on Indigenous peoples in Canada in light of Raphael Lemkin's original conception of the crime of genocide.[29] On the one hand, what Muller calls "the partial and political character" of the 1948 UN Genocide Convention refers in part to its silence on the matter of cultural genocide, despite Lemkin's own view that such a thing exists and that it is often an outcome of European colonialism. On the other hand, both Lemkin and the convention identified the "intent to destroy" as an essential element of genocide, which, in assessing the genocide committed against Indigenous people in Canada, has proven to be highly problematic. Muller, drawing on the work of such disparate authorities as the German jurist Kai Ambos and the Canadian genocide studies scholar Andrew Woolford, proposes a more nuanced understanding of intent in the commission of genocide—one that extends culpability beyond simply those who act with a specific genocidal purpose. In so doing, he not only makes a powerful case that the treatment of Indigenous people in Canada was indeed genocide, but also challenges the kind of forgetfulness that cultural historian Peter Burke, with whom Muller opens his chapter, described as a luxury enjoyed by history's victors.[30]

The prevalence and persistence of historical amnesia operates, however, in various ways, arising in some instances from the atrocities that constitute the tissue of the genocide itself. Outright denial is both the most common and the most extreme example of this—extreme in the sense that genocidal atrocity strikes us as something that ought to be undeniable, but which, thanks in part to what Stone calls "the merry-go-round of definitional debates," is in fact all too common.[31] Consequently, several papers in this volume speak to this issue directly by challenging denials. Only one concerns events—the Armenian genocide—that belong to the "canon" of genocides, while two others grapple with more contested atrocities—namely, the enslavement of black Americans, and settler-colonial genocide against Indigenous peoples in Canada. Raffi Sarkissian's study of the Toronto District School Board's struggle to integrate the history of the Armenian genocide into its high school history curriculum highlights the intractability of denialist arguments, while echoing the work of Geoffery Short and Samuel Totten in arguing convincingly for the broad educational value of teaching students about genocide and crimes against humanity using various examples, including that of the Armenians.[32] Steven Jacobs's essay below on William Patterson's 1951 petition to the United Nations, entitled *We Charge Genocide: The Crime of the Government against the Negro People*, traces the unfortunate fate of this remarkable document, and urges us to reconsider its significance for the field of genocide studies. Little studied (like the broader theme of North American slavery and genocide), this unsuccessful petition belongs nonetheless to the legacy of both Lemkin's denial that the African-American experience entailed the "destruction, death [and] annihilation" that distinguished genocide, and his views on Africans more generally.[33]

But it is Kristin Burnett, Lori Chambers, and Travis Hay's relentless interrogation of the media discourse concerning the 2012 state of emergency declared in several northern Ontario First Nations' communities in response to housing crises there that confronts most directly how historical amnesia and, in this case, deeply racist and sexist stereotypes help facilitate the denial of mass atrocities, such as the ongoing genocide of Indigenous peoples in Canada. Frankly acknowledging their own settler privilege (and, I would add, that enjoyed by every contributor to this volume), Burnett, Chambers, and Hay draw on the post-colonial arguments of Sherene Razack, Joyce Green, and Emma LaRocque, who have shown that the rhetorical strategies of settler colonialism have long been dedicated to the construction of Indigenous difference in order to dehumanize and marginalize Indigenous peoples; as well as Indigenous feminists such as Paula Gunn Allen and Andrea Smith, who locate the type of sexist and racist discourse used to describe Chief Theresa Spence's widely publicized 2012 protest in a larger constellation of gendered, heteropatriarchal thinking.[34]

Straddling the contested space between definition and denial are the histories of smaller groups (nations, peoples, etc.) who, while on the margins of events, can often get caught up nonetheless in the maelstrom of violence genocide unleashes. Israel Charny and Tessa Hoffman, drawing on the once contentious debate over just how widely the boundaries of the "Holocaust" should be drawn when it comes to identifying non-Jewish victim groups,[35] have both argued that genocide studies should adopt a more inclusive approach to the study of the victims of mass atrocity, including groups incidental to the genocidal project itself.[36] It is this perspective that informs Andrew Basso's contribution to this volume, in which he comparatively reassesses the Turkish destruction of Greek and Assyrian Christian minorities alongside the Armenians, and the victimization of Hutu and Twa populations in the Rwandan genocide. In so doing, Basso reveals that it may not always be perpetrators who engage in denial through the distortion of collective memory, as victims of genocide who assume control of post-conflict regimes may also seek to distort the historical record for their own political ends.

Representations of genocide provide us with perhaps the most direct means for investigating the genocide-as-atrocity formulation. The genocide studies literature described above considers historical, sociological, and anthropological representations of genocide, primarily with an eye to understanding how genocide happens, while the last three chapters in this volume consider the problem of representation from an artistic perspective, thereby aiming to bring us closer to understanding the *experience* of genocidal atrocity. Sarah Minslow, who has developed an undergraduate course on the subject of war and genocide in children's literature, struggled with how to get her students past the atrociousness of genocide to a place where they could to assess whether children's literature about genocide is "good" or "bad"—a task accomplished by complicating ideas of the "child," and then by locating the moral dilemmas faced by literary characters and how they respond to these within the specific, complex contexts in which they find themselves. In so doing, Minslow confronts the challenges of representing atrocity artistically, which, while necessary in children's literature,[37] is much harder to accomplish there than representations of genocide—and this latter fact, I would suggest, raises important questions about the necessity of their pairing in other genres. Lorraine Markotic's chapter on Bernhard Schlink's bestselling novel *The Reader*—a book, like the film *Schindler's List*, that's widely used to teach high school and university students about the Holocaust—argues that it is not enough to simply remember and represent atrocities past. Instead, we need to think about *how* we are remembering and representing, reflect upon what thoughts we might be excluding, what conceptions we might be considering only in a restricted or limited form, and how our thinking might, even in small ways, echo the very thinking of the time period of the atrocities. Schlink's writing here and elsewhere, like the *Historikerstreit* (or "historians' quarrel") of the 1980s, postwar filmic representations of German history such as *Heimat* (1984), and responses to *Europa Europa* (1990), indicates that coming to terms with their country's troubled past—*Vergangenheitsbewältigung*—remains a challenge for Germans.[38] What Markotic reveals is that *The Reader* effectively denies its readers the possibility of thinking outside the frame of its narrative structure, thereby circumscribing thinking itself in a way that not only mirrors the thoughts of the novel's main protagonist, but is also disturbingly reminiscent of the Nazi perspective both during and after the war. Markotic's analysis of *The Reader* illustrates the importance of thinking about how we think about the past, something the novel—despite its reflective protagonist—insidiously forecloses.

Over thirty years ago Lawrence Langer proposed that only artistic representations of the Holocaust "can lead the uninitiated imagination from the familiar realm of man's fate to the icy atmosphere of the death camps"—an accomplishment that becomes "ever more necessary as that event recedes in time and new generations struggle to comprehend why a civilized country in the midst of the twentieth century coolly decided to murder all of Europe's Jews."[39] It remains to be seen, however, if this is true. On the one hand, we're now more than twice as distant from those events as was Langer when he made his plea for this "necessary art," and so the poignancy of his remarks increases with the passing of the last few remaining survivors of the Holocaust. On the other hand, as genocidal atrocities have continued to occur, and as we've gradually come to recognize and acknowledge past atrocities as genocide, new arguments have emerged regarding the seductive power of art to represent violence in ways that history cannot.[40] Patrick Anderson and Jisha Menon, for example, claim that the spectacular quality of violent acts deepens their cultural impact, and they warn therefore that performative representations of violence may become constitutive of "the context in which violence is rationalized and excused." This resonates with Shoshana Felman's claim that trial testimony often re-enacts the trauma of violent acts, which can never truly be disclosed fully either through testimony or any other means.[41] Informed by this scholarship, Donia Mounsef examines here how some contemporary artistic performance, contrary to longstanding assumptions about both decorum on the stage and the dramatic unrepresentability of traumatic violence, is able to effect remarkably dense encounters with the ethical problems of atrocity. While the tension between atrocity and representation is as old as the Oresteia, the artists Mounsef discusses take their audiences beyond the trauma of atrocity to its survival, with the spaces of their performance thus becoming important sites of resistance.

◆◆◆

Langer, introducing a collection of essays dedicated to challenging the irrepressible human desire to find redemption in the horrors of the Holocaust, wrote:

> Our age of atrocity clings to the stable relics of faded eras, as if ideas like natural innocence, innate dignity, the inviolable spirit, and the triumph of art over reality were immured in some kind of immortal shrine, immune to the ravages of history and time. … As a result, the habit of discussing the past with a familiar discourse continues, while new models for dealing with mass murder intellectually, morally, historically, and philosophically do not proliferate.[42]

A dispiriting prediction indeed—and one that rings true when we consider how contemporary popular culture continues to fiercely resist facing up to the unsettling implications of the twentieth century's confrontation with what Primo Levi called the "Gorgon."[43] However, the essays contained here—and indeed, the expansive state of the field of genocide studies generally—give the lie to Langer's subsequent claim that scholars and activists working in this field are paralyzed by the darkness of their topic, becoming like Dante's fictional Dante, who can never again "return to the light" should he choose to look into the face of atrocity.[44] What follows is just such a confrontation—and the results, I would suggest, are both disquieting and encouraging, but never timid. In a similar vein, Susan Sontag, like Hannah Arendt, regarded the Holocaust as incomprehensible, and that ultimately "the only response is to continue to hold the event in mind, to remember it."[45] The goal of understanding atrocities, like efforts to understand the Holocaust, while aspirational, will surely remain as elusive as the USHMM's goal of ending genocide in the twenty-first century. Nevertheless, as with the study of the Holocaust, we understand the composition, causes, consequences, and experience of genocide better today than we did even just a decade ago, and this broader understanding of the phenomenon derives in large part from the adoption of new disciplinary perspectives and investigative methodologies. Our aim in this volume is to contribute to that project in the spirit of scholarly collaboration, and in so doing to continue to hold these tragic events in mind, and to remember them.

NOTES

1 Yehuda Bauer, "Editor's Introduction," *Holocaust and Genocide Studies* 1, no. 1 (1986): 1.

2 "From the Editor: *Apologia Rationalis*," *Journal of Genocide Research* 1, no. 1 (1999): 9–10.

3 Israel W. Charny and Roger W. Smith, "Why GSP?" *Genocide Studies and Prevention* 1, no. 1 (2006): i–ii.

4 "Imagine the Unimaginable: Ending Genocide in the 21st Century," United States Holocaust Memorial Museum, 24 July 2012, http://www.ushmm.org/confront-geno-cide/speakers-and-events/all-speakers-and-events/imagine-the-unimaginable-ending-genocide-in-the-21st-century/complete-symposium (accessed 1 July 2014).

5 Mark Penn, "Imagine the Unimaginable."

6 Jens Meierhenrich, "Introduction: the Study and History of Genocide," in *Genocide: A Reader*, ed. J. Meierhenrich (New York: Oxford University Press, 2014), 7–10.

7 "Resolutions," International Association of Genocide Scholars, http://www.genocides-cholars.org/resources/resolutions (accessed 15 July 2015).

8 A. Dirk Moses, "The Holocaust and Genocide," in *The Historiography of Genocide*, ed. Dan Stone (New York: Palgrave Macmillan, 2008), 547. For a similarly optimistic assessment of the state of the field, see Adam Jones, "Diffusing Genocide Studies, Defusing Genocides," *Genocide Studies and Prevention* 6, no. 3 (2011): 270–278.

9 See, for example, Mahmood Mamdani, "The Politics of Naming: Genocide, Civil War, Insurgency," *London Review of Books* 29, no. 5 (8 March 2007): 5–8.

10 Meierhenrich, "Introduction," 9.

11 Ibid. See, for example, Jürgen Zimmerer, *Von Windhuk nach Auschwitz? Beiträge zum Verhältnis von Kolonialismus und Holocaust* (Berlin: Lit Verlag, 2011); Donald Bloxham, *The Great Game of Genocide: Imperialism, Nationalism, and the Destruction of the Ottoman Armenians* (New York: Oxford University Press, 2007); Dan Stone, *The Holocaust, Fascism and Memory: Essays in the History of Ideas* (London: Palgrave Macmillan, 2013); Ben Kiernan, *Blood and Soil: A World History of Genocide and Extermination from Sparta to Darfur* (New Haven, CT: Yale University Press, 2007); Alexander Hinton, *Why Did they Kill? Cambodia in the Shadow of Genocide* (Berkeley: University of California Press, 2005).

12 Gabriel Schoenfeld, "Auschwitz and the Professors," *Commentary* 105, no. 6 (June 1998), https://www.commentarymagazine.com/articles/auschwitz-and-the-professors/ (accessed 1 October 2015); Herbert Hirsch, "Preventing Genocide and Protecting Human Rights: A Failure of Policy," *Genocide Studies International* 8, no.1 (2014): 4–5.

13 Charny and Smith, "Why GSP?" i.

14   Stone, "Introduction," *The Historiography of Genocide*, 2.

15   Doris Bergen, "Studying the Holocaust: Is History Commemoration?" in *The Holocaust and Historical Methodology*, ed. Dan Stone (New York: Berghahn Books, 2012), 158–159; Gavriel Rosenfeld, "The Politics of Uniqueness: Reflections on the Recent Polemical Turn in Holocaust and Genocide Scholarship," *Holocaust and Genocide Studies* 13, no. 1 (1999): 28–61.

16   William Gladstone, *Bulgarian Horrors and the Question of the East* (London: William Clowes and Sons, 1876), 31.

17   While Gary Bass has used the term "atrocitarian" to describe policy-makers inspired to intervene in international affairs on humanitarian grounds, Disraeli himself did not, as far I know, use the term to describe those whom he variously called the "infuriate and merciless humanitarians" and the "priests and professors" who rallied to Gladstone's call to action. Gary Bass, *Freedom's Battle: The Origins of Humanitarian Intervention* (Toronto: Random House, 2008), 6; as cited in George Buckle, *The Life of Benjamin Disraeli, Earl of Beaconsfield* (London: MacMillan, 1920), 6: 62, 194.

18   As quoted in Buckle, *The Life of Benjamin Disraeli*, 6: 61.

19   At the time of writing, the United States had declared that ISIS was "responsible for genocide against groups in areas under its control, including Yezidis, Christians, and Shia Muslims." John Kerry, "Remarks on Daesh and Genocide," US Department of State, 17 March 2016, http://www.state.gov/secretary/remarks/2016/03/254782.htm (accessed 1 July 2016). See also John Kerry, "To Defeat Terror, We Need the World's Help: The Threat of ISIS Demands a Global Coalition," *New York Times*, 29 August 2014; "Religious leaders say Isis persecution of Iraqi Christians has become genocide," *Guardian* (London), 9 August 2014; Stephen Harper, "Statement by the Prime Minister of Canada on passage of second ISIL motion in Parliament," Government of Canada, 30 March 2015, http://pm.gc.ca/eng/news/2015/03/30/statement-prime-minister-canada-passage-second-isil-motion-parliament (accessed 15 October 2015).

20   Zygmunt Bauman, *Modernity and the Holocaust* (Ithaca, NY: Cornell University Press, 1991); Ben Kiernan, *Blood and Soil*; Mark Levene, *Genocide in the Age of the Nation-State*, Vols. 1–2 (London: I. B. Tauris, 2005); Richard Rubenstein, "Afterword: Genocide and Civilization," in *Genocide and the Modern Age: Etiology and Case Studies of Mass Death*, eds. I. Wallimann, M. N. Dobkowski, and R. Rubenstein (Syracuse, NY: Syracuse University Press, 1987), 283–298.

21   Gregory Stanton, "The Ten Stages of Genocide," Genocide Watch, 2013, http://www.genocidewatch.org/genocide/tenstagesofgenocide.html (accessed 1 October 2015); Tony Barta, "Relations of Genocide: Land and Lives in the Colonization of Australia," in *Genocide and the Modern Age: Etiology and case studies of mass death*, eds. I. Wallimann and M. N. Dobkowski (New York: Greenwood, 1987), 237–252.

22   Helen Fein, *Accounting for Genocide: National Response and Jewish Victimization during the Holocaust* (New York: Free Press, 1979), 4.

23   "When Will They Get Justice? Failures of Sri Lanka's Lessons Learnt and Reconciliation Commission," Amnesty International, September 2011, http://www.amnesty.org/en/library/info/ASA37/008/2011/en (accessed 1 September 2015); John Baird, "Minister Baird Comments on Final Report of Sri Lanka's Lessons Learnt and Reconciliation Commission," Foreign Affairs and International Trade Canada, 11 January 2012, http://news.gc.ca/web/article-en.do?nid=650369 (accessed 1 September 2015); "EU Declaration on Sri Lanka's Lessons Learnt and Reconciliation Commission," European

Union Delegation to the United Nations, 23 February 2012, http://eu-un.europa.eu/ articles/en/article_11881_en.htm (accessed 1 September 2015); Alexander Laban Hinton, "Transitional Justice Time: Uncle San, Aunty Yan, and Outreach at the Khmer Rouge Tribunal," in *Genocide and Mass Atrocities in Asia: Legacies and Prevention*, eds. Deborah Mayersen, and Annie Pohlman (Abingdon, Oxon, UK: Routledge, 2013), 87.

24   Alexander Laban Hinton, ed., *Transitional Justice: Global Mechanisms and Local Realities after Genocide and Mass Violence* (New Brunswick, NJ: Rutgers University Press, 2010); Priscilla B. Hayner, *Unspeakable Truths: Transitional Justice and the Challenge of Truth Commissions* (New York: Routledge, 2010); Judy Barsalou and Victoria Baxter, *The Urge to Remember: The Role of Memorials in Social Reconstruction and Transitional Justice* (Washington, DC: United States Institute of Peace, January 2007). See also Paul Harvey Williams, *Memorial Museums: The Global Rush to Commemorate Atrocities* (Oxford: Berg, 2007).

25   Alexander Hinton, "Introduction: Toward an Anthropology of Transitional Justice," in *Transitional Justice*, 1–22. See also Hinton, "Transitional Justice Time," 94.

26   The Truth and Reconciliation Commission of Canada, *Honouring the Truth, Reconciling for the Future: Summary of the Final Report of the Truth and Reconciliation Commission of Canada* (2015), 240.

27   Ibid., 6.

28   On the TRC and cultural genocide, see Letters, "Setting the record straight on the TRC," *National Post* (Toronto), 5 June 2015, http://news.nationalpost.com/full-comment/letters/letters-setting-the-record-straight-on-the-trc (accessed 15 September 2015); David MacDonald, "Five reasons the TRC chose 'cultural genocide', " *Globe and Mail* (Toronto), 6 July 2015, http://www.theglobeandmail.com/opinion/five-reasons-the-trc-chose-cultural-genocide/article25311423/ (accessed 15 September 2015). On "cultural genocide" generally, and its application to the treatment of Indigenous peoples specifically, see Lawrence Davidson, *Cultural Genocide* (Piscataway, NJ: Rutgers University Press, 2012); Israel Charny, "Toward a Generic Definition of Genocide," in *Genocide: Conceptual and Historical Dimensions*, ed. G. J. Andreopoulos (Philadelphia: University of Pennsylvania Press, 1994), 64–94; William Schabas, *Genocide in International Law: The Crime of Crimes* (Cambridge: Cambridge University Press, 2009); *Colonial Genocide in Indigenous North America*, eds. Andrew Woolford, Jeff Benvenuto, and Alexander Laban Hinton (Durham, NC: Duke University Press, 2014); Andrew Woolford, "Ontological Destruction: Genocide and Canadian Aboriginal Peoples," *Genocide Studies and Prevention* 4 no.1 (2009): 81–97; David MacDonald and Graham Hudson, "The Genocide Question and Indian Residential Schools in Canada," *Canadian Journal of Political Science/Revue canadienne de science politique* 45, no. 2 (2012): 427–449; Ward Churchill, *Kill the Indian, Save the Man: The Genocidal Impact of American Indian Residential Schools* (San Francisco: City Lights Publishers, 2004); Robert van Krieken, "Cultural Genocide in Australia," in *The Historiography of Genocide*, ed. Dan Stone (New York: Palgrave Macmillan, 2008): 128–155; "United Nations Declaration on the Rights of Indigenous Peoples," 13 September 2007, http://www. un.org/esa/socdev/unpfii/documents/DRIPS_en.pdf. (accessed 1 September 2015).

29   The scholarship on Lemkin, once a neglected figure, is growing quickly: Raphael Lemkin, *Totally unofficial: the autobiography of Raphael Lemkin*, ed. Donna-Lee Frieze (New Haven, CT: Yale University Press, 2013); "Special Issue: New Approaches to Raphael Lemkin," *Journal of Genocide Research* 15, no. 3 (2013): 247–338; Steven Jacobs, *Lemkin on Genocide* (Lanthan, MD: Lexington Books, 2012); Dominik J. Schaller and

Jürgen Zimmerer, eds., *The origins of genocide: Raphael Lemkin as a historian of mass violence* (London: Routledge, 2009); John Cooper, *Raphael Lemkin and the struggle for the Genocide Convention* (London: Palgrave Macmillan, 2008); "Special Issue: Raphael Lemkin: the 'founder of the United Nation's Genocide Convention' as a historian of mass violence," *Journal of Genocide Research* 7, no. 4 (2005): 443–560; Samuel Totten and Steven L. Jacobs, eds., *Pioneers of genocide studies: confronting mass death in the century of genocide* (Westport, CT: Greenwood Press, 2002).

30   Kai Ambos, "What Does 'Intent to Destroy' in Genocide Mean?" *International Review of the Red Cross* 91, no. 876 (2009): 833–858; Andrew Woolford, "Nodal Repair and Networks of Destruction: Residential Schools, Colonial Genocide, and Redress in Canada," *Settler Colonial Studies* 3, no.1 (2013): 61–77.

31   Stone, "Introduction," *The Historiography of Genocide*, 2. I do not mean to suggest that scholars engaged in legitimate academic debates over the nature of genocide, which have been ongoing since Raphael Lemkin coined the term (and have arisen in part because of inconsistencies in Lemkin's own usage), are promoting genocide denial—but simply that deniers unfailingly seek to exploit differences among scholars as "proof" that the phenomena itself is fabricated. While the denial of specific genocides—the Holocaust and Armenian genocide in particular—have generated a large scholarly response, genocide denial as an activity has received relatively little scholarly attention, except from social justice organizations concerned with combatting genocide. See, for example, Israel W. Charny, "The psychology of denial: A contribution to the psychology of denial of genocide," *Journal of Armenian Studies* 4, nos. 1–2 (1992): 289–306; Israel W. Charny, "A classification of denials of the Holocaust and other genocides," *Journal of Genocide Research* 5, no. 1 (2003): 11–34; Gregory Stanton, "The 12 Ways to Deny a Genocide," Genocide Watch, 15 June 2005, http://www.genocidewatch.org/genocide/12waystodenygenocide.html (accessed 15 July 2015); Human Rights Watch, "Genocide Denial: Incitement or Hate Speech?" *HRW World Report 2007*, www.hrw.org/wr2k7/essays/shrinking/4.htm (accessed 15 July 2015); Yair Auron, *The Banality of Denial: Israel and the Armenian Genocide* (New Brunswick, NJ: Transaction Books, 2003); Sonja Biserko and Edina Becirevic, "Denial of genocide—on the possibility of normalising relations in the region," Bosnian Institute, 23 October 2009, http://www.bosnia.org.uk/news/news_body.cfm?newsid=2638 (accessed 1 June 2015); Deborah E. Lipstadt, *Denying the Holocaust: The Growing Assault on Truth and Memory* (New York: Free Press, 1993).

32   See, for example, Geoffrey Short, "Learning from Genocide? A study in the failure of Holocaust education," *Intercultural Education* 16, no. 4, (2005): 367–380; Samuel Totten, *Teaching about Genocide: Issues, Approaches, and Resources* (London: IAP, 2004).

33   Raphael Lemkin, "Nature of Genocide; Confusion With Discrimination Against Individuals Seen," *New York Times*, 14 June 1953. On *We Charge Genocide*, see Ann Curthoys and John Docker, "Defining Genocide," in *The Historiography of Genocide*, 15–21. On American slavery and genocide, see L. M. Thomas, *Vessels of Evil: American Slavery and the Holocaust* (Philadelphia: Temple University Press, 1993). On Lemkin's "inappropriate and racist" views of Africans, see D. J. Schaller, "Raphael Lemkin's view of European colonial rule in Africa: between condemnation and admiration," *Journal of Genocide Research* 7, no. 4 (2005): 531–538.

34   See, for example, Sherene Razack, *Looking White People in the Eye: Gender Race, Class and Culture in Courtrooms and Classrooms* (Toronto: University of Toronto Press,

1998); Joyce Green, "The Complexity of Indigenous Identity Formation and Politics in Canada: Self-Determination and Decolonisation, *International Journal of Critical Indigenous Studies* 2, no. 2 (2009): 36–46; Emma LaRoque, *When the Other Is Me: Native Resistance Discourse, 1850–1990* (Winnipeg: University of Manitoba Press, 2010); Paula Gunn Allen, *The Sacred Hoop* (Boston: Beacon Press, 1986); Andrea Smith, *Conquest: Sexual Violence and American Indian Genocide* (Brooklyn, NY: South End Press, 2005).

35   See, for example, Michael Berenbaum, ed., *A Mosaic of Victims: Non-Jews Persecuted and Murdered by the Nazis* (New York: New York University Press, 1990); Linda Altman, *The Forgotten Victims of the Holocaust* (Berkeley Heights, NJ: Enslow, 2003); Israel Gutman and Shmuel Krakowski, *Unequal Victims: Poles and Jews During World War Two* (New York: Holocaust Library, 1986); Guenter Lewy, *The Nazi Persecution of the Gypsies* (New York: Oxford University Press, 2000).

36   Israel W. Charny, "The Integrity and Courage to Recognize All the Victims of a Genocide," in *The Genocide of the Ottoman Greeks: Studies on the State-Sponsored Campaign of Extermination of the Christians of Asia Minor (1912–1922) and Its Aftermath: History, Law, Memory*, eds. Tessa Hofmann et al. (Scarsdale, NY: Melissa International Ltd., 2011), 21–38; Tessa Hofmann, "Cumulative Genocide: The Massacres and Deportations of the Greek Population of the Ottoman Empire (1912–1923)," in *The Genocide of the Ottoman Greeks*, 39–54.

37   Lawrence Langer, *The Holocaust and Literary Imagination* (New Haven, CT: Yale University Press, 1975); Kimberley Reynolds, *Radical Children's Literature: Future Visions and Aesthetic Transformations in Juvenile Fiction* (New York: Palgrave Macmillan, 2010); Susan Honeyman, *Elusive Childhood: Impossible Representations in Modern Fiction* (Columbus: Ohio State University Press, 2005); Adrienne Kertzer, " 'Do You Know What "Auschwitz" Means?' Children's Literature and the Holocaust," *The Lion and the Unicorn* 23, no. 2 (1999): 238–256.

38   On the *Historikerstreit*, see Charles Maier, *The Unmasterable Past: History, Holocaust, and German National Identity* (Cambridge, MA: Harvard University Press, 1988); Richard J. Evans, *In Hitler's Shadow: West German Historians and the Attempt to Escape from the Nazi Past* (New York: Pantehon, 1989); Peter Baldwin, ed., *Reworking the Past: Hitler, the Holocaust, and the Historians' Debate* (Boston: Beacon, 1990). On postwar German film, see Eric L. Santner, *Stranded Objects: Mourning, Memory, and Film in Postwar Germany* (Ithaca, NY: Cornell University Press, 1990); Anton Kaes, *From Hitler to Heimat: The Return of History as Film* (Cambridge, MA: Harvard University Press, 1989); Małgorzata Pakier, *The Construction of European Holocaust Memory: German and Polish Cinema after 1989* (Frankfurt am Main: Lang 2013). Schlink's other works that reflect his efforts at *Vergangenheitsbewältigung* include *Guilt about the Past* (Brisbane: Queensland University Press, 2009) and *Homecoming* (Toronto: Random House, 2008).

39   Lawrence Langer, "The Americanization of the Holocaust on Stage and Screen," in *Admitting the Holocaust: Collected Essays* (New York: Oxford University Press, 1995), 174–175. Langer later broadened his view to include recorded testimony, diaries, and memoirs as helping us "to interpret the various layers of memory through which the event was experienced by its victims and survivors." The key element here is "experience." See Langer, "Introduction," *Admitting the Holocaust*, 7. For a counterargument, see Inga Clendinnen, "Representing the Holocaust: The Case for History," *Michigan Quarterly Review* 37, no. 1 (1998): n.p.

40   Shoshana Felman and Dori Laub, *Testimony: Crises of Witnessing in Literature, Psycho-analysis and History* (New York: Routledge, 1991).

41   Patrick Anderson and Jisha Menon, "Introduction: Violence Performed," in *Violence Performed: Local Roots and Global Routes of Conflict*, eds. Patrick Anderson and Jisha Menon (New York: Palgrave Macmillan, 2009), 5–6; Shoshana Felman, *The Juridical Unconscious: Trials and Traumas in the Twentieth Century* (Cambridge, MA: Harvard University Press, 2002).

42   Langer, "Introduction," *Admitting the Holocaust*, 5.

43   Primo Levi, *The Drowned and the Saved*, trans. Raymond Rosenthal (New York: Vintage Books, 1988), 83.

44   "Turn your back and keep your eyes shut tight;

For should the Gorgon come and you look at her,

Never again would you return to the light."

Dante, *The Inferno*, trans. John Ciardi (New York: New American Library, 1954), canto 9, lines 52–54.

45   As cited in Michael Alan Signer, *Humanity at the Limit: The Impact of the Holocaust Experience on Jews and Christians* (Bloomington, IN: Indiana University Press, 2000), 40.

1

Atrocity and Proto-Genocide in Sri Lanka

Christopher Powell and Amarnath Amarasingam

Introduction

This paper discusses the concept of "proto-genocide." This concept adds clarity to studies of cultural genocide by helping to distinguish between situations where a collective identity is under violent attack and situations of full-blown genocide. The distinction between "genocide" and "proto-genocide" is analogous to the distinction, in the conservation status of species, between "endangered" or "critically endangered" and "vulnerable" or "near threatened."[1] Proto-genocide helps to define the boundaries of the genocide concept while still relating it to less totalizing forms of ethnic violence.

Our argument has three main components. First, we discuss the question of what distinguishes genocide from other atrocities, and hence what are the ultimate practical implications of a campaign against genocide. This discussion provides the rationale for a concept of proto-genocide. Second, we address the boundaries of the concept of genocide. Since cultures change all the time, it is important to distinguish cultural change, even in the context of violence and atrocity, from genocide per se. To this end we propose our notion of proto-genocide, in which enabling conditions for genocide are established but wholesale cultural extermination is not yet underway. Finally, we examine the current situation of Tamils in Sri Lanka. Although the historical pattern of severe atrocities against Tamil people has led some commentators to describe the situation as genocidal,[2] we argue that these events can be more precisely understood as an instance of proto-genocide. This analysis supports the view that tendencies toward genocide are a systemic feature of modern global society.

The Atrocity of Genocide

It seems a truism to point out that genocide is an atrocity. For many, it is the worst of all atrocities, the "crime of crimes."[3] The danger with this way of thinking is that the atrociousness of genocide becomes, implicitly, part of its definition so that one must prove an act is atrocious before one can establish that it is genocidal and, conversely, the atrocious quality of an act contributes to the case for its being considered genocidal. We propose that scholars should identify and set aside this kind of thinking wherever they encounter it. Just as atrocity cannot be its own explanation,[4] it cannot be its own definition either. This is because the label "atrocity" refers not to intrinsic properties of an act, but to our responses to it. To call something an "atrocity" expresses not only moral objection but an incalculable surplus of moral outrage. In other words, the concept of "atrocity" expresses a traumatized response. Traumatic experiences are those experiences which are so painful they cannot be assimilated normally.[5] Assimilating them, either personally or collectively, requires the expression and acknowledgement of the incalculable pain they cause, but it also requires that this pain be translated from an endlessly recurring lived experience to a perception which can be contained and which does not overwhelm our other faculties. The concept of genocide was born in the historical experience of traumatic violence, especially the trauma of the Nazi Holocaust. We must honour those experiences, especially as new or ongoing genocides continue to traumatize their victims and to create vicarious trauma in bystanders. But to understand the source of this trauma we must distinguish between genocide and the trauma it causes, between "genocide" and "atrocity." We must understand genocide as a structured social process.

If genocide is a structured social process, then it can be defined by its formal properties. Dispute over those formal properties has made genocide an essentially contested concept.[6] One crucial point of contention has been whether genocide essentially comprises or necessarily includes physical extermination implicitly,[7] or whether the eradication of a group's social and cultural existence should also be called genocide without qualification.[8] This question can be debated through the trading of moral intuitions, but it can also be advanced by considering what *purpose* we intend for the concept of genocide, what kind of practical difference in the world we are trying to make by using it.

Raphael Lemkin, who coined the term and campaigned for the criminalization of genocide in international law, stated clearly that his purpose, in part, was to protect human cultural diversity:

> The world represents only so much culture and intellectual vigor as are created by its component national groups. ... The destruction of a nation, therefore, results in the loss of its future contributions to the world.[9]

In contemporary terms, we can say that Lemkin was concerned with ethnodiversity.[10] The anthropologist Wade Davis uses the term "ethnosphere," in direct analogy to the term "biosphere," to refer to the global totality of all human cultures.[11] Different cultures enable different forms of human experience; different "ways of worldmaking"[12] at the conceptual level are articulated with different forms of practical relation among humans and between humans and the natural world.[13] This is valuable in itself, and may be necessary to the collective future of humanity. But human ethnodiversity is severely threatened. For instance, of approximately six thousand extant human languages, fully half are not being taught to infants and are therefore threatened with extinction, while only six hundred are spoken by a population base broad enough to be considered secure.[14] Genocide is therefore a global and systemic problem because it contributes to the drastic collapse of the ethnosphere.

A number of scholars have approached genocide as a *systemic* rather than a contingent feature of the modern state.[15] When genocide is treated as a contingent feature of the modern state, its causes are expected to appear in unique or at least unusual features of the perpetrator society, such as the distinctive ideologies associated with social revolutions, for instance. Systemic approaches recognize the unique features of each genocide, but also consider the ways in which conflicts or practices that are

common among modern states can contribute to the occurrence of genocide. Systemic analysis identifies the otherwise normal aspects of modern
social life which may need to be changed or compensated for in order to
eradicate genocide altogether. Powell's contribution to this literature focuses on how the institutional power of states is coupled with personal
social identity.[16] The modern sovereign state exists as a dynamic network
of relations of "deferentiation." In deferentiation, power struggles involving physical or symbolic violence are temporarily resolved when one party
performs deference towards the other, thereby deferring further violence
and establishing a hierarchical identity-difference relation. Through this
process, subjects obtain security for themselves while reproducing the
conditions of possibility for social violence. The practices of performing
deference, determined by the contingencies of local power struggles, are
fetishized as abstract social norms, while subjects are motivated to invest
their social identity in the figure of the sovereign. Genocide occurs when
social collectivities which have been partially but incompletely assimilated
into these networks (and therefore bear markers of social difference, including different identities, norms, and cultural practices), come to be positioned as radically Other, hence excluded from relations of identification
and moral solidarity, and when the interest and impunity exist to motivate
and enable the massive project of systematic group destruction. State formation, or what Norbert Elias called "the civilizing process," is therefore a
contradictory process, producing both human security and the conditions
for violence of varying degrees.[17]

In the context of this broad historical process, Lemkin's normative
entrepreneurship on behalf of the criminalization of genocide can be
understood as an expression of the contradictions of the state system
itself. It was possible for Lemkin to invent and successfully market the
concept of genocide because modern sovereignty simultaneously raises
and disappoints the hope of peace and security for all. Specifically, the
modern state raises the theoretical possibility of universal citizenship
and universal human rights, but also creates a new security dilemma
premised on the question of *whose* normative standards and cultural
identity will inform the relations of deferentiation on which state power
depends in practice. This strategic situation invites a distinctly modern
politics of "imagined communities" based on ethnic nationalism.[18] Thus
the genocide concept appears as a reaction against and resistance to the

over-coupling of state power with social identity, and the concept appears when it does in history precisely because this over-coupling can be perceived as a systemic problem.

The genocide concept, therefore, serves two purposes, which in the current historical formation are connected: the protection of the diversity of the ethnosphere, and a resistance to the over-coupling of state power with socio-cultural identity. From this perspective, what defines genocide is not so much the intentions of those engaged in its perpetration, or even the moral qualities of the acts involved, but its distinctive qualities as a process in which the use of violence tends towards the destruction of a socio-cultural collectivity as such. Thus, genocide does not always require a campaign of deliberate physical extermination; it can be perpetrated through what Tony Barta has called "relations of genocide" perpetrated by a "genocidal society" in which an entire people is "subject to remorseless pressures of destruction inherent in the very nature of the society."[19] These remorseless pressures can result from what Nancy Scheper-Hughes calls the "small wars" conducted in "the normative, ordinary social spaces of public schools, clinics, emergency rooms, hospital charity wards, nursing homes, city halls, jails and public morgues."[20] In these small wars, not all members of the perpetrator group need intend or even be aware of the overall genocidal trajectory of the actions in which they participate. Genocide may be achieved through a variety of measures that dissolve the social institutions and relationships necessary for the perpetuation of group life without featuring a coordinated program of mass killing.[21]

However, this conceptual approach may be objected to on the grounds that it makes the boundaries of the genocide concept unacceptably vague. Therefore, it is important to distinguish genocidal from non-genocidal attacks on collective life. We do this by investigating an important process at the boundary of genocide: proto-genocide.

The Boundaries of Genocide

The one constant of all culture is change, so what differentiates genocidal from non-genocidal situations where atrocities are being committed? Powell defines genocide as "an identity-difference relation of categorical obliteration."[22] This terse formulation makes several key points. First, social relations are understood as being practical. A genocidal relation is not a genocidal ideology or even a genocidal discourse (although it may include these), but a sustained flow of practice distinguished by the quality of transformation it effects in the actors involved.[23] As a process of practical transformation, genocidal relations, like all other social relations, involves power differentials. Power differentials can be mutually reciprocal; that is, in a situation of equality, all parties to the relation are mutually interdependent and can hold each other accountable. More often they are to some degree asymmetric, and at the furthest extreme of this asymmetry interdependence is transformed into impunity, a condition in which one party can do what they wish to the other(s) without being held accountable in return. Martin Shaw conceptualizes genocide precisely in terms of power dynamics and defines genocidal action as

> action in which armed power organizations treat civilian social groups as enemies and aim to destroy their real or putative social power, by means of killing, violence and coercion against individuals whom they regard as members of the groups.[24]

This conception goes to the heart of the matter: genocide involves a power struggle in which one group faces the realistic possibility of total destruction.

What does the destruction of a group involve, if not the physical annihilation of its members? Relational sociology conceptualizes groups as "figurations," ever-evolving dynamic networks of relations among individuals. Elias uses the metaphor of a dance to illustrate how the social institutions which we commonly describe in static terms—the family, the state, the church, and so on—can be more fully understood as patterns in the flow of action among individuals.[25] To destroy a figuration, therefore, is to disrupt this flow and sunder these relations. A group can be destroyed, as such, without killing a single member if the members are prevented from engaging in the practices which renew their connections to each other and are prevented from sustaining their shared distinctiveness from non-members.[26]

Powell proposes three conditions under which genocide can and will occur: identity-difference polarization, interest, and impunity. In essence, a network of actors joined together by common identity will pursue genocide across the boundary of difference if a sufficient interest exists to mobilize such a large-scale action and if the actors have the impunity to do so.[27]

First, identity-difference polarization allows perpetrators and victims to be defined as groups and for the former to define the latter as radically Other.[28] Defining groups as Other excludes the potential victims from what Helen Fein terms "the universe of obligation."[29] For Fein, individuals or groups inside this "universe" are people "toward whom obligations are owed, to whom rules apply, and whose injuries call for amends."[30] When individuals or groups are excluded from this universe, they become categories of people who are so radically Othered and excluded that they are rendered abject.[31] However, abjection is not a sufficient condition for genocide. Many oppressed groups—homosexuals, transgendered persons, African-Americans—have at various historical moments been rendered abject without being subjected to genocide. Given the resilience of social groups, genocide inevitably requires a sustained application of force. Such force can be applied incidentally, however, without genocide being a primary or even conscious motivation, but merely as a means to the realization of some other massive project such as colonialism. The second condition that must be present in order for genocide to take place is that there must be an interest motivating the genocidal action. Someone must benefit from the application of force which overcomes the resistance of the victims, even if this benefit is not explicitly recognized. And third, for genocide to take place, the capacity to resist it must be overcome; since this means the violent annihilation of the victim's "we" identity, which the victim will resist as a matter of life and death, the power relation between the two must be one of impunity.

These elements are dynamic and continue to take shape during the genocidal process itself. However, a non- or proto-genocidal situation may be distinguished from a genocidal situation by the absence of one or more of these elements. For instance, within a social configuration that includes potential perpetrator and potential victim, identity-difference relations may be substantially polarized without the potential perpetrator having either the interest or the impunity necessary to instantiate genocide. A proto-genocidal situation is one in which the developmental process of the whole configuration is tending towards the establishment of these three conditions. A non-genocidal situation is one in which one or more of the three conditions may be partially present, but in which there is no developmental tendency towards the establishment of all three.

Proto-Genocide in Sri Lanka

Sri Lanka is a small island off the southern coast of India, a little more than 25,000 square miles in size. While its close proximity to its larger neighbour has meant that religious, cultural, and social influences from India have always been present in the country, the Palk Strait that separates Sri Lanka and India has buffered the island-nation from shifts in the Indian political climate.[32] Sri Lanka's significant ethnic and religious diversity lies at the centre of its social and political history. Of the roughly twenty million people in Sri Lanka, the Sinhalese, who mostly identify as Buddhist, comprise the majority ethnic group, with 74 percent of the population. The Tamil community is made up of both Sri Lankan Tamils (12.6 percent) and Indian Tamils (5.6 percent), most of whom are Hindu, but with a significant number of Christians (mostly Catholic). The Muslims of Sri Lanka make up about 7 percent of the population.[33] And the smaller ethnic groups consist of the Burghers (0.4 percent), who are descendants of European settlers, and the Veddas, the Indigenous peoples of Sri Lanka.

Initially ethnic tensions, which became an intimate part of Sri Lankan society throughout the twentieth century, were for the most part about language and access to government services.[34] These tensions eventually spilled over into full-scale violence in the 1970s, increasingly coloured by Tamil demands for autonomy and territorial rights. While the Liberation Tigers of Tamil Eelam (LTTE, or Tamil Tigers) became the dominant, and often only, Sri Lankan Tamil fighting force, numerous other groups were active in the 1970s and 1980s. Over time, most of their leaders either were killed by the LTTE or crossed over to the government's side.[35] Beginning in the early 1980s, the LTTE launched a bloody campaign against the Sri Lankan government, fighting for a separate homeland for the Tamils, called Tamil Eelam. The civil war continued until May 2009, when the Sri Lankan armed forces defeated the Tigers in Mullivaikkal, a tiny spit of land in northeastern Sri Lanka. Civilian casualties were high, with the United Nations estimating that anywhere between forty and seventy thousand civilians lost their lives.[36] Since the war's end, the government of Sri Lanka often argues that the country did not have an ethnic problem—only a "terrorism problem"—and that there was in fact no "war" to speak about.[37] Such rewriting of the past, and lack of acknowledgement of Tamil grievances and demands, has coloured how the government has engaged with the people of the former war zones since the guns went silent.

As such, Sri Lankan Tamils' current situation provides, we argue, an example of a proto-genocidal situation. We assert that the numerous human rights violations committed against Tamils by the Sri Lankan government and the military, while atrocious, have not been specifically genocidal—so far. The decisive factor concerns the figuration of relational processes through which Sri Lankan Tamil culture and identity are (re) produced over time. Anti-Tamil atrocities in Sri Lanka has certainly affected how these processes have taken place, in ways that are very painful and destructive for individuals. The situation is one of grave human rights concern which deserves more international attention than it is getting. However, this persecution has not—so far—threatened to destroy the Tamil collective identity as such. This could change quickly, however. Since the collapse of Tamil military resistance to the Sri Lankan government in 2009, several developments have worked to systematically undermine Tamils' social power, and if these developments continue then Tamils could become acutely vulnerable to genocide. Indeed, many activists and academics already use the language of genocide to describe the plight of the Tamil community on the island since independence,[38] pointing to the 1981 burning of the Jaffna library, the numerous riots and pogroms since then, and the last stages of the civil war, as well as events in the postwar period, as clear evidence of genocide.

All three enabling conditions for genocide are *partially* fulfilled in this case. To begin with, identity-difference relations between Tamils and Sinhalese have been strongly polarized for many years, as evidenced below by the exclusionary mythology of Sinhalese nationalism. Meanwhile, incentives exist for further persecution of Tamils: ethnically exclusionary Sinhalese nationalism and anti-Tamil chauvinism has for many years provided political leaders with marginal returns, in the state and in civil society, while the appropriation of land and business opportunities in Tamil homelands provides economic incentives for Sinhalese soldiers. Finally, a number of developments push the power relations between Tamils and

Sinhalese within the Sri Lankan state further from a condition of reciprocal interdependence and towards a condition of impunity.

Identity-Difference Polarization

Sinhala-Buddhist nationalist ideology defines Tamils as historical oppres-
sors and enemies of the Sinhala nation. This ideology began to emerge
in the colonial period. In true Orientalist fashion,[39] the British occupiers
denied that the Sinhala people had any historical record until the "discovery," in the 1830s, of the *Mahavamsa*, a historical chronicle written in
the sixth century by the monk Mahanama, whereupon the *Mahavamsa*
was construed as the authentic historical document defining the essence
of the Sinhala people.[40] Modern interpretations of the text privileged the
role of the monarch Dutthagamini, who overthrew the Chola dynasty and
restored Buddhism to the island, thereby establishing Sinhalese and Tamils as historical enemies.[41] Through the work of anti-colonial leaders like
Anagarika Dharmapala (1864–1933) and Walpola Rahula (1907–1997),
this polarized view of Sinhala-Tamil relations was incorporated into the
Sri Lankan national narrative.[42]

This ideological framework began to be realized in practice after independence in 1948. After its profound defeat in the 1952 election, the Sri
Lanka Freedom Party (SLFP) under S. W. R. D. Bandaranaike aggressively
exploited communal tensions to win the 1956 election.[43] Declaring that Sri
Lanka's 1948 independence from Britain was not yet complete, Bandaranaike promised that, if the SLFP were elected, only Sinhala, and not Tamil, would be given official language status. Further developments in 1956,
including the celebration of the 2,500-year anniversary of the Buddha's
entry into nirvana and the publication of *The Betrayal of Buddhism* by the
All Ceylon Buddhist Congress, further asserted an essential bond between
Sinhala nationalism and the Buddhist religion. Bandaranaike's election
in 1956 "established a link between the government and the Buddhist religion that has been essential to the political and religious history of Sri
Lanka since that time."[44] Shortly after his victory, Bandaranaike proposed
the Official Language Act, which declared Sinhala to be the only official
language in Sri Lanka. This act would become a long-running symbol of
Sinhala nationalism and would solidify in the minds of many Tamils the
belief that the Sinhala leadership could not be trusted to uphold the rights

of minority populations.[45] There was an immediate backlash to the Language Act by Sri Lankan Tamils, represented by the Federal Party, who argued that the legislation placed their language, culture, and economic position in jeopardy.

After Bandaranaike's assassination in 1959 by a Buddhist monk, his widow, Sirimavo Ratwatte Dias Bandaranaike, carried forward many of her husband's policies and aggressively enforced the Sinhala-only act. What made matters worse was a government policy to hire Sinhala into government service. In May 1972, Bandaranaike and the United Front also used their overwhelming majority to introduce a new constitution. The new constitution made the country a republic, officially changed the name of the island from Ceylon to Sri Lanka, declared Sri Lanka to be a "Unitary State," gave Buddhism a "foremost place" in the country, and made it the state's duty to "protect and foster Buddhism." In the very same month that the constitution was passed, the Federal Party, the Tamil Congress, and the Ceylon Workers' Congress formed the Tamil United Front (TUF).

Perhaps the single most important issue which aggravated ethnic tensions, leading many Tamil youth to throw their support behind militant movements, was the matter of university admissions.[46] In the 1960s students were educated in one of three language streams: Sinhala, Tamil, or English. There existed, then, three different sets of entrance exams, which would be evaluated by three sets of examiners. In the late 1970s, critics began to allege (falsely) that Tamil students benefited from Tamil-language examiners' favouritism. To correct this alleged bias, a language-based system of standardization was introduced, which inevitably favoured Sinhalese students. The numerical scores of applicants in each of the three languages were adjusted to fit a common scale, which was based on the number of applicants in each language. As Sinhala youth were more numerous than Tamils, it meant that the scores of Sinhala students were raised in relation to Tamil and English applicants. "District quotas" introduced in 1974 further established the primacy of ethnicity over achievement in determining university entrance. "Under this system, residents of 'backward' districts were given preferential admissions treatment. Under criteria devised by the Education Ministry, these were mostly districts with heavy Kandyan and Muslim populations."[47] The district quotas had a significant impact on the number of Tamils admitted to university science programs. In a single year, the number of admissions dropped by a third.[48]

After these changes, existing Tamil political leaders lost legitimacy and militant movements like the LTTE began to emerge. Alongside this rise of Tamil militancy, the Tamil United Front made changes to its political objectives. In May 1976, a convention was held in the Northern Province constituency of Vaddukoddai, during which the TUF reconstituted itself as the Tamil United Liberation Front (TULF).[49] The insertion of the word "liberation" reflected the growing belief that fairness, political rights, and economic opportunities would not be guaranteed to Tamils as a minority population within a united Sri Lanka. The TULF manifesto for the 1977 elections makes it clear how far Tamil-Sinhala relations had deteriorated in the previous seven years:

> What is the alternative now left to the nation that has lost its rights to its language, rights to its citizenship, rights to its religions and continues day by day to lose its traditional homeland to Sinhalese Colonization? What is the alternative now left to a nation that lies helpless as it is being assaulted, looted and killed by hooligans instigated by the ruling race and by the security forces of the State? ... There is only one alternative and that is to proclaim with the stamp of finality and fortitude that we alone shall rule over our land our forefathers ruled. Sinhalese imperialism shall quit our homeland.[50]

As Richardson notes, "this manifesto marked a sea change in Tamil political organizations and attitudes in the short space of seven years—from Federal Party to Tamil United Liberation Front, from demands for language rights and devolution of power to demands for political independence."[51]

While a full examination of the course of the civil war cannot be undertaken here,[52] it should be sufficient to point out that following communal violence during the late 1970s and throughout the 1980s—including the riots of 1977 and 1981, the burning of the Jaffna library (and the subsequent loss of over ninety thousand rare Tamil manuscripts), the pogroms of Black July 1983, and subsequent Indian involvement in the training and funding of Tamil militant groups—the civil war reached unprecedented levels of destruction. Consequently, the LTTE became one of the most feared rebel groups of the twentieth century, equipped with an air force, a navy, an intelligence wing, an international propaganda and funding structure, as well as close to ten thousand well-trained cadres ready to die for the cause of national liberation.[53]

Interest in Persecution and Genocide

While ethnic tensions simmered in the country from the time of independence from the British in 1948, the riots of Black July 1983 fundamentally altered the course of ethnic tensions in the country. The shooting death of thirteen Sri Lankan soldiers in the north of the country by the LTTE set the stage for what would become one of the bloodiest decades in the country's history. Sri Lankan president J. R. Jayewardene tried to keep the funeral for the dead soldiers from turning into a political demonstration. However, the arrival of the bodies from Jaffna to Colombo on 24 July was delayed by several hours, and the funeral had to be cancelled. This provoked a riot which continued for a week. Hundreds of Tamil and Indian businesses were burned, homes were destroyed, and many were beaten, shot, or burned alive in their houses or vehicles. Many women were raped or forced to exhibit themselves in front of heckling crowds. Perhaps the most infamous incident occurred at the Welikade maximum security prison, about 4 miles north of Colombo. On the afternoon of 25 July, Sinhalese prisoners gained entry into the wing of the prison holding Tamil political detainees and killed thirty-seven of them with knives and clubs while guards stood idly by. Overall estimates of the number of people killed during Black July range from two hundred to two thousand, mostly Tamil. In addition to lives lost, the events of July 1983 also forced some one hundred thousand Tamils into refugee camps when their homes, vehicles, shops, and belongings were destroyed. Around thirty thousand people also became unemployed due to work sites being destroyed.

The events of Black July help to explain who benefits from ethnic persecution of Tamils, and how. It is no secret that the violence was highly organized, and that it greatly benefited the business class as well as certain political leaders.[54] Economic liberalization operated, and continues to operate, as a vehicle for this benefit:

Economic liberalisation, as a set of economic policies with asymmetrically distributed short-term effects, activates the individual's understanding of how ethnicity affects his material well-being because of pre-existing ethnic divisions of labour. Political entrepreneurs attempt to utilise this process in order to politicise ethnicity and transform it into a reliable and efficient basis for ethnic group cohesion and collective behaviour.[55]

As far back as the 1956 elections, Prime Minister Bandaranaike "combined the promise of selective incentives along ethnic lines with the use of mobilizational resources."[56] From 1970 to 1977, Biziouras argues, Sri Lanka experienced a low level of economic liberalization during which Sinhalese political entrepreneurs could selectively allocate to segments of the Tamil population the various incentives they would receive. With increasing economic liberalization after 1977, and ethnic tensions already simmering, a kind of ethnic outbidding became prominent. During this period, the

> Sinhalese UNP political entrepreneurs, cognisant of the need to outbid their SLFP opponents in terms of selective incentives, actively distributed selective incentives to their ethnic brethren: public-sector jobs, public investment in infrastructural projects in Sinhalese-majority areas, preferential access to policy-makers, and tailored policies to meet specific demands by the Sinhalese critical masses.[57]

The 1983 Black July pogrom was not, therefore, a case of deep-seated enmity between Sinhalese and Tamil people finally erupting onto the streets, but rather an expression of the connections between state power, ethno-religious identity, and economic incentives, and the need for this power to translate into economic incentives as well. As Biziouras notes,

> the Sinhalese who participated in the Colombo riots demanded material resources, jobs and access to state subsidies and were led by Sinhalese UNP leaders. … [These attacks] were actively organised and implemented on the basis of attacking the Tamils' economic resources. These attacks were implemented by rank-and-file JSS (Jathika Sevaka Sangamaya, or National Workers Association) members, coordinated by the UNP Minister of Industry Cyril Matthew, often targeting the properties of Colombo-area Tamil merchants.[58]

More recent attacks, not against Tamils but against the Muslim population in Colombo—such as the attacks on mosques and Muslim-owned businesses in 2013 and 2014—have similar undertones.

Slide Towards Impunity

Suppression of Political Representation

As respected political scientist A. J. Wilson noted, from the beginning of British rule in Sri Lanka, Tamils "remained a community apart … [who] did not wish to be assimilated, and maintained a group consciousness as a separate community and civilization with their own language, culture and territory, and the Hindu faith as their distinguishing characteristics."[59] There has, however, always been a debate in the country about whether minorities can be "Sri Lankan too" while practising their respective religious and cultural traditions, and whether the structure of the state is able to include other national identities within its borders. As Karthigesu Sivathamby once asked, "Cannot a Tamil be a Sri Lankan too? Does being a Sri Lankan Tamil imply that his/her Tamilness cannot be as publicly stated as his or her 'Sri Lankaness'? Cannot Tamilness and the Sri Lankaness coexist? For Sri Lankan Tamils, these are soul-shattering questions."[60] As Sivathamby points out, whatever internal debates once existed, this identity, as shown above, has been increasingly at risk since independence, and particularly since the outbreak of civil war in the 1980s. We argue here, however, that even with the end of the war in May 2009, the preservation of Tamil collective identity remains at risk.

One of the most pernicious aspects of postwar Sri Lanka has been the continued attack on Sri Lankan, and particularly Tamil, civil society. For instance, on 10 January 2012, Gotabaya Rajapaksa, President Mahinda Rajapaksa's brother and secretary of the Defence and Urban Development Ministry, delivered a lecture to the Sri Lanka Foundation Institute and Associated Newspapers of Ceylon Limited. The president's brother, arguably the second most powerful man in Sri Lanka, began his lecture by stating that the country still faces "several threats" following the end of protracted civil war. The very first threat he mentioned, and which he discussed at length, was the "reorganization of the LTTE in the international arena."[61] Mentioning several Tamil diaspora groups by name, he argued that even after the defeat of the LTTE, "the rump of the LTTE's global establishment is still active." Rajapaksa argued, for example, that the "unwavering intent" of LTTE-linked groups overseas "is the division of Sri Lanka and the establishment of a separate state." He went on to note: "Most of them say they engage only in political activism and not violence. Almost all of them pretend to have a democratic face. But make no mistake. The Tiger has not changed its stripes."[62]

While the defense secretary's remarks do not necessarily reflect in essence the views of mainstream Sri Lankans or the broader international community, such a stark verdict on diaspora activism by someone as powerful as the president's brother and defense minister is worrisome to say the least. To make matters worse, in April 2014, the government of Sri Lanka proscribed as "terrorist fronts" sixteen organizations and released the names of more than four hundred individuals who were banned from entering the country.[63] The timing of the proscription, occurring concurrently with the twenty-fifth session of the United Nations Human Rights Council, signalled to many that the government decision was, as Human Rights Watch stated, "aimed at restricting peaceful activism by the country's Tamil minority" against the government.[64] Many things were worrisome about this decision. For example, it made it difficult for Tamil political parties on the island to receive support and funding from abroad, it made it impossible for many diaspora activists associated with these banned organizations from visiting family and friends in the country, and it made it quite dangerous for NGO groups and aid workers to receive support, financially or otherwise, from diaspora organizations who have a vested interest in the country.[65] The full ripple effect of the Sri Lankan government's actions remains to be seen, but it is clear that the government is increasingly worried about diaspora activists and organizations, and that it is not shy about targeting them.

However, the government has not only targeted overseas diaspora organizations. Many civil society organizations in the former war zones struggle to function under government interference and surveillance. A case in point is the Northern Provincial Council (NPC). In the diaspora and the former war zones of Sri Lanka following the war, there was much talk about the potential for the establishment of such a council to move the country towards a modicum of devolution and power-sharing. As Kumaravadivel has written, however, the NPC, even after the elections were finally held in September 2013, continues to suffer from interference and heavy-handedness from the government in Colombo as well as the governor of the Northern Province (who is appointed by the president).[66] As Kumaravadivel notes, "In the South, the Governors are dormant. They do not interfere with the Provincial Council administrations. However in the North and East, wherein the Governor's chair is occupied by two retired army personnel, the Governors make maximum use of their constitutionally granted power. The 13th amendment gives the Governor a choice as to whether s/he wants to be active or not. In the North and East the Governors act like Viceroys from an alien land."[67]

In addition to its crackdown on diaspora organizations and its interference in the affairs of the NPC, the defence ministry, in July 2014, "banned non-governmental organizations from holding press conferences, awareness campaigns, training for journalists, workshops and disseminating press releases on everything from voter rights to exposing corruption."[68] While this ban applies to NGOs across the country, it has of course had a chilling effect in the former war zones of the north as well. Attacks on journalists have also been on the rise. As the civil war was again raging after 2006, Keith Nohayr of the *Nation* was kidnapped and beaten before being released, J. S. Tissanayagam was detained and went through arduous court proceedings before being pardoned, and Lasantha Wickrematunge, a prominent anti-government journalist and editor of the *Sunday Leader*, was killed by four armed assassins on 8 January 2009.[69] As the Committee to Protect Journalists noted, at least twenty-six journalists have been driven into exile between 2008 and 2013, Tamil journalists in the north and east of the country have been continuously attacked and targeted for their reporting,[70] and the offices of respected Tamil newspapers have been targeted by arsonists.[71]

Militarization, the Loss of Economic Livelihood, and Women's Insecurity

As the International Crisis Group (ICG) pointed out, the issue of livelihood and economic development in the north has been intimately tied to the continued militarization of the former war zones.[72] According to the ICG, "Since the war ended in 2009, hundreds of millions of dollars have poured into the province, but the local populations, mostly left destitute by the conflict, have seen only slight improvements in their lives.

Instead of giving way to a process of inclusive, accountable development, the military is increasing its economic role, controlling land and seemingly establishing itself as a permanent occupying presence."[73] Even as the Northern Province is among the least densely populated, the number of military troops stationed there is very substantial. According to some estimates, sixteen of the Sri Lankan army's nineteen brigades are located in Tamil-dominated areas, with a soldier-to-civilian ratio of 1:11—one of the highest in the world.[74]

To be sure, militarization does not refer only to the presence of the military in the north and east.[75] Unlike in the years immediately following the end of the war, soldiers are not always seen wandering the city streets of the north. Rather, militarization persists in a more sustained and routinized kind of way. The economic aspects of militarization, in addition to security issues, are becoming increasingly worrisome to people in the former war zones. As scholars and activists have noted, the military has been involved with a variety of economic initiatives in the country: running security companies, a catering service, hotel chains, farming, and conducting whale watching tours.[76] The military is often accused by people in the north of flooding the market with their own goods at reduced prices since they have virtually no overhead costs. This frustration extends to land rights as well.[77] Many people interviewed in the north by Amarasingam are distressed by the fact that the military is being given lands in the former war zones. This is being done, as one activist put it, to "purposefully redraw the demographic makeup of the region" and to eventually nullify the argument that the north is a "Tamil homeland" with a unique culture and tradition, which deserves to govern itself with a sense of autonomy.[78] As Fonseka and Jegatheeswaran point out, "Four years after the war, the military continues to play a major role in the acquisition and alienation of land in the North and East … [and] the large-scale acquisitions happening in the North and East appear to be directed by the central government and the military with limited information available to local officials and affected populations."[79]

Within the broader context of militarization and postwar insecurity, it is women who struggle most at the hands of both the military and members of the Tamil population. Three decades of civil war has resulted in over forty thousand female-headed households, with husbands and older male children having been killed in the war. This, combined with inadequate housing and limited livelihood options, has put many women in situations of vulnerability.[80] During research visits to the north, Amarasingam was often told that women were much safer during the time of the LTTE. Under the LTTE, sexual violence was apparently harshly dealt with, which served as a deterrent. In the postwar environment, women's vulnerability has increased drastically in the context of militarization. As Fonseka and Raheem point out, most roads in the north have significant military presence in one form or another, and this "has had a bearing on women who continue to live with host families or in displacement camps as a result of their lands being occupied. For instance, in households in areas of the Vanni but also in Jaffna and Mannar, consisting largely of women with no adult male presence, the residents even sleep the night in other houses for safety reasons."[81] As such, the issue of land—and secure housing—is also intimately tied to women's security and vulnerability. For example, a recent report by Yasmin Sooka, the executive director of the Foundation for Human Rights, argued that abductions, arbitrary detention, torture, rape and sexual violence have increased since the end of the war in 2009. More damningly, the report argued that "these widespread and systematic violations by the Sri Lankan security forces occur in a manner that indicates a coordinated, systematic plan approved by the highest levels of government."[82]

Sinhalization of the Tamil Areas and Tamil Mourning

When Navi Pillay, the UN High Commissioner for Human Rights, visited Sri Lanka in August 2013, she attempted to visit Mullivaikkal and the Nandikadal Lagoon, the tiny spit of land where the civil war came to an end, and where the LTTE leader Velupillai Prabhakaran was killed. The government argued that Pillay was attempting to "pay tribute" to the LTTE, and that no more evidence of the UN's biased stance against the Sri Lankan government was needed. While this particular incident made headlines, it is certainly not an isolated example of the ways in which the Sri Lankan government attempts to dictate how the war should be remembered. For the government, the thirty year civil war was not an ethnic conflict but a terrorism problem. As such, the government has seen fit to destroy the childhood home of the LTTE leader, as well as raze to the ground a series of LTTE cemeteries that used to dot the north and east of the country, often installing army camps directly on top of them.[83] The mothers and fathers of the LTTE combatants who were buried at these cemeteries have been traumatized by these actions.

In addition to the destruction and desecration of LTTE cemeteries, public acts commemorating the war's end have been banned by the military every year since May 2009. While the celebratory pageantry is well planned in Colombo for "Victory Day," Tamils in the Northern Province are not allowed to publicly mourn their dead. As military spokesman Ruwan Wanigasuriya said in May 2014, "Any persons trying to hoist black flags, distribute leaflets or put up posters will be considered as supporting of terrorism and such persons will be taken into custody under the Prevention of Terrorism Act."[84] Any act of public remembrance, in other words, will be interpreted and treated as a kind of tribute to the LTTE. Despite the ban, however, over two thousand students and faculty at the University of Jaffna observed Mullivaikkal Remembrance Day in 2014. Each attendee stood silently holding a candle, while military personnel and police kept watch outside. Through such bans and surveillance, the government attempts to stifle communal strategies for coping with the immense losses suffered over the last three decades, and therefore contributes to feelings of isolation and dislocation already rampant in the former war zones. As Tissainayagam writes,

> May 18 has come to symbolise different things in different parts of Sri Lanka. This precisely is the reason why the restrictions on mourning apply only to the Northern Province—the only Tamil-dominated province in the country. In areas outside the North, the government holds huge victory day celebrations, replete with militaristic symbols—marching columns, parading of military hardware and speeches reinforcing national unity and victory over terrorism and division of the country. These events have strong overtones of racism: the triumph of Sinhala nationalism, embodied by the government of President Mahinda Rajapakse and his family, over the Tamils by crushing their aspiration for dignity, rights and equality. ... By criminalising northern Tamils mourning their dead as an act of terrorism, which can be punished by arrest and detention under the Prevention of Terrorism Act (PTA), Rajapakse hopes he can contain the Tamils' moves to cohere as a community once again.[85]

In addition to the attacks on public mourning and the lack of acknow-ledgement of Tamil lives lost in the war, the Sri Lankan government is also engaging in a broad project aimed at "Sinhalizing" Tamil areas of the north. As The Social Architects, an anonymous group of activists based in Sri Lanka, recently noted, "Since 1958, the names of ancient Tamil vil-lages and streets have surreptitiously been given Sinhalese names." Close to one hundred important Tamil villages and cities, which continue to have deep emotional significance for Tamils all over the world, have been "Sinhalized": Vattukoddai has been changed to Battakote, Manipay has been changed to Mampe, and the island of Nainatheevu has been changed to Nagatheeba.[86]

The government is also redrawing the boundaries of Tamil border villages and incorporating them into predominantly Sinhalese districts. It is quite obvious that this is being done to reduce Tamil representation in various areas, again in an attempt to undermine and eliminate the argument that there are "majority" Tamil areas or Tamil "homelands" throughout the country.[87] What is more hurtful for many Tamils in the country, as well as those in the diaspora, has been the continued destruc-tion of Hindu temples in the former war zones, and the building of Bud-dhist shrines in their place. One of the clearest examples of this change is the hot spring wells in Kanniya, in the eastern district of Trincomalee. When Amarasingam visited the site in January 2014, the statue of Hindu god Ganesha was being kept under a tin shed, and a giant Buddha shrine had been erected close to the springs.

Conclusion

Our notion of proto-genocide complements and partly overlaps with Gregory Stanton's concept of the ten stages of genocide.[88] It differs in that Stanton's work is oriented to physical genocide where ours is oriented to cultural genocide. Our notion of proto-genocide also owes much to Tony Barta's concept of "relations of genocide" and a "genocidal society." As Barta has written,

> My conception of a genocidal *society*—as distinct from a genocid-al state—is one in which the bureaucratic apparatus might offi-cially be directed to protect innocent people but in which a whole

race is nevertheless subject to remorseless pressures of destruction inherent in the very nature of the society.[89]

While we do not suggest that the Sri Lankan state is officially directed to protect Tamil culture—quite the contrary—Barta's key point is that cultural extermination can be accomplished through a relatively decentralized collection of institutional practices and structural relations. Similarly, Keith Doubt's discussion of "sociocide"[90] shows how even physical genocide involves violent attacks on the social institutions through which a group maintains its solidarity and shared identity. Furthermore, Sri Lanka's colonial history enables us to situate its proto-genocide on a continuum with the subaltern genocides examined by Robins and Jones.[91] The concept of proto-genocide therefore helps to define a field of inquiry which up to this point has been suggested but not focally explored by genocide scholars.

Powell has argued that modern genocides are a systemic by-product of the globalizing expansion of Western civilization.[92] The imposition of the nation-state through colonialism has increased the stakes of local struggles over collective identity and created new incentives for mass violence. Under these conditions, we can expect to find proto-genocidal situations alarmingly common. Many of these might involve tribal or Indigenous peoples with small populations,[93] but the condition of Tamils in Sri Lanka is nonetheless illustrative of the structural qualities of a proto-genocidal situation.

Since independence, and especially during the civil war, Sri Lankan Tamils have suffered severe atrocities. While some of these atrocities have affected vital Tamil cultural institutions, they have not amounted to a coherent program (intended or otherwise) of cultural extermination. However, that could change. Sinhala nationalist ideology excludes Tamils from the universe of moral obligation; this ideology, along with Sri Lankan policies towards Tamils, and the civil war itself, have contributed to what Hinton calls "genocidal priming,"[94] pushing Sinhala-Tamil relations towards the kind of polarization which enables perpetrators to legitimate genocide.[95] Economic and political incentives exist for the progressive disenfranchisement of Tamils, potentially up to and including their total abjection. Militarily and otherwise, Tamils have demonstrated the capacity to resist abjection and to defend the social institutions which maintain their coherence as a people. But the ongoing suppression of Tamil politics and civil society, the colonization and Sinhalization of Tamil areas by Sinhalese military officers, the loss of economic livelihood by Tamil families, and restrictions placed on Tamil mourning have the potential to gradually erode Tamil society. If this erosion goes far enough, Tamils could be unable to effectively resist more thoroughgoing measures such as the complete prohibition of Tamil language, forced conversion to Buddhism, economic expropriation, and forced dispersion—measures that could amount to a program of cultural extermination. With the election of Maithripala Sirisena in January 2015, many in the country and abroad expressed hope that the postwar situation would change. Indeed, there are many positive signs that change is afoot: the military governor of the Northern Province was replaced with a civilian, and President Sirisena expressed some interest in inviting exiled journalists back to the country. However, Sirisena has not yet expressed a commitment to the demilitarization of the former war zones. Only time will tell whether a change in leadership will result in a change in political culture. In language analogous to that of ecological conservation, Sri Lankan Tamils are not yet critically endangered, but they are threatened. This is an issue of interest to genocide scholars, and of concern to genocide and human rights activists.

NOTES

1   International Union for the Conservation of Nature, *IUCN Red List Categories and Criteria, Version 3.1, Second Edition* (2014): 14–15, http://s3.amazonaws.com/iucnredlist-newcms/staging/public/attachments/3097/redlist_cats_crit_en.pdf (accessed 9 September 2016).

2   See for example Francis Boyle, *The Tamil Genocide by Sri Lanka: The Global Failure to Protect Tamil Rights Under International Law* (Atlanta: Clarity Press, 2013); Rosie DiManno, "Sri Lanka's Hidden Genocide" *Toronto Star*, 4 November 2013; A. Sivanandan, "Ethnic cleansing in Sri Lanka," *Race & Class* 51, no. 3 (2010): 59–65.

3   William Schabas, *Genocide in International Law: The Crime of Crimes* (Cambridge: Cambridge University Press, 2009).

4   Mahmood Mamdani, *When victims become killers: colonialism, nativism, and the genocide in Rwanda* (Princeton, NJ: Princeton University Press, 2001), 228.

5   Judith Lewis Herman, *Trauma and Recovery: From Domestic Abuse to Political Terror* (London: Pandora, 2001).

6   W. B. Gallie, "Essentially Contested Concepts," *Proceedings of the Aristotelian Society* 56 (1956): 167–198; Christopher Powell, "What do genocides kill? A relational conception of genocide," *Journal of Genocide Research* 9, no. 4 (2007): 527–547; For summaries of the definitional debate see Adam Jones, *Genocide: A Comprehensive Introduction* (London: Routledge, 2010), 16–20; Martin Shaw, *What is Genocide?* (Cambridge: Polity, 2007).

7   See for instance Frank Robert Chalk and Kurt Jonassohn, *The history and sociology of genocide: analyses and case studies* (New Haven, CT: Yale University Press, 1990); Israel W. Charny, "Toward a Generic Definition of Genocide," in *Genocide: Conceptual and Historical Dimensions*, ed. G. J. Andreopoulos (Philadelphia: University of Pennsylvania Press, 1994), 64–94; Pieter N. Drost, *The Crime of State*, 2 vols. (Leyden: A. W. Sythoff, 1959); Helen Fein, *Genocide: a sociological perspective* (London: Sage, 1993); Barbara Harff and Ted R. Gurr, "Toward empirical theory of genocides and politicides: identification and measurement of cases since 1945," *International Studies Quarterly* 37, no. 3 (1988): 359–371; Irving Louis Horowitz, *Taking Lives: Genocide and State power* (New Brunswick, NJ: Transaction Publishers, 2002); Steven T. Katz, *The Holocaust in Historical Context*, vol. 1. (New York: Oxford University Press, 1994).

8   Tony Barta, "Relations of Genocide: Land and Lives in the Colonization of Australia," in *Genocide and the Modern Age: Etiology and case studies of mass death*, ed. I. Wallimann and M. N. Dobkowski (New York: Greenwood, 1987), 237–252; Jeff Benvenuto, "What Does Genocide Produce? The Semantic Field of Genocide, Cultural Genocide, and Ethnocide in Indigenous Rights Discourse," *Genocide Studies and Prevention: An International Journal* 9, no. 2 (2015): 26–40; Barbara Cassidy, "Getting Rid of the Indian Problem: Aboriginal Suicide as a Manifestation of Genocide," PhD diss., York University, Toronto, 2002; Roland Chrisjohn, Sherri Young, and Michael Maraun, *The Circle Game: Shadows and Substance in the Indian Residential School Experience in Canada* (Penticton, BC: Theytus Books, 2006); Ward Churchill, "Genocide By Any Other Name: North American Indian Residential Schools in context," in *Genocide, War Crimes and The West*, ed. A. Jones (New York: Zed Books, 2004), 78–115; Ward Churchill, *Kill the Indian, Save the Man: The Genocidal Impact of American Indian Residential Schools* (San Francisco: City Lights Publishers, 2004); Robert Davis and Mark Zannis, *The Genocide Machine in Canada: The Pacification of the North* (Montreal: Black Rose Books, 1973); Peter E. Dawson, "The Relocation of Aboriginal People in Canada, 1952 to 1967: A United Nations Human Rights Analysis From a Cultural Perspective, Cultural Genocide," PhD diss., York University, Toronto, 2001; Anges Grant, *No End of Grief: Indian Residential Schools in Canada* (Winnipeg: Pemmican Publications, 1996); Bonita Lawrence, *"Real" Indians and Others: Mixed-Blood Urban Native Peoples and Indigenous Nationhood* (Vancouver: UBC Press, 2004); Manitoba Review Committee on Indian and Metis Adoptions and Placements, "No quiet place: final report to the Honourable Muriel Smith, Minister of Community Services" (Winnipeg: M. C. Services, 1985); Dirk A. Moses, "An antipodean genocide? The origins of the genocidal moment in the colonization of Australia," *Journal of Genocide Research* 2, no. 1 (2000): 89–106; Dean Neu and Richard Therrien, *Accounting for Genocide: Canada's Bureaucratic Assault on Aboriginal People* (Winnipeg: Fernwood Publishing, 2003); Eric Robinson and Henry Bird Quinney, *The Infested Blanket: Canada's Constitution-Genocide of Indian Nations* (Winnipeg: Queenston House Publishing, 1985); Roseau River Anishnabe First Nation Government, *Genocide in Canada*. Manitoba: Roseau River Anishnabe First Nation, 1997; Andrea Smith, *Conquest: Sexual Violence and the American Indian Genocide* (Cambridge: South End Press, 2005); Andrew Woolford, "Ontological Destruction: Genocide and Canadian Aboriginal Peoples," *Genocide Studies and Prevention* 4, no. 1 (2009): 81–97; Andrew Woolford and Jasmine Thomas, "Genocide and Aboriginal Peoples in Canada: A Dialogue in Waiting," in *Genocide of Indigenous Peoples: A Critical Bibliographic Review*, eds. S. Totten and R. K. Hitchcock (Edison, NJ: Transaction Publishers, 2010): 61–86.

9   Raphael Lemkin, *Axis rule in occupied Europe: laws of occupation, analysis of government, proposals for redress* (Washington, DC: Carnegie Endowment for International

Peace Division of International Law, 1944), 91. For a more detailed discussion of the importance of cultural destruction in Lemkin's conception of genocide, see Adam Muller's contribution to this volume, "Troubling History, Troubling Law: The Question of Indigenous Genocide in Canada." Also in this volume, Steven Leonard Jacobs's " 'We Charge Genocide': An Historical Petition All But Forgotten and Unknown" discusses anti-black racism in the United States as a form of systematic social and cultural oppression which Lemkin knew about but did not treat as genocide.

10   Hans-Dieter Evers, Anis Yusoff, and A. BB. Shamsul, "Ethno-diversity and bio-diversity: Methods and measurement," *Munich Personal RePEc Archive*, MPRA Paper No. 24429 (2010).

11   Wade Davis, *Light at the Edge of the World: A Journey Through the Realm of Vanishing Cultures*: (Toronto: Douglas & Mcintyre, 2007).

12   Nelson Goodman, *Ways of Worldmaking* (Indianapolis: Hackett, 1978).

13   Davis, *Light At The Edge Of The World*.

14   Ibid.

15   Zygmunt Bauman, *Modernity and the Holocaust* (Ithaca, NY: Cornell University Press, 1991); Ben Kiernan, *Blood and Soil: A World History of Genocide and Extermination* (New Haven, CT: Yale University Press, 2007); Mark Levene, *Genocide in the Age of the Nation-State*, vols. 1–2 (London: I. B. Tauris, 2005); Michael Mann, *The Dark Side of Democracy: Explaining Ethnic Cleansing* (Cambridge: Cambridge University Press, 2005); Dirk A. Moses and Dan Stone, eds., *Colonialism and Genocide* (London: Taylor & Francis, 2008); Richard Rubenstein, "Afterword: Genocide and Civilization," in *Genocide and the Modern Age: Etiology and Case Studies of Mass Death*, eds. I. Wallimann, M. N. Dobkowski (Syracuse, NY: Syracuse University Press, 1987), 283–298; Robert van Krieken, "The barbarism of civilization: cultural genocide and the 'stolen generations'," *British Journal of Sociology* 50, no. 2 (1999): 297–315.

16   Christopher Powell, *Barbaric Civilization: A Critical Sociology of Genocide* (Montreal: McGill-Queen's University Press, 2011).

17   Norbert Elias, *The Civilizing Process: The History of Manners and State Formation and Civilization*, trans. E. Jephcott (Oxford: Blackwell, 2000).

18   Benedict Anderson, *Imagined Communities: Reflections on the Origins and Spread of Nationalism* (London: Verso, 1991).

19   Barta, "Relations of Genocide," 239–240.

20   Nancy Scheper-Hughes, "Specificities: Peace-Time Crimes," *Social Identities* 3, no. 3 (1997): 472.

21   Christopher Powell and Julia Peristerakis, "Genocide in Canada: A Relational View," in *Colonial Genocide and Indigenous North America*, eds. A. Woolford, J. Benvenuto, and A. L. Hinton (Durham, NC: Duke University Press, 2014).

22   Powell, *Barbaric Civilization*, 84

23   Powell, "What do genocides kill?"; Powell and Peristerakis, "Genocide in Canada: A Relational View."

24   Martin Shaw, *What is Genocide?* (Cambridge: Polity, 2007): 154.

25   Elias, *The Civilizing Process*, 482

26 Powell, "What do genocides kill?"; Powell and Peristerakis, "Genocide in Canada: A Relational View."

27 Powell, *Barbaric Civilization*, 12

28 Note that the definition of the victim group can be a product of the perpetrator's ideology: partly, as in the Nazis' racialized definition of Jews, or almost entirely, as in the Khmer Rouge's definition of the bourgeoisie. See Powell, *Barbaric Civilization*, 63

29 Helen Fein, "Scenarios of Genocide: Models of Genocide and Critical Responses," in *Toward the Understanding and Prevention of Genocide: Proceedings of the International Conference on the Holocaust and Genocide*, ed. I. W. Charny. (Boulder: Westview Press, 1984): 3–31.

30 Ibid., 4

31 Powell, *Barbaric Civilization*, 216–219.

32 Chandra De Silva, *Sri Lanka: A History* (New Delhi: Vikas Publishing House, 1997), 9.

33 Ibid., 3–5; Dennis McGilvray, *Crucible of Conflict: Tamil and Muslim Society on the East Coast of Sri Lanka* (Durham, NC: Duke University Press, 2008).

34 Stanley Tambiah, *Sri Lanka: Ethnic Fratricide and the Dismantling of Democracy* (Chicago: University of Chicago Press, 1986), 74; A. Jeyaratnam Wilson, *The Break-Up of Sri Lanka: The Sinhala-Tamil Conflict* (Honolulu: University of Hawaii Press, 1988).

35 de Silva, *Sri Lanka*.

36 UN Panel of Experts, *Report of the Secretary-General's Panel of Experts on Accountability in Sri Lanka*, 31 March 2011, www.un.org/News/dh/infocus/Sri_Lanka/POE_Report_Full.pdf (accessed 12 April 2013).

37 Neil DeVotta, "The Liberation Tigers of Tamil Eelam and the Lost Quest for Separatism in Sri Lanka," *Asian Survey* 49, no. 6 (2009): 1021–1051; Andi Schubert, "Victorious Victims: An Analysis of Sri Lanka's Post-War Reconciliation Discourse," ICES Research Paper No. 6. (Colombo: ICES, 2013), http://www.ices.lk/victorious-victims/ (accessed 4 January 2015).

38 See for example Guruparan Kumaravadivel and Sivakami Rajamanoharan, "Four Years On, Genocide Continues Off the Battlefield," *OpenSecurity*, 20 May 2013, https://www.opendemocracy.net/opensecurity/kumaravadivel-guruparan-sivakami-rajamanoharan/four-years-on-genocide-continues-off-bat (accessed 22 May 2013).

39 Edward Said, *Orientalism* (New York: Vintage Books, 1978).

40 Anne Blackburn, *Locations of Buddhism: Colonialism and Modernity in Sri Lanka* (Chicago: University of Chicago Press, 2010), 71–78; Nira Wickramasinghe, *Sri Lanka in the Modern Age: A History of Contested Identities* (London: Hurst & Company, 2006), 89; Steven Kemper, *The Presence of the Past: Chronicles, Politics, and Culture in Sinhala Life* (Ithaca, NY: Cornell University Press, 1991); Pradeep Jeganathan, "Authorizing History, Ordering Land: The Conquest of Anuradhapura," in *Unmaking the Nation: The Politics of Identity and History in Modern Sri Lanka*, eds. Pradeep Jeganathan and Qadri Ismail (Colombo: Social Scientists' Association, 1995), 112; Sudharshan Seneviratne, " 'Peripheral Regions' and 'Marginal Communities': Towards an Alternative Explanation of Early Iron Age Material and Social Formations in Sri Lanka," in *Tradition, Dissent and Ideology: Essays in Honour of Romila Thapar*, eds. R. Champakalakshmi and S. Gopal. (New Delhi: Oxford University Press, 1996); Elizabeth Nissan, "History in the Making: Anuradhapura and the Sinhala Buddhist Nation," *Social Analysis*, 25 (1989): 68.

41 Alice Greenwald, "The Relic on the Spear: Historiography and the Saga of Dutthag-amini," in *Religion and Legitimation of Power in Sri Lanka*, ed. Bardwell L. Smith (Chambersburg, PA: Amina Books, 1978), 13–35; Neil DeVotta, *Blowback: Linguistic Nationalism, Institutional Decay, and Ethnic Conflict in Sri Lanka* (Stanford: Stanford University Press, 2004), 26; Patrick Grant, *Buddhism and Ethnic Conflict in Sri Lanka* (Albany, NY: SUNY Press, 2009), 48–50.

42 Walpola Rahula, *The Heritage of the Bhikku* (New York: Grove Press, 1974); DeVotta, *Blowback*, 31–32; Grant, *Buddhism and Ethnic Conflict in Sri Lanka*, 81; H. L. Sene-viratne, *The Work of Kings: The New Buddhism in Sri Lanka* (Chicago: University of Chicago Press, 1999), 191.

43 John Richardson, *Paradise Poisoned: Learning about Conflict, Terrorism and Devel-opment from Sri Lanka's Civil Wars* (Kandy: International Center for Ethnic Studies, 2005), 144.

44 George Bond, *The Buddhist Revival in Sri Lanka: The Religious Tradition, Reinterpreta-tion, and Response* (Columbia: University of South Carolina Press, 1988): 90.

45 Neil DeVotta, "Illiberalism and Ethnic Conflict in Sri Lanka," *Journal of Democracy* 13, no.1 (2002): 84–98; DeVotta, *Blowback*.

46 de Silva, *Sri Lanka*, 130–132.

47 Richardson, *Paradise Poisoned*, 297.

48 For a detailed analysis of the university admissions issue, see Chandra De Silva, "The Politics of University Admissions: A Review of Some Aspects of the Admissions Policy in Sri Lanka, 1971–1978," *Sri Lanka Journal of Social Science* 1, no. 2 (1978): 85–123.

49 Robert Kearney, "Ethnic Conflict and the Tamil Separatist Movement in Sri Lanka," *Asian Survey* 25, no. 9 (1985): 898–917; W. I. Siriweera, "Recent Developments in Sinhala-Tamil Relations," *Asian Survey* 20, no. 9 (1980): 903–913.

50 Quoted in Richardson, *Paradise Poisoned*, 294.

51 Ibid.

52 But see for example A. Jeyaratnam Wilson, *Sri Lankan Tamil Nationalism: Its Origins and Development in the Nineteenth and Twentieth Centuries* (Vancouver: University of British Columbia Press, 2000); M. R. Narayan Swamy, *Tigers of Lanka: From Boys to Guerillas* (Colombo: Vijitha Yapa Publications, 1994).

53 Dagmar Hellmann-Rajanayagam, "The 'Groups' and the Rise of Militant Secessionism," in *The Sri Lankan Tamils: Ethnicity and Identity*, eds. Manogaran Chelvadurai and Bryan Pfaffenberger (Boulder, CO: Westview Press, 1994).

54 L. Piyadasa, *Sri Lanka: The Holocaust and After* (London: Marram Books, 1984).

55 Nikolaos Biziouras, "The Political Economy of Ethnic Mobilization: Comparing the Emergence, Consolidation, and Radicalization of Ethnic Parties in Post-Colonial Sri Lanka and Malaysia," *Commonwealth & Comparative Politics* 51, no. 4 (2013): 482.

56 Ibid., 486.

57 Ibid., 490.

58 Ibid., 491.

59 Wilson, *Sri Lankan Tamil Nationalism*, 1.

60 Kartigesu Sivathamby, *Being a Tamil and Sri Lankan* (Colombo: Aivakam, 2005), xxi.

61   Gotabaya Rajapaksa, "LTTE Linked Overseas Groups Want Armed Struggle to Resume in Sri Lanka," 11 January 2012, http://dbsjeyaraj.com/dbsj/archives/3587 (accessed 11 January 2012).

62   Ibid.

63   D. B. S Jeyaraj, "Sri Lanka Proscribes 15 Suspected LTTE Front Organizations Abroad as Foreign Terrorist Entities Under UN Resolution 1373," 2 April 2014, http://dbsjeyaraj.com/dbsj/archives/29147 (accessed 3 April 2014).

64   Human Rights Watch, "Sri Lanka: Asset Freeze Threatens Peaceful Dissent," April 2014, http://www.hrw.org/news/2014/04/07/sri-lanka-asset-freeze-threatens-peaceful-dissent (accessed 6 January 2015).

65   Ibid.

66   Guruparan Kumaravadivel, "Much Ado About Nothing," *Colombo Telegraph*, 21 April 2013, https://www.colombotelegraph.com/index.php/much-ado-about-nothing-2/ (accessed 6 January 2015).

67   Ibid.

68   Amal Jeyasinghe, "Sri Lanka's NGO Crackdown Woes," *China Post* (Taipei), 21 July 2014, http://www.chinapost.com.tw/commentary/afp/2014/07/21/412869/Sri-Lankas.htm (accessed 24 July 2014).

69   See Gordon Weiss, *The Cage: The Fight for Sri Lanka and the Last Days of the Tamil Tigers* (London: Bodley Head, 2011), 147–157; Raine Wickrematunge, *And Then They Came for Me: The Lasantha Wickrematunge Story* (Bloomington, IN: AuthorHouse, 2013).

70   Reporters Without Borders, "Army Surrounds Tamil Daily's Headquarters in Jaffna," 20 May 2014, http://en.rsf.org/sri-lanka-army-surrounds-tamil-daily-s-19-05-2014,46308.html (accessed 23 July 2014).

71   "Tamil Paper Uthayan attacked in Northern Sri Lanka," *BBC News Asia*, 3 April 2013, http://www.genocidewatch.org/srilanka.html (accessed 30 April 2013).

72   International Crisis Group, "Sri Lanka's North II: Rebuilding Under the Military," 2012, http://www.crisisgroup.org/en/regions/asia/south-asia/sri-lanka/220-sri-lankas-north-ii-rebuilding-under-the-military.aspx (accessed 1 April 2014).

73   Ibid., i.

74   Eric Ellis, "The Smugglers' Prey," *The Global Mail*, 2013, https://markfinger.github.io/recent-work/sri-lanka/smugglers-prey.html (accessed 20 December 2013).

75   Minority Rights Group, *No War, No Peace: The Denial of Minority Rights and Justice in Sri Lanka*, 2011, http://minorityrights.org/publications/no-war-no-peace-the-denial-of-minority-rights-and-justice-in-sri-lanka-january-2011/ (accessed 6 January 2015).

76   Brenden Brady, "Soldiers at Your Service," *Slate*, 30 August 2013, http://www.slate.com/articles/news_and_politics/roads/2013/08/sri_lankan_army_goes_into_tourism_business_after_crushing_the_tamil_tigers.html (accessed 30 August 2013).

77   Bhavani Fonseka and Dharsha Jegatheeswaran, "Politics, Policies and Practices With Land Acquisitions and Related Issues in the North and East of Sri Lanka," (Colombo: Centre for Policy Alternatives, 2013), http://www.cpalanka.org/policy-brief-politics-policies-and-practices-with-land-acquisitions-and-related-issues-in-the-north-and-east-of-sri-lanka/ (accessed 6 January 2015); Bhavani Fonseka and Mirak Raheem,

"Land Issues in the Northern Province: Post-War Politics, Policy and Practices" (Colombo: Centre for Policy Alternatives, 2011), http://www.cpalanka.org/land-issues-in-the-northern-province-post-war-politics-policy-and-practices/ (accessed 6 January 2015).

78 See The Social Architects, *Salt on Old Wounds: The Systematic Sinhalization of Sri Lanka's North, East and Hill Country* (Colombo: The Social Architects, 2012), http://www.internationalpolicydigest.org/2012/03/20/salt-on-old-wounds-post-war-sri-lanka/ (accessed 6 January 2015).

79 Fonseka and Jegatheeswaran, "Politics, Policies and Practices," 8.

80 Amantha Perera, "Single Mothers Battle on in Former War Zone," *Inter Press Service*, 7 July 2014, http://www.ipsnews.net/2014/07/single-mothers-battle-on-in-former-war-zone/ (accessed 30 July 2014).

81 Fonseka and Raheem, "Land Issues in the Northern Province," 111.

82 Yasmin Sooka, "An Unfinished War: Torture and Sexual Violence in Sri Lanka, 2009–2014," *Stop Torture*, 2014: 6. http://www.stop-torture.com/ (accessed 6 January 2015).

83 Jennifer Hyndman and Amarnath Amarasingam, "Touring 'Terrorism': Landscapes of Memory in Post-War Sri Lanka," *Geography Compass* 8, NO. 8 (2014): 560–575.

84 Quoted in J. S. Tissainayagam, "From Tiananmen to Jaffna: Banning Community Commemoration," *Asian Correspondent*, 15 May 2014, http://asiancorrespondent.com/author/js-tissainayagam/ (accessed 20 May 2014).

85 Tissainayagam, "From Tiananmen to Jaffna."

86 The Social Architects, *Salt on Old Wounds*, 42–43.

87 Ibid., 24.

88 Gregory Stanton, "The Ten Stages of Genocide," 2013, http://www.genocidewatch.org/genocide/tenstagesofgenocide.html (accessed 6 January 2015).

89 Barta, "Relations of Genocide," 239–240.

90 Keith Doubt, *Understanding Evil: Lessons from Bosnia* (New York: Fordham University Press, 2006).

91 Nicholas A. Robins and Adam Jones, *Genocides by the Oppressed: Subaltern Genocide in Theory and Practice* (Bloomington, IN: Indiana University Press, 2009).

92 Powell, *Barbaric Civilization*.

93 See for example Survival International, "Annual Report 2014," http://www.survivalinternational.org/info/annualreview (accessed 25 September 2014); Davis, *Light At The Edge Of The World*.

94 Alexander Laban Hinton, "The Dark Side of Modernity: Toward an Anthropology of Genocide," in *Annihilating Difference: The Anthropology of Genocide*, ed. Alexander Laban Hinton (Berkeley: University of California Press, 2002), 1–42.

95 See for comparison Powell, *Barbaric Civilization*, 250–271.

Finding Global Justice Locally at Sites of Atrocity: The Case for the Srebrenica-Potočari Memorial Center and Cemetery

Laura Beth Cohen

Introduction

Signed by all parties in November 1995, the General Framework Agreement on Peace (also known as the Dayton Peace Agreement) brought an end to the 1992–1995 Bosnian War.[1] Trials for accused war criminals continue to be heard by courts at the international, national, entity, and canton levels for a wide range of war crimes and mass atrocities. Importantly, though, while the carnage wrought by armies and militias may have ended, the wars over human rights, history, memory, and commemoration continue to be waged in the fragile socio-political terrain that now defines contemporary Bosnia i Herzegovina (Bosnia). These issues are, in many ways, painful reminders that the conflict is still ongoing between Bosnia's three constituent peoples—Bosnian Muslims (Bošniaks), Bosnian Serbs, and Bosnian Croats—having shifted from a physical war with guns to a political war over memories.

The battle over the memorialization of the 1995 Srebrenica genocide is a potent example of how this process is navigated by local stakeholders. As opposed to trials of high-ranking officers held by the International

Criminal Tribunal for the former Yugoslavia (ICTY)—the primary global justice mechanism for trying those involved in the genocide (in addition to other crimes committed in the region during the 1990s)—lower-ranking perpetrators may never be indicted. Some still reside alongside survivors in their pre-war communities, where they retain positions of political and municipal power. This painful contradiction is apparent in the communal and national battles over the creation of memorials at former sites of atrocity. Given that many outside-imposed transitional justice mechanisms, especially criminal prosecutions, have not lived up to victims' expectations, local justice is interpreted differently and contested frequently at these locations, such as the Srebrenica-Potočari Memorial Center and Cemetery to the Victims of the 1995 Genocide (henceforth Srebrenica Memorial).[2] At their most basic level, the battles about commemoratively marking these sites of atrocity showcase how survivors have sought other avenues to secure justice locally.

I contend that sites of atrocity reveal the ways communities with divisive wartime memories orient themselves to the past, and in so doing shed light on how traumatized post-conflict populations collectively try to rebuild their communities and lives. In the case of Srebrenica, I argue that there has been a positive translation of global justice at the local level in the form of the Srebrenica Memorial. Specifically, I focus upon how the Srebrenica Memorial delivers global justice locally in straightforward as well uncanny ways to reveal the site's subtle contradictions, juxtapositions, and ironies. Importantly, the international community approved the mandate for the Srebrenica Memorial in response to intense lobbying by Srebrenica's survivors, and it is therefore unique. All other Bosnian memorialization initiatives at sites of atrocity are led—and disputed—by the communities in which they are located.

An assessment of the Srebrenica Memorial is therefore rooted in the strategic importance of memorial sites as locally symbolic and practical locations of global justice. Sites of atrocity are particularly important in studying the complexities of nationalized and localized processes of transitional justice in post-conflict societies where the past remains highly contested.[3] Traditional transitional justice scholars emphasize the importance of restoring truth and justice to the victims via state institutions, legal mechanisms, and reconciliation commissions.[4] In contrast, sites of atrocity remain embedded in the community where the crimes happened and where the past is temporally omnipresent.[5] Sites of atrocity are thus an important arena for understanding not only individual but also communal and national memory in the aftermath of war.

This chapter begins with a brief overview of the Srebrenica genocide and the ensuing legal responses, including those of the ICTY and the International Court of Justice (ICJ). In part 2, I analyze the differing ways that "justice" itself is defined as well as the challenges that arise when transitional justice programs, as envisioned by outside actors, are implemented at the local level. In part 3, I examine the problematic nature of contested memory, including the roles that divisive mnemonic communities play during struggles to create memorials at local sites of atrocity. In part 4, I theorize how the "transitional justice imaginary" plays out at local sites of atrocity, simultaneously keeping these communities stuck in the past yet unable to move forward. I conclude with reflections about the ways the Srebrenica Memorial contributes both to the positive and negative aspects of the genocide's memorialization. This includes some thoughts about the significance and challenges of these kinds of site-specific memorialization projects in relationship to other post-conflict transitional justice mechanisms.

Methodology

The primary source material for this chapter was gathered during my ethnographic fieldwork in Bosnia during 2011 and subsequent visits in 2012 and 2015. (Subsequent data from fieldwork conducted in 2016 has not been included in this chapter.) My qualitative data included site visits, photographic documentation, and property mapping of the Srebrenica Memorial and other 1992–1995 Bosnian War sites of atrocity located elsewhere in the Srebrenica municipality. I also documented and conducted participant observation at public commemorative events related to the Srebrenica genocide (in Bosnia) as well as alternative commemorative events held by the Bosnian Serb community. My research encompassed numerous visits to the Srebrenica Memorial, including a review of its daily operations as well as independent investigations and guided tours with survivors, staff members, and former Dutch United Nations (UN) Peacekeepers.

I interviewed thirty-two individuals across six different groups using purposive and snowball sampling. These included meetings with the

Srebrenica Memorial's staff; domestic academics, experts, and representatives of civil society organizations; national staff members and government ministers; staff members from national and international non-governmental organizations; international staff members of the Bosnian War Crimes Chamber; residents of Srebrenica; and members of local victims associations. I visited seven of the Srebrenica genocide execution sites on 13 July 2012 with the three different groups of Mothers of Srebrenica,[6] and in July 2015 I attended the twentieth anniversary commemoration of the Srebrenica genocide, where I was able to investigate renovations currently underway at the Srebrenica Memorial. I used a grounded theory approach to analyze my findings, having organized them using various qualitative coding schemes to identify topics and patterns related to the study.

Part 1: War, Genocide, and Aftermath

The Bosnian War began on 6 April 1992 in Sarajevo. It followed the Socialist Republic of Bosnia i Herzegovina's 1992 referendum to formally secede from the Socialist Federal Republic of Yugoslavia—thus becoming the Republic of Bosnia i Herzegovina.[7] This declaration galvanized Serbia, led by then prime minister Slobodan Milosević, to declare war,[8] using the Yugoslav People's Army (JNA) as Serbia's proxy along with the Bosnian Serb Army (VRS) and independent Serbian and Bosnian Serb militias, led by Ratko Mladić and Radovan Karadžić.[9] The Drina Valley (Podrinje) is the eastern part of Bosnia that borders Serbia, and it is here that the VRS and its associated militias first began their campaign of ethnic cleansing (*etničko čišćenje*) upon the war's outbreak.[10] Formerly home to 37,000 residents of various ethnicities with a majority of Bošniak inhabitants, the VRS sought to ethnically cleanse the entire Srebrenica municipality (*opština*) and other neighbouring areas of all Bošniaks.[11]

In 1993 the Srebrenica enclave was declared one of six humanitarian "Safe Areas" by UN Security Council Resolutions 819 and 824.[12] On 11 July 1995, the enclave, theoretically under the protection of the Dutch UN Peacekeeping Battalion (or "DutchBat"), was overrun by the VRS. Between 11 and 22 July 1995, nearly half of the Bošniak men and boys who fled through the forest, and nearly all the men and boys gathered in the exterior surroundings of the former Yugoslav-era battery factory (the UN's peacekeeping headquarters)—approximately 8,372 in total—were

2.1 Plaque inside the cemetery portion of the Srebrenica Memorial, Laura Beth Cohen, July 2012.

systematically executed.[13] Women and girls were forcibly bused to Tuzla, located in the then free territory controlled by the Army of Bosnia i Herzegovina (ARBiH).

These killings became the single largest massacre to take place on the European continent since World War Two,[14] and the ICTY formally declared them genocide during the Radislav Krstić case.[15] A controversial debate has long raged about whether the DutchBat leadership knew what was happening right in front of their eyes.[16] Separately, in 2007, the ICJ followed up with its own ruling regarding Serbia's involvement in the Srebrenica genocide. The ICJ held that, while Serbia was not responsible for actually committing the genocide, the country did, in fact, violate its obligations under the UN Convention on the Prevention and Punishment of the Crime of Genocide (Genocide Convention).[17] Most significantly, following the signing of the Dayton Peace Agreement in 1995, the Srebrenica *opština* was assigned to the entity of the Republika Srpska (RS) governed by Bosnian Serb authorities.[18]

Part 2: Interpreting Global Justice Locally

In the wake of the unimaginable human slaughter committed by the Nazis during World War Two, the quest for justice continues to take centre stage, a legacy of the International Military Tribunal at Nuremberg.[19] Modern iterations of these international criminal tribunals (ICT), such as the International Criminal Court, the International Criminal Tribunal for Rwanda, and the ICTY, as well as hybrid international-national courts (such as the Special Court for Sierra Leone and the Extraordinary Chambers in the Courts of Cambodia), have been created in the aftermath of such wanton and intentional brutality. They focus on the identification and prosecution of war criminals when governments commit massive human rights violations and atrocities—such as crimes against humanity, genocide, and war crimes—against their own populations (depending upon an individual ICT's mandate). Simultaneously, these ICTs can also be interpreted as an attempt to assuage the guilt of these same international actors for not having prevented the atrocities in the first place.[20] As they relate to the adjudication of genocide, crimes against humanity, and other crimes of war in the international arena, ICTs, according to David Koller, are a blend of both *legal doctrine* (i.e., holding perpetrators legally accountable by the standards of international criminal and humanitarian law) and *realpolitik* (i.e., the political decisions, considerations, and negotiations of state actors involved in their creation).[21] The establishment of these ICTs is premised on the twin beliefs that, by bringing accused senior-level criminals to trial, this may both act as a deterrent to future crimes and deliver some sort of justice to the aggrieved population.[22]

Yet what exactly defines justice? The "justice" literature is immense in its scope, offering diverse legal and normative interpretations as well as alternative conceptions, especially as it relates to transitional justice mechanisms.[23] For example, Kingsley Chiedu Moghalu explains that justice, in its most basic and conceptual form, can be interpreted in two ways. The first is through the lens of *equality*: "The equal distribution and application of rights and privileges" among all peoples in a given society.[24] The second is through the lens of *formality*: "The specific context of the equality of such rights and privileges before the law."[25] Moghalu then describes three normative and interconnected levels of justice that also exist within international society. These include *international/interstate justice* (i.e., "the rights and duties of sovereign states in international relations on the basis of sovereign equality"); *individual or human justice* (i.e., "the rights and duties of individuals as subjects, not just objects, of international law"); and *cosmopolitan or world justice* (i.e., that which "embodies a radical transnational extension of individual justice").[26]

Jeremy Webber offers another typology—this one on the different types of justice in actual practice. He argues there are three kinds of justice operating at various times: "retrospective (backward-looking); prospective (forward-looking); and the adjustment of contending legal and political orders."[27] *Retrospective* justice is retributive in nature and deals with the legal righting of past wrongs, mostly through criminal trials.[28] *Prospective* justice (also known as *restorative* or *distributive* justice) is community-oriented and seeks to repair post-conflict damage through trials and other non-judicial forms, including truth-telling commissions, reparations, restitution, and memorialization projects, among others.[29] The third form of justice, *reforming the "legal and political order,"* refers to institutional reforms as well as other democracy building and rule of law initiatives that aim to rebuild the formal structure of the post-conflict society so that both retrospective and prospective justice can flourish within the domestic context.[30] What is referred to as *transitional justice* may include a combination of initiatives, including criminal prosecutions; memorialization/memory projects, memorials and commemorations; truth-telling/truth commissions; monetary reparations; institutional reform and lustration; and restitution.[31] However, there are a range of concerns about and issues with the ways that transitional justice is envisioned, translated, and administered, as I will show.

Another way of conceiving of justice is how it plays out in the courtroom. Here, too, there are differing interpretations. At one end of the spectrum is Hannah Arendt's belief that justice, as delivered through criminal trials, should strictly follow the law to the exclusion of all other considerations, including the background context of the crimes and why things unfolded as they did.[32] This view, known as *legal formalism*, is founded upon a strict interpretation of the way the law is supposed to function in democratic societies: using only primary evidence and concrete facts to determine the accused's guilt or innocence through an established set of rules, procedures, and relationships between the defendant, prosecution, lawyers, and judges.[33] Legal formalists believe that these decisions should be made without reference to social, political, historical, philosophical, or moral considerations.[34]

For Pierre Bourdieu, however, there is a sociological aspect to the practice of law that does, in fact, influence how it is interpreted, communicated, and practised. This "juridical field" includes the implicit social conventions, values, and traditions followed by those who work within it. As Richard Terdiman explains, "[This] internal politics of the profession exercises its own specific and pervasive influence on every aspect of the law's functioning outside the professional body itself."[35] Moreover, when we take account of the differences between systems of civil and common law, as well as the socio-cultural, legal, and political variances in individual countries, it is little wonder that the definition of justice remains so elusive.[36]

Beyond the emphasis on criminal trials, victims and survivors continue to call for these investigations to illuminate the truth of what happened and to increase efforts to locate their still-missing loved ones so they are able to bury and commemorate them.[37] This dichotomy between, on the one hand, the international community's desire to "help" traumatized populations rebuild in the aftermath of war and, on the other hand, the need for survivors to reclaim their agency, humanity, and voice, creates resistance.[38] This struggle reflects the differing priorities and methods of outside actors, national governments, and local communities all struggling to make sense of what has happened and to provide recourse. It also includes the challenges of top-down approaches, often led by outsiders, and bottom-up initiatives conceived of at the grassroots level. Anna Lowenhaupt Tsing defines such "friction" as "the awkward, unequal, unstable, and creative qualities of interconnection across difference."[39]

The prevailing assumption is that these transitional justice mechanisms—specifically ICTs—have a positive influence on survivors by delivering justice.[40] However, according to Miklos Biro et al., "For many survivors, justice may not mean trials but a much more personal sense of what they need in order to move on with their lives."[41] Eric Stover further posits that justice is not a monolithic concept; in fact, it must consist of several components in order to resonate with survivors. These include consultations between internal and external actors, including victims; clearly defined aims; a mixture of international and national judicial solutions; implementation of additional transitional justice mechanisms, such as truth commissions and memorials; and social justice considerations to help survivors move on with their present-day lives.[42] Hugo van der Merwe's postulation about the fuzzy definition of justice is equally illuminating. He notes that

> a number of factors may feed into a sense that justice has been done. At a simplistic level is the issue of whether victims feel that perpetrators have been sufficiently punished. But a more inclusive approach could also consider the sense of vindication provided by the punishment, whether victims have a better understanding of how they came to be victimized, their ability to regain a sense of power relative to the perpetrator, or the reestablishment of a sense of meaning in society, which may have been destroyed by the victimization.[43]

These competing visions of what defines post-conflict transitional justice programs complicate the meaning of justice for local survivors.[44] Calls for reparations, as well as social justice (including economic reforms), and/or locally relevant interpretations of justice, can also offer meaningful and practical alternatives.[45] For example, John Torpey advances the argument that "reparation politics" are a more comprehensive way of envisioning and achieving transitional justice's aims. His typology of reparations emphasizes "communicative history" (i.e., "memory, memorials, and historical consciousness") as the overarching mechanism, followed by apologies, reparations, and, finally, transitional justice. He also argues that demands for reparations occur in both post-conflict societies as well as those of long-established liberal democracies (such as, for example, calls for reparations by indigenous populations).[46]

Centred in between these disparate perspectives is the oft-ignored positive impact of memorialization. Beyond the pro-democratic efforts to bring the rule of law and justice to societies in the aftermath of collective violence, the role of memorialization allows survivors to have a voice in the rebuilding of their society, according to Rosalind Shaw and Lars Waldorf.[47] This is because memorials function on a broader socio-political plane, rather than within the "narrow definition of symbolic reparation."[48] Additionally, because so much of the debate is negotiated at the local level, what shall be remembered and what shall be forgotten must be negotiated there since it is the community itself that must find a way to achieve civil relations. Outside actors with memorialization expertise must therefore be respectful of the community's needs, regardless of the outcome.[49]

Localizing Global Justice in Srebrenica

The ICTY is the primary international criminal justice mechanism for trying high-level perpetrators of crimes committed during the wars in the Balkans during the 1990s, including the Srebrenica genocide.[50] While the Tribunal's prosecutors included the count of genocide in several different cases concerning massacres committed throughout Bosnia, Krstić was the first man to be convicted of the crime of genocide in Srebrenica.[51] A large discursive body of literature has focused on the myriad issues related to all aspects of the ICTY, including its Western-derived emphasis on the rule of law and delivery of justice as a form of democracy promotion. Issues have been raised about which cases it decided to pursue; its outreach programs and treatment of victims before, during, and after the trials; its acquittals, convictions, and sentencing of perpetrators; its inability to generate a comprehensive factual history of the Bosnian War; its handling of evidence; and its often conflicting judicial decisions for similar crimes in different cases.[52] While the ICTY is set to permanently close down in 2017, its ongoing critical functions will be transferred to the United Nations Mechanism for International Criminal Tribunals.[53]

As it relates to the Srebrenica genocide, the case against Mladić is still underway. Mladić is currently in custody in The Hague, indicted for both his role in masterminding the Srebrenica genocide and "persecutions, extermination, murder, deportation, inhumane acts, terror, unlawful attacks, [and the] taking of hostages."[54] His case is expected to conclude before the ICTY closes down. In March 2016, Karadžić was convicted of "genocide, crimes against humanity and violations of the laws or customs of war committed by Serb forces during the armed conflict in Bosnia ... from 1992 until 1995" and received a sentence of forty years imprisonment.[55] Despite all of its issues and controversies, the ICTY still remains the single most influential global justice mechanism related to the Srebrenica genocide. Yet for the majority of Srebrenica's survivors, the justice the ICTY has delivered remains hollow.[56]

However, as Sarah Wagner has argued, a second global justice mechanism was also created at the behest of the American president Bill Clinton in the form of the International Commission on Missing Persons (ICMP).[57] Upon discovery of the hundreds of mass graves littered throughout the Podrinje, the ICMP eventually took up the role of exhuming these human remains while simultaneously developing an extensive DNA forensic identification process to identify the victims; providing evidentiary documentation to the ICTY; and eventually returning the mortal remains of the victims to their surviving families.[58] However, as is the case with the ICTY, the ICMP's work, despite its mandate of neutrality and its emphasis on recovering the remains of all persons killed regardless of their ethnicity, has also been controversial.[59]

Ongoing issues relating to the exhumations and DNA analyses notwithstanding, I argue that the creation of the Srebrenica Memorial is a tangible translation of global justice at the local level. The story of how the Srebrenica Memorial came into existence is one of devotion, perseverance, fearlessness, and, ultimately, hope, etched into a hostile landscape by grieving families in honour of their loved ones killed during the genocide. Upon the horrifying realization that their male relatives were dead, the Mothers became insistent on finding out the truth.[60] As the mass graves were discovered and the bones of the dead exhumed and identified, the Mothers wanted these mortal remains to receive a dignified burial. Nor did they want the cemetery to be located in the Federation of Bosnia i Herzegovina, far away from their original homes, even though the Federation is where many of Srebrenica's survivors now reside.[61] Between 1997 and 2003, and with the financial support of the ICMP as well as from other individual countries, over ten thousand petitions from the surviving women were collected to pressure the international community and the Office of the High Representative (OHR) to designate the land for the Srebrenica Memorial in Potočari.[62] Potočari is the manufacturing village located 9 kilometres from Srebrenica (also in the RS) where the battery factory is located and, thus, where the fleeing refugees last saw their relatives alive.

Between 1997 and 2000, the families of the victims decided that they wanted to commemorate the dead and mark the location of Potočari with their presence at least once a year. Between 2001 and 2007, a series of decrees and laws took effect to realize the Srebrenica Memorial's creation.[63] The most significant and high profile event takes place each 11 July to commemorate the day the Srebrenica enclave was "cleansed." These surviving women—grandmothers, mothers, wives, daughters, sisters, aunts, and nieces—have become the international face of the genocide's aftermath. They have garnered tremendous political agency, lobbying international and national politicians on behalf of their dead, which has aided the community's recovery.[64]

Vernacularization in Practice

The Srebrenica Memorial, as defined by Srebrenica's surviving female population, is a concrete example of how global justice can be translated into a locally relevant expression and mechanism of justice. Its success is due to what Peggy Levitt and Sally Merry refer to as "vernacularization," which they define as "the process of appropriation and local adoption of globally generated ideas and strategies."[65] The Srebrenica Memorial's distinctiveness is derived from its synthesis of a cemetery, the battery factory, and memorial room (*Spomen Soba*). It is a site of atrocity, a site for interring, visiting, mourning, remembering, reflecting, and teaching. With support from the international community—weighed down by its guilty conscience—Srebrenica's survivors fought and secured the land and buildings in Potočari. They struggled to prove that their loved ones existed, to ensure they would never be forgotten, and to create a place where memory of the genocide would be evoked for generations to come—a place of unimaginable sadness, but also of perpetual remembrance.

Driving up the mountain into Srebrenica, you are surrounded by forests and rebuilt houses. You see many devastated buildings but also a community attempting to come back to life amidst a challenging economic environment. Srebrenica's natural beauty aside, the eye is constantly drawn to the mixture of rebuilt and bombed-out homes. The tall yellow building that used to be Srebrenica's main hotel is abandoned to its fate of crumbling ruins. Many of the houses sit silently unoccupied since their inhabitants were expelled, moved away, or murdered. The Bosnian War's legacy continues to cast a shadow over nearly every aspect of the population's lives, regardless of ethnicity. In Srebrenica, the war's lingering aftermath, as well as the ensuing political, economic, and socio-cultural problems, are further shrouded by the town's infamy. Most significantly, the differing narratives and interpretations of the Srebrenica genocide hover just below the surface, despite the fact that residents get along and cooperate with one another on a daily basis.[66] While the creation of the Srebrenica Memorial represents global justice translated locally, an ethno-nationalized

2.2 Contemporary Srebrenica, Laura Beth Cohen, July 2011.

atmosphere, including genocide denial, is very much alive, especially in the days and weeks leading up to the annual 11 July commemoration as well as during elections, when politicians dredge up the war's wounds for their own personal gain. Seeing the Srebrenica Memorial through a different lens—one that acknowledges the complex political environment in which it operates and contributes—is therefore key.

Part 3: Contested Memories and Memorialization at the Srebrenica Memorial

It is important to understand the dynamics underlying contested memories in post-conflict settings where war pits different groups against each other. This kind of catastrophic and life-altering breakdown of communal relations during the conflict can all too easily resurface in the postwar environment as complex yet stereotypical categorizations of, for example, victims, survivors, perpetrators, and bystanders, become entrenched.[67] To understand how these polarized interpretations of what transpired take hold, we first need to understand how collective memories are formed. Our individual memories become fused with those of our wider social circle throughout the course of our lives. United through shared memories and perspectives, a new sort of grouping—what Benedict Anderson calls an "imagined community"—is formed.[68] "Community", though, does not necessarily have to be based upon members of the same group living in the same territory. To Hannah Arendt, for example, the concept of nation

> relates not so much, and not primarily, to a piece of land as to the space between individuals in a group whose members are bound to and at the same time separated and protected from, each other by all kinds of relationships, based on common language, religion, a common history, customs, and laws. Such relationships become spatially manifest insofar as they themselves constitute the space wherein the different members of a group relate to and have intercourse with each other.[69]

Moreover, as Yael Zerubavel argues, "The power of collective memory does not lie in its accurate, systematic, or sophisticated mapping of the past, but in establishing basic images that articulate and reinforce a particular ideological stance."[70] Finding common ground between opposing groups with different and highly charged interpretations of the past becomes all the more challenging. These manipulated historical narratives are translated into invented myths around which ethnic groups organize their identity, often becoming replacements for the facts.[71]

In other words, when it comes to highly polarized memories about mass atrocities, what one mnemonic community (such as victims and survivors) believes and/or remembers to be true is refuted or inverted by the other mnemonic group (such as the community to which the perpetrators belong but who may also be victims and survivors in their own right). In this binary, identifying with the victims would mean a negation of the opposing group's own methods of self-protection and preservation—denying the crimes committed in their name; their deeply held convictions about what took place; and their own mythologized, perceived and/or real suffering. As Eviatar Zerubavel observes, "Each of the different parties waging such heated mnemonic battles tends to regard its own historical narrative, which is normally based on its own typically one-sided 'time maps,' as the only correct one, which is quite understandable given the unmistakably partisan political agenda it is specifically designed to promote."[72] These debates over contested memories reinforce the fact that memory is personal and subjective. For even when the "facts" have been proven, what is considered the "historical truth," according to Iwona Irwin-Zarecka, "is being contested ... and the otherwise quiet presence of the past is disturbed."[73]

The discourse about the creation of memorial sites at sites of atrocity emphasizes their historic, symbolic, forensic, and educational significance. Nora fashioned the term *lieux de mémoire* as the difference between a nation's historical consciousness (*millieux de mémoire*) and "objects [that] are part of everyday experience: cemeteries, museums, commemorations."[74] In post-conflict countries where history is contested, these *lieux de mémoire* take on a new significance: they act as locations for grieving, for remembrance, for closure, for historical memory, for documentation, for artistry, for reinterpretation, for communal dialogue, for collective identity, for healing, for education, and sadly, for political manipulation.[75] The distortions of ethnic narratives and myths frequently play out where the mass atrocities took place, easily becoming a front line of aggression.[76] The singling out of a particular perpetrator group, if they are included, can further fuel the creation of a hostile counter-narrative to deflect blame.[77] And yet, as Martha Minow notes, "Public disputes over proposed and existing memorials may occasion the productive if painful kind of struggle for memory as do rights over reparations."[78] The need to memorialize a difficult past as well as counteract the vicious denial and contestation it elicits is therefore a critical component of transitional justice and memorialization initiatives at both the macro and micro levels.[79]

The Srebrenica Memorial through the Looking Glass

Despite the war having ended two decades ago, memorialization remains contentious in Bosnia.[80] Regardless of ethnicity, the war has exacted a painful toll upon the population and memories of the conflict are still raw and divisive. What stands out about the innumerable local memorials across the country is the way they commemorate the dead and missing by emphasizing the victimhood of each ethnic group, further reinforcing that "they did this to us," and fortifying the seeds of future discontent, conflict, and revenge.[81] In this way memory, including whose memory should be preserved, is vigorously contested—and this includes battles over whether the genocide even took place. These mnemonic battles directly affect the climate in which the Srebrenica Memorial exists. This is likely one of the reasons that the memorial's steering committee, in an attempt to avoid drawing any further attention to the site, has tried to maintain its primary purpose as a cemetery where the dead are buried and whose identities are ascertained through DNA analysis each year. Ironically, the Srebrenica Memorial's modus operandi winds up mimicking the silence surrounding the crimes and the related taboo of speaking about them that is prevalent in the community the other 364 days of the year (the exception being the annual 11 July commemoration). This is especially true since the site is already a metaphorical battlefield of traumatic collective memory.[82] Moreover, while the Srebrenica Memorial is open to visitors of all religious backgrounds, the cemetery's design showcases that it is first and foremost Muslim in its orientation. (The role of religion at the site, including the designation of all victims buried there as martyrs (*šehidi*), has also caused debate among the surviving community as well, and is an important issue in its own right.)[83]

The site, according to its mandate,[84] focuses on the facts of the Srebrenica genocide (as "proven" by the ICTY).[85] All parts of the Srebrenica Memorial reinforce this; only the plight of the Srebrenica enclave's fleeing refugees and their subsequent deportation and execution beginning in July 1995 are described. Bosnian Serb citizens are not vilified. The *Spomen Soba's* installations were updated in advance of the twentieth anniversary of the genocide. There are informational placards describing the crimes committed by various Bosnian Serb military leaders who were convicted by the ICTY; a variety of wartime pictures of fleeing refugees, the exhumations of mass graves, controversial DutchBat graffiti; aerial footage of the property during July 1995; and boards explaining the complexities of conducting DNA identifications on the human remains found in primary, secondary, and tertiary mass graves. A documentary film, numerous photographs of personal artifacts found in the graves, and biographies of twenty of the victims underscore the genocide's scale as well as individual familial loss.[86] A separate building located in the cemetery includes information on how to locate specific graves as well as a small conference room featuring photographs of the exhumations of mass graves taken by the Bosnian photographer Tarik Samarah.[87] In addition, in 2014 a new multimedia room,

2.3 Green temporary grave markers, Srebrenica, Laura Beth Cohen, July 2011.

the Documentation Center Srebrenica, was created in partnership with the SENSE News Agency. It features interactive displays and computer terminals for students to conduct research about the Srebrenica genocide and related ICTY trials.[88]

Because of the site's strict interpretation of its decree, it is difficult for a visitor to get a broader picture of life in Srebrenica *opština* from the start of the war onward. Posing this question brings up a larger controversy of whether or not it is possible for the Srebrenica Memorial to extend its narrative to include the larger story of what happened in the enclave between 1992 and 1995. This includes the extensive civilian suffering in the few hundred Bošniak villages razed to the ground and ethnically cleansed during the first months of the war; conflicting interpretations about DutchBat's role before and during the genocide; and attacks against Bosnian Serb villages during the ARBiH's defence of Srebrenica—all of which remain vigorously contested.[89]

Part 4: The Srebrenica Memorial as Unmistakably Uncanny

The same transitional justice mechanisms designed, in part, to help survivors and victims find closure and justice often exacerbate the societal conundrums they profess to resolve and the healing processes they aim to foster. Alexander Hinton refers to this as the "transitional justice imaginary," which he defines as "normative (i.e., it is associated with certain truth claims and moral-laden assumptions); performative (i.e., through its enactment, people constitute an imagined community); and productive (i.e., the imaginary produces certain subject positions and types of being)."[90] One key aspect of the transitional justice imaginary, according to Hinton, is the creation of "transitional justice time" that is "premised on a value-laden pre-post state of conflict and teleological movement between them."[91] In other words, transitional justice mechanisms, such as criminal prosecutions and truth commissions, often narrow their scope to a particular period of time, excluding everything that happened before and after the conflict. As a result, broader historical circumstances leading up to the hostilities, ongoing contestations of memory between clashing mnemonic communities, and continuing human rights violations in the post-conflict society go unrecognized. Taken together, this impacts the aggregate community's ability to come to terms with what happened while ensuring that traumatic memories keep survivors frozen in time, unable to move on (to the degree they are able) with their lives.[92]

As such, psychic trauma and transitional justice time blur the lines between the past and present so that life becomes a state of unending liminality.[93] Time in the lives of traumatized populations and individuals can therefore take on uncanny characteristics. According to Sigmund Freud, "The 'uncanny' is that class of the terrifying which leads back to something long known to us, once very familiar. ... On the other hand, everything is uncanny that ought to have remained hidden and secret, yet comes to light."[94] Another way of conceiving how the uncanny is omnipresent in survivors' lives is Franz Kafka's concept of "Odradek" in his short story, "The Cares of a Family Man":

> One is tempted to believe that the creature [Odradek] once had some sort of intelligible shape and is now only a broken-down remnant. Yet this does not seem to be the case; at least there is no sign of it; nowhere is there an unfinished or unbroken surface to suggest anything of the kind; the whole thing looks senseless enough, but in its own way perfectly finished. In any case, closer scrutiny is impossible, since Odradek is extraordinary nimble and can never be laid hold of. Often for months on end he is not to be seen; then he has presumably moved into other houses; but he always comes faithfully back to our house again.[95]

Taken together, the concepts of transitional justice time, the uncanny, and "Odradek" are highly relevant to how the Srebrenica genocide's traumatic legacy continues to haunt survivors and perpetrators—thus directly impacting the Srebrenica Memorial. For as John Borneman comments,

> Loss that becomes traumatic is characterized by not having been experienced at the time of the occurrence. During an ethnic cleansing, some central aspect of the loss remains unregistered and escapes recognition at the actual time of happening; language and the ordering mechanisms of the symbolic order fail to register what is often called "the unspeakable." In other words, the event

is only, if at all, experienced later as it returns to the victim, unbidden, frequently as a horrifying silence that cannot be spoken.[96]

The Uncanny Lurks in Srebrenica

For the survivors still searching for the mortal remains of their family members, the annual 11 July commemoration does not provide closure. The lack of knowledge about their loved ones—what, specifically, happened to them—still haunts the survivors. Without a body (or body parts) to bury, the person is still considered missing and not yet officially dead.[97] Because community records were also destroyed during the war, there is no tangible proof that the missing person ever existed.[98] There is not a single place that the families can go to mourn for those still missing, something acutely felt by those Bošniaks who believe that their dead must receive a proper religious burial in accordance with their faith.[99] In the past several years, Bošniak women continue the commemoration on 13 July by visiting other Srebrenica genocide massacre sites across the Podrinje. Local Bosnian Serb inhabitants and the RS authorities make it difficult for the Mothers of Srebrenica to visit these buildings and fields located in Branjevo, Orahovac, Kravica, Petkovici, Grbavci, Pilica, Kozluk, and Nova Kasaba. Visiting these sites is complicated, made difficult since their locations are deep within the countryside where many are accessible only by dirt roads.

These sites are located within a two-hour drive from Srebrenica, and in the intense heat of July you are eerily reminded of the terror that the victims must have experienced while being driven to their deaths—to utterly remote locations, far from their homes, in which the silence of the landscape belied their very existences. Upon reaching these locations, the uncanny takes hold. Residents stare ominously. While a single RS police officer has been assigned to escort two tour buses transporting the Mothers, a few other RS police officers are posted in some of the communities ostensibly to keep residents from antagonizing the mourners. The presence of these officers does not provide a level of comfort judging from the way they tend to glare at the mourners; in fact, at the former Petkovici aluminum factory dam, the men standing atop the imposing gravel structure staring down at the Mothers were local guards who control access to the site—and not the police.[100] It is as if all this happened once before. But we are in the present day. The bus to Kravica is delayed for over an hour by the local authorities, who attempt to prevent this small commemoration from taking place (in both 2015 and 2016, the Mothers were allowed inside the property). In the case of Grbavci, the school has been renovated and is now used, once again, by local schoolchildren.

Other sites, such as the cultural centre (*dom kulture*) in Pilica, have been left as they were when the massacres were committed. Bullet holes still riddle the walls and the building decays while flowers from the Mothers' previous visit lay rotting on the floor. (In 2016, graffiti glorifying Mladić and Milosević as well as other hostile messages were sprayed onto the walls.) The field where the Branjevo pig farm used to be is surrounded by newly rebuilt homes filled with young, mostly Bosnian Serb, families. In the case of the above-mentioned dam, miscellaneous shell casings can still be found lying on the ground amidst the growing foliage. Of all these sites, only one—Nova Kasaba, a former soccer field—has a small yet somewhat obscure memorial plaque.[101] And yet, without the Mothers' insistence upon commemorating these sites every year, they would, in fact, be utterly forgotten. As Lara Nettelfield and Sarah Wagner note, "The act of visiting these sites was even more important given that the effort to deny the crimes in Srebrenica [has] increased in recent years."[102]

Odradek Skulks at the Srebrenica Memorial

Once a year on 11 July the world remembers the genocide and tens of thousands of people gather at the Srebrenica Memorial to participate in the annual commemoration. But the next day, the masses leave and Srebrenica's residents go back to the quiet routine of life in this small town. Yet, you can still sense the silence—that which is not talked about. The uncanny blows through the air as "Odradek" makes his presence felt yet again. One of the biggest questions hovering over the Srebrenica Memorial concerns the dwindling number of remains being identified and laid to rest each year; at some point soon there may no longer be anyone left to bury. It is a prospect few in Srebrenica's survivor community are willing to tolerate, but nonetheless, it too lingers over the survivors as yet another incarnation of the way their traumas and fears keeps them frozen in time. As Isaias Rojas-Perez observed during his work among traumatized populations in post-conflict villages in Peru, "Perhaps no other figure than the *desaparecido* [the missing] so clearly inhabits the temporality of the finished/

unfinished past of the post-conflict state."[103] Acute trauma is also a theme in Linda Green's research on Guatemala's post-conflict female survivors:

> Fear, like pain, is overwhelmingly present to the person experiencing it but it may be barely perceptible to anyone else and almost defies objectification. Subjectively, the mundane experience of chronic fear wears down one's sensibility to it. … The routinization of fear undermines one's confidence in interpreting the world.[104]

As it relates to the Srebrenica genocide, the liminal aspect of this contested memory may actually keep both communities locked into a specific period of time: that which is most painful and controversial and less focused on the here and now. For those survivors still hoping that their beloved's mortal remains will be found, the Srebrenica Memorial is first and foremost a site of remembrance. Because the property includes both the cemetery and the battery factory, the preservation of the genocide's "material remains" works as a powerful method for its survivors to "etch" their memory into the landscape.[105] In addition, the Srebrenica Memorial's significance as a site of atrocity, combined with the survivors' need to find closure on their pre-war lands, strengthens the site's importance for future generations.[106] However, the site cannot be depoliticized unless the society finds a way to separate out the war's facts, including the suffering of the entire population, from prevailing ethno-political beliefs about what took place and who did what to whom.[107]

Concluding Thoughts

In war's aftermath, a post-conflict country struggles to find a balance between sincere attempts to articulate the past and assertions that are founded upon falsities and denial—a balance that must be achieved if a single encompassing narrative is to be forged.[108] Localized transitional justice mechanisms, including non-prosecutorial initiatives led by outside actors, are essential, since the process, which can take a long time to accomplish (if ever), requires a concerted effort by national politicians, civil-society actors, and the general populace.[109] The battle over the truth takes centre stage because there are many conflicting versions of the past. Two decades is still a relatively short period of time for Bosnian society to recover politically, economically, and socio-culturally. The acute ethnocentric climate as well as the numerous destroyed buildings and villages that still dot the countryside are painful reminders that the war is still going on—just in a different expression. Lower-level war criminals still reside within some of the villages in the Srebrenica municipality, and in some locations Mladić is celebrated as a war hero.[110]

The Srebrenica Memorial remains on the front lines of this battle between history and memorialization: it is a visceral reminder of the 1995 genocide and the horrors of the 1992–1995 Bosnian War. Crucially, though, the memory it keeps alive can only go so far. For Srebrenica's survivors, whose loved ones remain missing, the physical pain and psychic limbo continues. Without mortal remains to bury, it is as if these victims never existed, except within the hearts and souls of those who loved them most. These survivors continue to commemorate their dead and missing by visiting remote fields and buildings where executions took place. For survivors, the war remains very much alive in their society because justice, as delivered through the transitional justice framework of criminal prosecutions, has not yet been served and may very well never be. Nonetheless, the Srebrenica Memorial and the annual 11 July commemoration continue to raise awareness and keep the memory of the genocide alive as part of Bosnia's struggle to address the war's horrific past. So although the pursuance of justice through the ICTY remains fraught, the reality is that a locally relevant and vernacularized version of global justice has, in fact, been delivered in the form of the Srebrenica Memorial despite the complexities it embodies.

Looking at the mnemonic battles waged at the Srebrenica Memorial allows us to appreciate the complexities and challenges that both survivors and perpetrators face in reconciling the war's traumatic and contested legacy. Memorial sites are but one integral transitional justice mechanism that post-conflict societies may embrace in order to reconcile the past with the present. Memorials at sites of atrocity around the world, including the Srebrenica Memorial, are locations where post-conflict countries confront the harshest realities of war and tyranny. These symbolic and highly charged memorialized sites are locations where past animosities are confronted, including the reasons why the conflict erupted in the first place.[111] Essential, then, is the linkage between memorials and other transitional justice endeavours, undertaken by all actors involved, in order to support rather than destabilize each other.[112]

As one of the original expressions of localized justice within Bosnia, the Srebrenica Memorial sits at the forefront of the society's painful reckonings as they attempt to clear the past and find their way to a more peaceful—or, at the very least, empathetic—future together. The site's foundation remains a constructive, albeit complicated, spot, even though its very existence directly challenges those who continue to deny that the genocide took place. Unfortunately, until politicians in Bosnia's two entity-level governments as well as that of the Bosnian federal state embark upon more concerted and integrated efforts to delve into the war's horrors and to provide some tangible measure of justice and healing for the population, the Srebrenica Memorial's growth in this area will remain stilted. And until things change, "Odradek" will continue hovering over Srebrenica's darkest spaces.

NOTES

1   Laura Silber and Allan Little, *The Death of Yugoslavia* (London: Penguin, 1995); US Department of State, *General Framework Agreement for Peace in Bosnia and Herzegovina*, Dayton, Ohio, 21 November 1995.

2   Joanna Mannergren Selimović, "Perpetrators and Victims: Local Responses to the International Criminal Tribunal for the Former Yugoslavia," *Focaal: Journal of Global and Historical Anthropology* 57 (2010): 50–61; Gentian Zyberi and Jernej Letnar Černič, "Transitional Justice Processes and Reconciliation in the Former Yugoslavia: Challenges and Prospects," *Nordic Journal of Human Rights* 33, no. 2 (2015): 132–157.

3   Brandon Hamber, "Utopian Dreams or Practical Possibilities? The Challenges of Evaluating the Impact of Memorialization in Societies in Transition," *International Journal of Transitional Justice* 4, no. 3 (2010): 397–420; Marita Sturken, "Pilgrimages, Reenactment and Souvenirs: Modes of Memory Tourism," in *Rites of Return: Diaspora Poetics and the Politics of Memory*, eds. Marianne Hirsch and Nancy K. Miller (New York: Columbia University Press, 2011), 283.

4   Roger Duthie, "Afterword: The Consequence of Transitional Justice in Particular Contexts," in *Transitional Justice: Global Mechanisms and Local Realities after Genocide and Mass Violence*, ed. Alexander Laban Hinton (New Brunswick, NJ: Rutgers University Press, 2010), 249; Siri Gloppen, "Roads to Reconciliation: A Conceptual Framework," in *Roads to Reconciliation*, eds. Elin Skaar, Siri Gloppen, and Astri Suhrke (Lanham, MD: Lexington Books, 2005), 38; Priscilla B. Hayner, *Unspeakable Truths: Transitional Justice and the Challenge of Truth Commissions* (New York: Routledge, 2010), 8.

5   Judy Barsalou and Victoria Baxter, *The Urge to Remember: The Role of Memorials in Social Reconstruction and Transitional Justice* (Washington, DC: United States Institute of Peace, 2007), 6; Kjetil Sandvik, "Crime Scenes as Augmented Reality: Models for Enhancing Places Emotionally by Means of Narratives, Fictions and Virtual Reality,"

in *Re-Investing Authenticity: Tourism, Place and Emotions*, eds. Britta Timm Knudsen and Anne Marit Waade (Bristol: Channel View Publications, 2010), 138; Paul Harvey Williams, *Memorial Museums: The Global Rush to Commemorate Atrocities* (Oxford: Berg, 2007), 39.

6   The three groups of Mothers associations are the Mothers of the Enclaves of Srebrenica and Žepa, led by Munira Subašić (based in Sarajevo); the Women of Srebrenica, led by Hajra Ćatić (based in Tuzla); and the Mothers of Srebrenica, led by Hatidža Mehme-dović (based in Srebrenica). Throughout this chapter, I refer to them collectively as the Mothers.

7   Susan L. Woodward, *Balkan Tragedy: Chaos and Dissolution after the Cold War* (Washington, DC: Brookings Institution, 1995), 235.

8   Milosević was indicted for crimes against Bošniaks in Bosnia, Croatia, and Kosovo. On 11 March 2006, he died of a natural death before a verdict was reached. ICTY, "Case Information Sheet: 'Kosovo, Croatia & Bosnia' IT 02-54-Slobodan Milošević," http://www.icty.org/x/cases/slobodan_milosevic/cis/en/cis_milosevic_slobodan_en.pdf (accessed 16 February 2016).

9   Gerard Toal and Toal Dahlman, *Bosnia Remade: Ethnic Cleansing and its Reversal* (Oxford: Oxford University Press, 2011), 7; Woodward, *Balkan Tragedy*, 262.

10 Sarah E. Wagner, *To Know Where He Lies: DNA Technology and the Search for Srebreni-ca's Missing* (Berkeley: University of California Press, 2008), 27.

11 Jan Willem Honig, *Srebrenica: Record of a War Crime* (London: Penguin, 1996), xvii.

12 United Nations Security Council Resolution S/RES/819 (1993) and UNSC Resolution S/RES/824 (1993), http://www.un.org/docs/scres/1993/scres93.htm (accessed 26 February 2016).

13 Honig, *Srebrenica: Record of a War Crime*, 49.

14 The ICTY was established by the UN in 1993 and was the first European war crimes tribunal since the International Military Tribunal in Nuremberg. See ICTY, "About the ICTY," http://www.icty.org/en/about (accessed 16 February 2016).

15 In 2004, Krstić was sentenced to thirty-five years in prison for his role in "aiding and abetting genocide, murders, extermination, and persecutions in Srebrenica." ICTY, "Case Information Sheet: 'Srebrenica-Drina Corps' IT-98-33-Radislav Krstić," http://www.icty.org/x/cases/krstic/cis/en/cis_krstic_en.pdf (accessed 16 February 2016).

16 In 2013, a Srebrenica survivor, Mr. Hasan Nuhanović, won a case against the Dutch government which stated that the latter was responsible for the deaths of the former's brother and father, as well as a third man, in July 1995 because they were evicted by DutchBat from the peacekeeping compound when it was clear that doing so would put their lives in danger. Nuhanović buried his father in July 2011. See International Crimes Database, *The State of the Netherlands v. Hasan Nuhanović*, 6 September 2013, http://www.internationalcrimesdatabase.org/Case/1005/The-Netherlands-v-Nuha-novi%C4%87/ (accessed 16 February 2016). Additionally, in 2014 the Dutch government was found responsible for the deaths of three hundred people during the 1995 Srebren-ica genocide by a civil court in The Hague. See "Dutch State Liable for 300 Srebrenica Massacre Deaths," *Guardian* (London), 16 July 2014, http://www.theguardian.com/world/2014/jul/16/dutch-liable-srebrenica-massacre-deaths (accessed 16 February 2016). An extensive analysis of DutchBat's role during the Srebrenica genocide is outside the scope of this chapter.

17   ICJ, "Case Concerning Application of the Convention on the Prevention and Punish-
      ment of the Crime of Genocide (Bosnia and Herzegovina v. Serbia and Montenegro)
      Judgment," 26 February 2007, http://www.icj-cij.org/docket/files/91/13685.pdf (accessed
      16 February 2016).

18   The Dayton Agreement split the country in half between the three warring groups.
      Postwar Bosnia is one state with two political entities: the Federation of Bosnia i
      Herzegovina (Federation), led by Bošniaks and Bosnian Croats, and the Republika
      Srpska (RS), led by Bosnian Serbs. The Bosnian government's office of the president
      was divided into three seats, requiring an elected official from each of the three ethnic
      groups. Moreover, the country has fourteen separate governments (one for the federal
      government; one for the entity of the RS; one for the entity of the Federation; ten
      cantonal-level ones within the Federation; and a multi-ethnic partnership in the city of
      Brčko). Upon the war's conclusion, the country was administered by the Office of the
      High Representative (OHR) leading to numerous steps toward national integration.
      However, there remain separate entity-level telecommunication companies, fire depart-
      ments, and utility services, as well as divided schools ("two schools under one roof") in
      certain cities.

19   Martii Koskenniemi, "Between Impunity and Show Trials," in *Max Planck Yearbook
      of United Nations Law*, eds. J. A. Frowein and R. Wolfrum (The Hague: Kluwer Law
      International, 2002), 6: 1–35.

20   Howard Ball, *Prosecuting War Crimes and Genocide: The Twentieth-Century Experience*
      (Lawrence, KS: University Press of Kansas, 1999), 223; Frédéric Mégret, "Not Lambs to
      the Slaughter: A Program for Resistance to Genocidal Law," in *Confronting Genocide*,
      eds. René Provost and Payam Akhavan (Dordrecht: Springer, 2011), 197; Karen E.
      Smith. "Acculturation and the Acceptance of the Genocide Convention," *Cooperation
      and Conflict* 48, no. 3 (2013): 359.

21   David S. Koller. "The Global as Local: The Limits and Possibilities of Integrating
      International and Transitional Justice," in *Contested Justice: The Politics and Practice
      of International Criminal Court Interventions*, eds. Christian de Vos, Sara Kendall, and
      Carsten Stahn (Cambridge: Cambridge University Press, 2015); Kingsley Chiedu Mo-
      ghalu, *Global Justice: The Politics of War Crimes Trials* (Stanford: Stanford University
      Press, 2008); Eric Stover and Harvey M. Weinstein, "Conclusion: A Common Objective,
      A Universe of Alternatives," in *My Neighbor, My Enemy: Justice and Community in the
      Aftermath of Mass Atrocity*, eds. Eric Stover and Harvey M. Weinstein (Cambridge:
      Cambridge University Press, 2004), 334.

22   K. Annan, UN Secretary-General, *Report of the Secretary General: The Rule of Law and
      Transitional Justice in Conflict and Post-Conflict Societies* (New York: United Nations,
      2004), 224; Kathryn Sikkink and Hun Joon Kim, "The Justice Cascade: The Origins
      and Effectiveness of Prosecutions of Human Rights Violations," *Annual Review of Law
      and Social Science* no. 9, (2013): 269–285; Ruti G. Teitel, "Transitional Justice Genealo-
      gy," *Harvard Human Rights Journal* 16, (2003): 69–94.

23   A comprehensive analysis of the "justice" literature is outside the scope of this chapter.

24   Moghalu, *Global Justice*, 5.

25   Ibid.

26   Ibid., 5–6.

27   Jeremy Webber. "Forms of Transitional Justice," in *Transitional Justice*, eds. Melissa S.
      Williams, Rosemary Nagy, and John Elster (New York: New York University Press, 2012), 6–7.

28   See also Hugo van der Merwe, "Delivering Justice during Transition: Research Challenges," in *Assessing the Impact of Transitional Justice: Challenges for Empirical Research*, eds. Hugo van der Merwe, Victoria Baxter, and Audrey R. Chapman (Washington, DC: United States Institute of Peace, 2008), 119; Eric Stover, *The Witnesses: War Crimes and the Promise of Justice in The Hague* (Philadelphia: University of Pennsylvania Press, 2005), 119.

29   Webber, "Forms of Transitional Justice," 6–7, and Stover, *The Witnesses*, 118.

30   Webber, "Forms of Transitional Justice," 6–7.

31   Annan, *Report of the Secretary General*; Duthrie, "Afterword"; Gloppen, "Roads to Reconciliation"; and Hayner, *Unspeakable Truths*.

32   Hannah Arendt, *Eichmann in Jerusalem: A Report on the Banality of Evil* (New York: Viking Press, 1964), 253.

33   Kieran McEvoy, "Beyond Legalism: Towards a Thicker Understanding of Transitional Justice," *Journal of Law and Science* 34, no. 4 (2007): 411–440.

34   Ibid. See also J. Shklar, *Legalism* (Cambridge, MA: Harvard University Press, 1964); Ernest J. Weinrib, "The Jurisprudence of Legal Formalism," *Harvard Journal of Law and Public Policy* 16, no. 3 (1993): 583–595.

35   Pierre Bourdieu and Richard Terdiman, "The Force of Law: Toward a Sociology of the Juridical Field—Translator's Introduction," *Hastings Law Journal* 38, (July 1987): 806–808.

36   Laurel E. Fletcher, "Refracted Justice: The Imagined Victim and the International Criminal Court," in *Contested Justice: The Politics and Practice of the International Criminal Court Interventions*, eds. Christian de Vos, Sara Kendall, and Carsten Stahn (Cambridge: Cambridge University Press, 2015), 314; Merwe, "Delivering Justice during Transition," 121–122.

37   Stover, *The Witnesses*, 15.

38   See also Fletcher, "Refracted Justice."

39   Anna Lowenhaupt Tsing, *Friction: An Ethnography of Global Connection* (Princeton, NJ: Princeton University Press, 2005), 4. See also Alexander Laban Hinton, "Introduction: Toward an Anthropology of Transitional Justice," in *Transitional Justice: Global Mechanisms and Local Realities after Genocide and Mass Violence*, ed. Alexander Laban Hinton (New Brunswick, NJ: Rutgers University Press, 2010), 9.

40   Duthie, "Afterword"; Gloppen, "Roads to Reconciliation"; David C. Gray, "Extraordinary Justice," *Alabama Law Review* 62, no. 1 (2010): 55–109; Hayner, *Unspeakable Truths*; Mathias Hellman, "Challenges and Limitations of Outreach from the ICTY to the ICC," in *Contested Justice: The Politics and Practice of International Criminal Court Interventions*, eds. Christian de Vos, Sara Kendall, and Carsten Stahn (Cambridge: Cambridge University Press, 2015).

41   Miklos Biro, Dean Adjuković, Dinka Corkalo, Petar Milin, and Harvey M. Weinstein, "Attitudes Toward Justice and Social Reconstruction in Bosnia and Herzegovina and Croatia," in *My Neighbor, My Enemy: Justice and Community in the Aftermath of Mass Atrocity*, eds. Eric Stover and Harvey M. Weinstein (Cambridge: Cambridge University Press, 2004), 201. See also Roberta Culbertson and Béatrice Pouligny, "Re-Imagining Peace after Mass Crime: A Dialogical Exchange between Insider and Outsider Knowledge," in *After Mass Crime: Rebuilding States and Communities*, eds. Béatrice Pouligny,

Simon Chesterman, and Albrecht Schnabel (Tokyo: United Nations University Press, 2007), 280.

42 Stover, *The Witnesses*, 145. See also Rosemary Nagy, "Transitional Justice as Global Project: Critical Reflections," *Third World Quarterly* 29, no. 2 (2008): 275–289.

43 Merwe, "Delivering Justice during Transition," 123; see also Hinton, "Introduction," 1.

44 See Paige Arthur, "How 'Transitions' Reshaped Human Rights: A Conceptual History of Transitional Justice," *Human Rights Quarterly* 31, (2009): 321–367; Richard Ashby Wilson, *Writing History in International Criminal Trials* (Cambridge: Cambridge University Press, 2011).

45 Hinton, "Introduction," 1; Nagy, "Transitional Justice as Global Project"; Dustin N. Sharp, "Emancipating Transitional Justice from the Bonds of the Paradigmatic Transition," *International Journal of Transitional Justice* 1, (2015): 150; Tsing, *Friction*, 13.

46 John Torpey, "Introduction: Politics and the Past," in *Politics and the Past: On Restoring Historical Injustices*, ed. John Torpey (Oxford: Rowan & Littlefield, 2003), 8–9. See also Martha Minow, *Between Vengeance and Forgiveness: Facing History after Genocide and Mass Violence* (Boston: Beacon Press, 1998), 93.

47 Rosalind Shaw and Lars Waldorf, "Introduction: Localizing Transitional Justice," in *Localizing Transitional Justice: Interventions and Priorities after Mass Violence*, eds. Rosalind Shaw, Lars Waldorf, and Pierre Hazan (Stanford: Stanford University Press, 2010), 7.

48 Louis Bickford and Amy Sodaro, "Remembering Yesterday to Protect Tomorrow: The Internationalization of a New Commemorative Paradigm," in *Memory and the Future: Transnational Politics, Ethics and Society*, eds. Yifat Gutman, Adam D. Brown, and Amy Sodaro (Houndmills, Basingstoke, Hampshire: Palgrave Macmillan, 2010), 2. See also Joanna Mannergren Selimović, "Making Peace, Making Memory: Peacebuilding and Politics of Remembrance at Memorials of Mass Atrocities," *Peacebuilding* (2013): 2–15.

49 Barsalou and Baxter, "The Urge to Remember," 18.

50 ICTY. "About the ICTY," http://www.icty.org/en/about (accessed 16 February 2016).

51 ICTY, "Case Information Sheet: 'Srebrenica-Drina Corps' IT-98-33-Radislav Krstić," http://www.icty.org/x/cases/krstic/cis/en/cis_krstic_en.pdf (accessed 16 February 2016).

52 Ramesh Chandra Thakur, *The United Nations, Peace and Security: From Collective Security to the Responsibility to Protect* (Cambridge: Cambridge University Press, 2006), 121. See also Lara Nettelfield, *Courting Democracy in the Balkans: The Hague Tribunal's Impact in a Postwar State* (Cambridge: Cambridge University Press, 2012); Leslie Vinjamuri and Jack Snyder, "Advocacy and Scholarship in the Study of International War Crime Tribunals and Transitional Justice," *Annual Review of Political Science* 7, no. 3 (2004): 345–362. A full analysis of the ICTY's positive and negative impact is outside the scope of this chapter.

53 United Nations Mechanism for International Criminal Tribunals, "About the MICT," http://www.unmict.org/en/about (accessed 7 March 2016).

54 ICTY, "Case Information Sheet: IT-09-92: Ratko Mladić," http://www.icty.org/x/cases/mladic/cis/en/cis_mladic_en.pdf (accessed 25 February 2016).

55 ICTY, "Judgement Summary for Radovan Karadžić," http://www.icty.org/x/cases/karadzic/tjug/en/160324_judgement_summary.pdf and http://www.icty.org/en/press/

tribunal-convicts-radovan-karadzic-for-crimes-in-bosnia-and-herzegovina (both accessed 5 September 2016).

56   Stover, *The Witnesses*, x–xi. This point was reiterated to me in the interviews I conducted with all three groups of Mothers.

57   International Commission on Missing Persons (ICMP), "About Us—History," http://www.icmp.int/about-us/history/ (accessed 16 February 2016); Sarah E. Wagner, "Identifying Srebrenica's Missing: The 'Shaky Balance' of Universalism and Particularism," in *Transitional Justice: Global Mechanisms and Local Realities after Genocide and Mass Violence*, ed. Alexander Laban Hinton (New Brunswick, NJ: Rutgers University Press, 2010), 28.

58   For more information about how the ICMP assumed this role as well as why the term "mortal remains" is a more accurate term for the exhumed bodies, see Wagner, *To Know Where He Lies*. In 2005, the Missing Persons Institute of Bosnia and Herzegovina (MPI) was founded as an independent state-level institution to continue these exhumations and DNA identifications. The creation of MPI was highly politicized as it replaced the individual commissions that each of Bosnia's three constituent ethnic groups initially created. See also Kristen Juhl, "The Politicisation of the Missing Persons Issue in Bosnia and Herzegovina," *International Journal of Human Rights* 20, no. 1 (2016): 1–32.

59   Many of these remaining victims are still considered missing or cannot be fully identified due to the lack of forensic material (i.e., the majority of the bones have not been exhumed from mass graves and subsequently identified through DNA analysis). This is due, in part, to the vast areas of Bosnia that still contain active landmines as well as the refusal/hesitancy of people who may know where these graves are located to come forward. The situation is made more complicated due to the lack of international funding to support de-mining missions as well as the chance that the bones may have moved as a result of the heavy flooding that occurred across the country in the spring of 2014. See also Michael Biach, "Bosnia Mines Still Kill 20 Years Later," *Al Jazeera*, 12 February 2014, http://www.aljazeera.com/indepth/features/2014/02/bosnia-mines-still-kill-20-years-later-201425131626160304.html (accessed 27 February 2016); Kristen Chick, "Bosnia's Flood Clean-up Brings a Hazardous Wrinkle: Land Mines," *Christian Science Monitor* (Boston), 5 July 2014, http://www.csmonitor.com/World/Europe/2014/0705/Bosnia-s-flood-clean-up-brings-a-hazardous-wrinkle-land-mines (accessed 27 February 2016); "Bosnia Floods Unearth Grim Wartime Mass Grave," *Reuters*, 3 June 2014, http://www.reuters.com/article/us-balkans-floods-grave-idUSKBN0EE1YW20140603 (accessed 27 February 2016).

60   Hajra Ćatić (Women of Srebrenica), interview, 18 August 2011.

61   Ibid.; Hasan Nuhanović (Srebrenica Memorial), interview, 22 August 2011.

62   Munira Subašić (Mothers of the Enclaves of Srebrenica and Žepa), interview, 5 September 2011; Nura Begović (Women of Srebrenica), interview, 18 August 2011; Kathryne Bomberger (ICMP), interview, 6 September 2011. For a more extensive analysis of the Mothers' efforts to secure Potočari as the location of the cemetery and memorial, see Wagner, *To Know Where He Lies*; Olivera Simić, "Remembering, Visiting and Placing the Dead: Law, Authority and Genocide in Srebrenica," *Law Text Culture* 13, no. 1 (2009): 273–310.

63   OHR, List of key decisions and decrees related to Srebrenica, http://www.ohr.int/?ohr_archive_taxonomy=srebrenica-potocari-memorial-and-cemetery&lang=e and http://www.ohr.int/?p=65883&lang=en (accessed 26 February 2016).

64   T. G. Ashplant, Graham Dawson, and Michael Roper, "The Politics of War Memory and Commemoration: Contexts, Structures and Dynamics," in *The Politics of War, Memory and Commemoration*, eds. T. G. Ashplant, Graham Dawson, and Michael Roper (London: Routledge, 2000), 49; Marcelo M. Suárez-Orozco and Antonius C. G. M. Robben, "Interdisciplinary Perspectives on Violence and Trauma," in *Cultures Under Siege: Collective Violence and Trauma*, eds. Antonius C. G. M. Robben and Marcelo M. Suárez-Orozco (Cambridge: Cambridge University Press, 2000), 22.

65   Peggy Levitt and Sally Merry, "Vernacularization on the Ground: Local Uses of Global Women's Rights in Peru, China, India and the United States," *Global Networks* 9, no. 4 (2009): 441.

66   This point was reiterated in the majority of my interviews in 2011 as well as in interviews currently underway in 2016. Srebrenica to the world may be an international symbol of the genocide but for local people who live there, they are concerned with the challenges of daily existence, such as securing and maintaining employment, creating a good life for their children, and creating opportunities for younger adults in the community.

67   Mégret, "Not Lambs to the Slaughter," 206. See also Fletcher, "Refracted Justice"; Stover, *The Witnesses*; Eric Stover and Harvey M. Weinstein, eds., *My Neighbor, My Enemy: Justice and Community in the Aftermath of Mass Atrocity* (Cambridge: Cambridge University Press, 2004).

68   Benedict Anderson, *Imagined Communities: Reflections on the Origin and Spread of Nationalism* (London: Verso, 1996), 6.

69   Arendt, *Eichmann in Jerusalem*, 262–263.

70   Yael Zerubavel, *Recovered Roots: Collective Memory and the Making of Israeli National Tradition* (Chicago: University of Chicago Press, 1995), 8.

71   Jasna Dragović-Soso, "Conflict, Memory and Accountability: What Does Coming to Terms with the Past Mean?" in *Conflict and Memory: Bridging Past and Future in (South East) Europe*, eds. Wolfgang Petritsch, Vedran Džihić, and Franz-Lothar Altmann (Baden-Baden: Nomos, 2010), 32. See also Eviatar Zerubavel, *Time Maps: Collective Memory and the Social Shape of the Past* (Chicago: University of Chicago Press, 2003); Y. Zerubavel, *Recovered Roots*,

72   E. Zerubavel, *Time Maps*, 109. See also Elizabeth A. Cole and Judy Barsalou, *United or Divide: The Challenges of Teaching History in Societies Emerging from Violent Conflict* (Washington, DC: United States Institute of Peace, 2006), 9.

73   Iwona Irwin-Zarecka, *Frames of Remembrance: The Dynamics of Collective Memory* (New Brunswick, NJ: Transaction Publishers, 1994), 140.

74   Pierre Nora, "General Introduction: Between Memory and History," in *Realms of Memory: Re-Thinking the French Past*, eds. Pierre Nora and Lawrence D. Kritzman (New York: Columbia University Press, 1996), 1, 6, 18.

75   Peter Carrier, *Holocaust Monuments and National Memory Cultures in France and Germany since 1989: The Origins and Political Function of the Vél' d'Hiv' in Paris and the Holocaust Monument in Berlin* (New York: Berghahn Books, 2005), 23; Jenny

Edkins, "Remembering and Rationality: Trauma, Time and Politics," in *Memory, Trauma and World Politics: Reflections on the Relationship between Past and Present*, ed. Duncan Bell (Houndmills, Basingstoke, Hampshire: Palgrave Macmillan, 2006), 176; J. E. Turnbridge and G. J. Ashworth, *Dissonant Heritage: The Management of the Past as a Resource in Conflict* (Chichester: J. Wiley, 1996), 118 and 128.

76   Barsalou and Baxter, *The Urge to Remember*, 17; Sebastian Brett, Louis Bickford, Liz Sevčenko, and Marcela Rios, "State Policy and Civic Action," in *Memorialization and Democracy Conference* (Santiago: International Coalition of Sites of Conscience, International Center for Justice, and FLASCO-Chile/Latin American School of Social Sciences, 2007), 23; Edin Hajdarpašić, " 'But My Memory Betrays Me': National Master Narratives and the Ambiguities of History in Bosnia and Herzegovina," in *Conflict and Memory: Bridging Past and Future in (South East) Europe*, eds. Wolfgang Petritsch, Vedran Džihić, and Franz-Lothar Altmann (Baden-Baden: Nomos: 2010), 202; Larry Ray, "Mourning, Melancholia and Violence," in *Memory, Trauma and World Politics: Reflections on the Relationship between Past and Present*, ed. Duncan Bell (Houndmills, Basingstoke, Hampshire: Palgrave Macmillan, 2006), 42; Liz Ševčenko, "Sites of Conscience: Lighting Up Dark Tourism," in *Rites of Return: Diaspora Poetics and the Politics of Memory*, eds. Marianne Hirsch and Nancy K. Miller (New York: Columbia University Press, 2011), 120; Dacia Viejo-Rose. "Destruction and Reconstruction of Heritage: Impacts on Memory and Identity," in *Heritage, Memory and Identity*, eds. Helmut Anheier and Yudhishthir Raj Isar (London: Sage, 2011), 58.

77   Turnbridge and Ashworth, *Dissonant Heritage*, 109–110.

78   Minow, *Between Vengeance and Forgiveness*, 140.

79   Barsalou and Baxter, *The Urge to Remember*, 13.

80   Pete van der Auweraert, *Reparations for Wartime Victims in the Former Yugoslavia: In Search of the Way Forward* (Geneva: International Organization for Migration, 2013). See also Dragan M. Popovič, *Transitional Justice Guidebook: Executive Summary* (Sarajevo: United Nations Development Program, 2009); Graeme Simpson, Edin Hodžić, and Louis Bickford, *"Looking Back, Looking Forward": Promoting Dialogue through Truth-Seeking in Bosnia and Herzegovina* (Sarajevo: United Nations Development Programme, 2012).

81   Mirsad Tokača, "The Bosnian Culture of Commemorative Memory: Why and How?" in *Conflict and Memory: Bridging Past and Future in (South East) Europe*, eds. Wolfgang Petritsch, Vedran Džihić, and Franz-Lothar Altmann (Baden-Baden: Nomos, 2010), 226; see also Ivana Franović and Nenad Vukosavljević, eds., *War of Memories: Places of Suffering and Remembrance of War in Bosnia-Herzegovina* (Sarajevo-Belgrade, Center for Non-Violent Action, 2016).

82   See also Selimović, "Making Peace, Making Memory."

83   Sarah E. Wagner, "Tabulating Loss, Entombing Memory: The Srebrenica-Potočari Memorial Centre," in *Memory, Mourning, Landscape: At the Interface/Probing the Boundaries*, eds. Elizabeth Anderson, Avril Maddrell, Kate McLoughlin, and Alana Vincent (Amsterdam: Rodopi, 2010), 69. See also Xavier Bougarel, "Death and the Nationalist: Martyrdom, War Memory and Veteran Identity among Bosnian Muslims" in *The New Bosnian Mosaic: Identities, Memories and Moral Claims in a Post-War Society*, eds. Xavier Bougarel, Elissa Helms, and Ger Duijzings (Aldershot, Hamshpire: Ashgate, 2007).

84   The mandate of the Srebrenica Memorial is to "educate people of all ages and back-grounds to ensure that the Srebrenica message be heard by the whole world so as to avert future genocides." Its purpose is to construct and maintain the site; receive and disburse funds for the site; cooperate with similar centres, foundations, and asso-ciations worldwide; and conduct other related activities. OHR, "Decision Enacting the Law on the Center for the Srebrenica-Potočari Memorial and Cemetery for the Victims of the 1995 Genocide," 25 June 2007, http://www.ohr.int/?p=64715&print=pdf (accessed 26 February 2016); OHR, "Statute of the Foundation of Srebrenica-Po-točari Memorial and Cemetery," 20 September 2001, http://www.ohr.int/?ohr_ar-chive=statute-of-the-foundation-of-srebrenica-potocari-memorial-and-ceme-tery&lang=en&print=pdf (accessed 26 February 2016).

85   ICTY, "Facts about Srebrenica," http://www.icty.org/x/file/Outreach/view_from_ hague/jit_srebrenica_en.pdf (accessed 16 February 2016).

86   Leslie Woodhead, Stephen Segaller, and Krishan Arora, *Srebrenica: A Cry from the Grave*, http://www.pbs.org/wnet/cryfromthegrave/about/intro.html (accessed 16 February 2016). The film in the *Spomen Soba* was produced by these filmmakers, and includes footage from their original film.

87   Tarik Samarah, http://tariksamarah.com/en/ (accessed 27 February 2016).

88   The SENSE News Agency is based in The Hague and reports on the ICTY. The agency also created the online portal "Srebrenica: Genocide in Eight Acts." See "SENSE-Sre-brenica Documentation Center Opened," http://www.sense-agency.com/icty/ sense-%E2%80%93-srebrenica-documentation-center-opened.29.html?news_id=16137 and http://srebrenica.sense-agency.com/en/ (both accessed 5 September 2016).

89   The defence of Srebrenica was led by the ARBiH's commander, Naser Orić, who was previously acquitted by the ICTY for allegations about crimes committed in the *opština* under his leadership. See ICTY, "IT-03-68 Appeals Chamber Judgment 2008," http:// www.icty.org/x/cases/oric/acjug/en/080703.pdf (accessed 27 February 2016). On 10 June 2015—just weeks before the twentieth annual commemoration of the Srebrenica geno-cide—Switzerland acted on an outstanding arrest warrant for Orić issued by Serbia. After negotiations, Orić was extradited to Bosnia instead of Serbia. His arrest enraged the organizers of the Srebrenica commemoration who, in turn, threatened to cancel the event. See *B92*, 25 June 2015, http://www.b92.net/eng/news/region.php?yyyy=2015&m-m=06&dd=25&nav_id=94559 (accessed 28 February 2016). Orić's trial at the Bosnian War Crimes Chamber, which began in September 2015, remains ongoing. For more information, see Court of Bosnia and Herzegovina, "S1 1 K 014977 15 Kri - Orić Naser et al.," http://www.sudbih.gov.ba/predmet/3473/show (accessed 5 September 2016). For more information on the ARBiH's defence of Srebrenica, see Honig, *Srebrenica: Record of a War Crime*.

90   Alexander Laban Hinton, "Transitional Justice Time: Uncle San, Aunty Yan, and Outreach at the Khmer Rouge Tribunal," in *Genocide and Mass Atrocities in Asia: Legacies and Prevention*, eds. Deborah Mayersen and Annie Pohlman (Abingdon, Oxon: Routledge, 2013), 87.

91   Ibid.

92   Ibid., 96.

93   See also Alexander Laban Hinton, "Justice and Time at the Khmer Rouge Tribunal: In Memory of Vann Nath, Painter and S-21 Survivor," *Genocide Studies and Prevention* 8, no. 2 (2014): 7–17.

94 Sigmund Freud, "The 'Uncanny'," in *The Standard Edition of the Complete Psychological Works of Sigmund Freud, Volume XVII (1917–1919): An Infantile Neurosis and Other Works*, ed. Sigmund Freud (London: Vintage, 2001), 219 and 224.

95 Franz Kafka, *Franz Kafka: The Complete Stories* (New York: Schocken, 1971).

96 John Borneman, "Reconciliation After Ethnic Cleaning: Listening, Retribution, Affiliation," *Public Culture* 14, no. 2 (Spring 2002): 283.

97 Isaias Rojas-Perez, "Inhabiting Unfinished Pasts: Law, Transitional Justice, and Mourning in Post-War Peru," *Humanity: An International Journal of Human Rights, Humanitarianism, and Development* 4, no. 1 (Spring 2013): 161; Wagner, *To Know Where He Lies.*

98 Munira Subašić (Mothers of the Enclaves of Srebrenica and Žepa), interview, 5 September 2011.

99 Wagner, "Tabulating Loss, Entombing Memory."

100 See also Linda Green, "Fear as Way of Life," *Cultural Anthropology* 9, no. 2 (1994): 239.

101 On 13 July 2012, I accompanied the Mothers to seven of the Srebrenica genocide killing sites and experienced firsthand the incomprehensible terror of making this journey. In 2013, the commemorative visit to the Kravica warehouse was successfully prevented by the local authorities; however in 2015 and again in 2016, the group was permitted access to the property.

102 Lara Nettelfield and Sarah Wagner, "The Fifteenth Anniversary of the Srebrenica Genocide: Memorial Visit to Srebrenica's Crimes Scenes—Part Three of a Series," *The Blog of Cambridge University Press, North America*, http://www.cambridgeblog.org/2010/10/the-fifteenth-anniversary-of-the-srebrenica-genocide-memorial-visit-to-srebrenicas-crimes-scenes-part-three-of-a-series/ (accessed 16 February 2016); See also Lara Nettelfield and Sarah Wagner, *Srebrenica in the Aftermath of Genocide* (Cambridge: Cambridge University Press, 2014).

103 Rojas-Perez, "Inhabiting Unfinished Pasts," 152.

104 Green, "Fear as Way of Life," 230.

105 Isabel Wollaston, *A War against Memory? The Future of Holocaust Remembrance* (London: SPCK, 1996), 37.

106 Craig E. Pollack, "Intentions of Burial: Mourning, Politics, and Memorials Following the Massacre at Srebrenica," *Death Studies* 27, (2003): 125–142, See also Nettelfield and Wagner, *Srebrenica in the Aftermath of Genocide.*

107 Ger Duijzings, "Commemorating Srebrenica: Histories of Violence and the Politics of Memory in Eastern Bosnia" in *The New Bosnian Mosaic: Identities, Memories and Moral Claims in a Post-War Society,* eds. Xavier Bougarel, Elissa Helms, and Ger Duijzings (Aldershot, Hamsphire: Ashgate, 2007).

108 Hayner, *Unspeakable Truths*, 189; Minow, *Between Vengeance and Forgiveness*, 119.

109 Harvey M. Weinstein, Laurel E. Fletcher, Patrick Vinck, and Phuong N. Pham, "Stay the Hand of Justice: Whose Priorities Take Priority?" in *Localizing Transitional Justice: Interventions and Priorities after Mass Violence*, eds. Rosalind Shaw, Lars Waldorf, and Pierre Hazan (Stanford: Stanford University Press, 2010), 33.

110 A commemorative plaque to Ratko Mladić was installed in the hills above Sarajevo in July 2014. David Pettigrew, "Mladić Plaque in East Sarajevo: A Continuation of the

Genocide," Institute for Research of Genocide Canada, August 2014, http://institute-forgenocide.org/?p=8490.20 (accessed 16 February 2016).

111   Hamber, "Utopian Dreams or Practical Possibilities," 2010.

112   Brett et al., "State Policy and Civic Action."

Troubling History, Troubling Law: The Question of Indigenous Genocide in Canada

Adam Muller

> I mean, there is no truth on this matter of what is a genocide.
>
> —Samantha Power[1]

> Why is there such a sharp contrast in attitudes to the past in different cultures? It is often said that history is written by the victors. It might also be said that history is forgotten by the victors. They can afford to forget, while the losers are unable to accept what happened and are condemned to brood over it, relive it, and reflect on how different it might have been. Another explanation might be given in terms of cultural roots. When you have them you can afford to take them for granted but when you lose them you search for them.
>
> —Peter Burke[2]

In July 2014, members of the International Association of Genocide Scholars (IAGS), the world's largest organization devoted to the interdisciplinary study of historical and contemporary genocide, met in Winnipeg, Manitoba, for a conference organized under the broad theme of "Genocide Studies and Indigenous Peoples." Unusually for the IAGS, which typically meets every second year, the Winnipeg conference was held in an off year, sandwiched between the organization's 2013 event in Siena, Italy, and a meeting scheduled for 2015 in Yerevan, Armenia, in order to coincide with ceremonies honouring the centenary of the Armenian genocide. The decision to break with tradition and have the IAGS meet in 2014 was not uncontroversial, but it ended up being justified by the IAGS executive for three primary and overlapping reasons:[3] the opening in Winnipeg of the Canadian Museum for Human Rights (CMHR), which was originally scheduled to take place in July; the expected conclusion in June of the work of the Truth and Reconciliation Commission of Canada (TRC), which had looked into the abuses occurring in Canada's Indian Residential School (IRS) system;[4] and the opening at the University of Manitoba later in 2014 of the National Research Centre on Indian Residential Schools, whose archive contains TRC testimony and other key documentation pertaining to the history and legacy of Canada's IRS system.

Converging in Winnipeg in the summer of 2014, then, were four distinct but importantly overlapping processes: one nurturing scholarly inquiry into genocide and its aftermaths; a second attempting to engage the general public in the story of human rights struggles and successes; a third collecting testimony pertaining to Canada's historically atrocious treatment of Indigenous peoples; and a fourth working to preserve this testimony and develop effective means for sharing it. Responding to this convergence, an article entitled "The Genocide Test," written by veteran public policy reporter Mary Agnes Welch, appeared in July in the *Winnipeg Free Press*. It was intended to elucidate some of the issues arising in virtue of the IAGS conference's theme, and in it Welch raised the question of whether or not Canadian settler colonialism was genocidal. In exploring the implications of this question, Welch solicited statements mainly from Indigenous and non-Indigenous scholars and activists who agree that it was so. She also noted the resistance of average Canadians to the idea that their country was founded on such a heinous crime,[5] even as she acknowledged recent advances in genocide scholarship that, over time, continue to shift the public's understanding of Indigenous history and the role played by genocide in shaping it. Summarizing the view of Charlene Bearhead, currently the education lead at the National Centre for Truth and Reconciliation, Welch concluded that "If nothing else, the next generation, armed with a fuller historic picture, will lead the change."[6] Significantly, and not for the first time, Welch singled out the CMHR for failing to embrace this change and formally designate Canadian settler colonialism as genocidal—a failure that, since at least the summer of 2013, has caused the museum to come under sustained fire from scholars, Indigenous peoples, and their allies nationwide.

In what follows I propose using Welch's article as the point of departure for a reflection on the underpinnings and scope of the change to which Welch and Bearhead refer, and on behalf of which they advocate. Along the way I will be considering specific aspects of the argument that there has been genocide committed against Aboriginal peoples in Canada. I will begin by considering what "genocide" means, exactly, by focusing on the text of the United Nations General Assembly Resolution 260, the Convention on the Prevention and Punishment of the Crime of Genocide (henceforth the "Genocide Convention"), which I will work to locate more precisely in its historical context. Any account of this context requires reference to the life and work of the convention's primary framer, Raphael Lemkin, about whom more later. Rereading Lemkin allows us to comprehend the extent to which critical concern over the language of the Genocide Convention is justified. It also shows how the convention remains weakened by a set of political compromises that in crucial ways caused it to depart markedly from Lemkin's original conception and hopes. By specifying difficulties with the convention's dependence on an overly stringent notion of "special" genocidal intention, I provide substantial reasons for adopting a broader view of genocide. Such a view is, I conclude, much better suited to accounting for the destructive effects of European settler colonialism, in Canada and elsewhere in the world. It is also much more responsive to, and reflective of, the perspectives of Indigenous peoples themselves.

What is Genocide?

Debate over whether or not genocide occurred in Canada hinges on at least two underlying issues: what we understand genocide to be, and whether or not the Canadian case—Canada's historical treatment of Indigenous peoples—is special, and therefore unlike other instances of settler colonialism elsewhere in the world that seem more straightforwardly genocidal. For many Canadians it seems impossible to reconcile what is generally known of Aboriginal Canadians' relatively more pacific experience of European settlement and governance with the experiences documented, say, by Bartolomé de las Casas in his shocking *A Short Account of the Destruction of the Indies* (1552), in which the Dominican monk and first-hand observer of Spain's brutally annihilatory conquest of South and Central America and the Caribbean is described in all its horror.

Both of these issues may be seen at work in the responses to Welch's article published subsequently by the *Winnipeg Free Press*. For example, in his opinion piece entitled "Canadian Policies Don't Meet Genocide Test," Michael Melanson, who has commented frequently on this issue, always in the same vein, proffers the view that the conceptual limits of genocide have been indisputably established by the United Nations through its adoption of the Genocide Convention on 9 December 1948. Melanson views attempts to conceive of genocide outside of the frame of the convention's language and relevant case law as distorting and counterproductive, not least since the United Nations is unlikely to revise the text of the agreement any time soon. For Melanson and many others, the Genocide Convention is the decisive authority in matters genocidal; although individual countries, including Canada, have laws prohibiting genocidal acts, these commentators consider the convention more authoritative since it speaks for an international consensus.[7] More than this, Melanson contends that whatever violence has been directed against Aboriginal Canadians, as with the case of missing and murdered Aboriginal women, was undertaken not by the state acting with genocidal intent, but by those personally acquainted with the victims, and that even the seizing of Aboriginal children and their relocation to residential schools and subsequent mistreatment was accomplished not by the Canadian state in a coordinated effort at group destruction, but by more and less beneficent groups often affiliated with Aboriginal communities, and for the most part functioning independently. Speaking for many Canadians, Melanson writes that in the Canadian case there is no clear evidence of genocidal intent: "The RCMP showed most of the murdered aboriginal women were killed by people they knew. Southern Chiefs Organization Grand Chief Terry Nelson said recently the high number of aboriginal children in CFS care was 'the definition of genocide.' Since devolution, those seizures have been undertaken by aboriginal agencies. Groups do not target themselves for genocide and suicides, by definition, are not genocide, but wholesale judgment seems to be the point."[8]

In his published reply to Melanson, IAGS vice president Andrew Woolford points out that overreliance on the international legal architecture that gives the genocide concept its coherence and institutional force, and which remains crucial to our capacity to recognize genocide on the ground, has the undesirable effects of actually weakening the concept's integrity and limiting its relevance to contexts wherein groups violently clash. In advancing this claim Woolford, a sociologist, acknowledges that he is "a genocide scholar working in the tradition of Raphael Lemkin,"[9] and indeed his perspective has in important ways been shaped by (even as Woolford has contributed importantly to) a reassessment of Lemkin's work and legacy. This reassessment is currently underway in the field of genocide studies and cognate disciplines such as law, history, and political science, and I will be referring to it as the "Lemkinian Turn." Raphael Lemkin (1900–1959) was the Polish-Jewish jurist who coined the term "genocide" and brought the idea of this singular crime to the broader public's attention, not least through the publication of his influential study of Nazi wartime conduct, *Axis Rule in Occupied Europe* (1944). Following the Second World War, Lemkin almost singlehandedly drafted the text of the Genocide Convention, and shepherded its passage through the byzantine committee structures of the United Nations, driven then as now by parochial national interests. Speaking of Lemkin's struggle to see the genocide concept incorporated into international law, Woolford writes that "Although Lemkin drafted the United Nations' Genocide Convention, his definition was diluted by the nations of the world, sometimes for what were practical reasons, but other times for clearly political reasons."[10]

This is not a trivial point. Over the course of its transnational institutionalization, Lemkin's foundational idea of genocide was shorn of much of its breadth and complexity, generally in response to the desire of the victorious postwar powers (most notably the Soviet Union and Great Britain) not to leave themselves open to legal challenges to their own occasionally genocidal, colonial, and imperial conduct.[11] It is therefore striking in this regard that chief among the alterations to Lemkin's original text was the removal of any reference to cultural genocide, a key component of Lemkin's original conception of the crime and the idea most directly indebted to the jurist's reading of the history of European colonialism. According to the standard view of the evolution of his ideas, such as that provided by Michael Ignatieff in a recent essay in the *New Republic*,[12] Lemkin's formulation of the genocide concept is held to have been primarily influenced by the Holocaust, an extermination event that was particularly conspicuous to him given his Polish and Jewish origins, and which still looms large over accounts of the evolution of postwar justice and human rights talk of the period—notwithstanding the recent appearance of persuasive revisionist historiography by Samuel Moyn, Marco Duranti, and others.[13]

The centrality of the destruction of culture to Lemkin's original formulation of the genocide concept cannot be denied. For Lemkin, genocide was a crime centring on a group's destruction, an idea retained in article 2 of the Genocide Convention, which defines genocide as "acts committed with intent to destroy, in whole or in part, a national, ethnical, racial or religious group." According to Peter Balakian, who has recently published work arising from research into hitherto unknown documents contained in Lemkin's archive, Lemkin understood groups to be sustained by three main attributes or capacities: the physical existence of their members; their ability to remain biologically reproductive (i.e., their wherewithal to produce new members of the group, and thus to renew themselves); and their capacity for "spiritual" or cultural expression. According to Lemkin, genocide occurs when one or all three of these capacities is destroyed, rendering a group unable to persist and its members unable to recognize one another as the same kinds of beings-in-the-world. Balakian argues that "Lemkin focuses on how the destruction of religious institutions and objects, for example, eliminates the 'spiritual life' through which a human group finds defining expression; when a group's culture (schools, treasures of art and culture, houses of worship, and the like) is destroyed, he argues, 'the forces of spiritual cohesion' are torn apart and the group 'starts to disintegrate.' "[14]

As an indication of how far it departs from Lemkin's original intentions, nowhere in the Genocide Convention is this cohesion that Balakian refers to identified as something worth protecting. Instead, the United Nations agreement targets threats to a group's biological and reproductive integrity, as may be witnessed by article 2's itemization of genocidal conduct, which entirely concerns physical harms or constraints:

a) Killing members of the group;

b) Causing serious bodily or mental harm to members of the group;

c) Deliberately inflicting on the group conditions of life calculated to bring about its physical destruction in whole or in part;

d) Imposing measures intended to prevent births within the group;

e) Forcibly transferring children of the group to another group.[15]

This list makes no mention of the fact that a group may cease to exist for reasons other than the application of massive physical violence; and nowhere in the convention is culture identified as worthy of preservation in virtue of its role in sustaining group life. It should be remembered that culture serves as the expression (i.e., the outer form) of a group's inner life, and it is thus a mechanism through which group integrity may be maintained and renewed, and the identities informed by it sustained. With this in mind, Lemkin clearly states that there are two distinct but often overlapping modes of genocidal destruction. One of these he labels "barbarism," the other "vandalism."[16] While barbaric acts are those directed against human bodies in various ways, vandalism targets culture by seeking to destroy monuments, sites of conscience, works of art, and the like. Such destruction is the essence of what Lemkin understands "cultural genocide" to be, since in his view culture is the essence of a people. In an unpublished 1948 essay on genocide in international law, he writes:

> Cultural genocide can be accomplished predominately in the religious and cultural fields by destroying institutions and objects through which the spiritual life of a human group finds its expression, such as houses of worship, objects of religious cult, schools, treasures of art and culture. By destroying spiritual leadership and institutions, forces of spiritual cohesion within a group are removed and the group starts to disintegrate.[17]

To be clear, what Lemkin terms cultural genocide is criminal as well as immoral for precisely the same reason as what he calls "physical" or "biological" genocide. For all of these forms of destruction have the same object in common: the annihilation of a group.[18]

This particular object is the defining feature of genocide, and the source of its primary harms. What makes genocide different from, say, varieties of mass murder, is not its conspicuous production of bodies, but rather the attempted destruction of what might be called "human kinds." The signal casualty of genocide is not people, but *a people*, and thus a highly morally and politically charged form of (and capacity for) belonging. I agree with Christopher Powell and Amarnath Amarasingam in their contribution to this volume insofar as, like them, I see genocide as targeting "the social institutions and relationships necessary for the perpetuation of group life,"[19] what I want to call the "groupness" of groups—the corporeal, social, ideological, and institutional preconditions of social life, the people and structures through and against which our identities are shaped and our world comes to make sense. For Lemkin, the loss of cultures should be a matter of universal concern, since it results in the reduction of human diversity and with it our permanent alienation from distinctive repertoires of human achievement from which we might learn a great deal. He writes that "When a nation is destroyed, it is not the cargo of the vessel that is lost, but a substantial part of humanity with a spiritual heritage in which the whole world partakes."[20]

Lemkin and Colonialism

In their landmark account of Lemkin's understanding of colonial history, historians Michael A. McDonnell and Dirk Moses show that, contrary to the standard view, Lemkin's conception of genocide was profoundly marked by his encounter with colonialism's destructive excesses, which he experienced primarily through his reading of works of history and autobiography, though also first-hand while living in pre–World War Two Poland. More than this, they argue that "the very notion [of genocide] is colonial in nature because it entails occupation and settlement,"[21] two hallmarks of colonialism. In their analysis, McDonnell and Moses scrupulously review Lemkin's research notes and show how his thinking drew heavily from reference works on the European conquest of North and South America, including several by las Casas, whose descriptions of the mass murder of Indigenous populations he found harrowing. In addition to work documenting Spanish crimes, Lemkin also delved deeply into texts on the withering effects of European oppression in North America, Australasia, East Asia, and Africa.

For Lemkin, European colonialism's brutality was in some cases clearly genocidal, and his conception of genocide was deeply indebted to his attempt to understand the nature of colonialism's harms. Prominent amongst these harms was the destruction of Indigenous cultures. Lemkin worked tirelessly to ensure the inclusion of cultural genocide in the Genocide Convention, but failed to do so principally owing to resistance from world powers fearful that their own colonial pasts might leave them vulnerable to indictment, a fear heightened by the postwar intensification of liberation struggles in Europe's remaining colonies. McDonnell and Moses are correct to see the displacement of Indigenous peoples and the eradication of important (by their lights) features of their traditional lives as intrinsic to colonialism.[22] Lemkin's failure to get language on culture included in the Genocide Convention severely compromises the international community's ability to confront colonial abuses, and to determine which of them might or might not be genocidal. It therefore makes some sense to view the convention, notwithstanding all the good it has done, as in some sense continuing to labour in colonialism's shadow.

Michael Melanson and others aside, appealing to international law in response to the question of whether or not genocide occurred in colonial contexts is hardly straightforward. On the contrary, while cases such as that of the Herero in Namibia, who had their villages and food supplies destroyed by troops acting in support of German settlers, before being driven off into the desert to die, may seem more obviously criminal by the light of the Genocide Convention (i.e., because they concern state-sanctioned mass murder in the context of an attempted ethnocide), other examples, such as that of settler colonialism in Canada, which lacks both the high levels of violence and degrees of coordination and state involvement found in the German case, are harder to categorize. Not, however, that the experience of the Herero proved all that easy to formally designate a genocide. It was not until the appearance of the UN's *Whitaker Report* in 1985, more than eighty years after the fact, that German actions in Southwest Africa received their proper label, and not until 2004 that the German government issued a formal apology for earlier crimes, even as it refused to provide financial compensation for the descendants of the genocide's original victims.

So then, acknowledgement of the partial and political character of the Genocide Convention attunes us to the contingency of international law in determinations of whether or not genocide has occurred. Notwithstanding how well it works in some cases where physical violence figures prominently, the convention works less well in others where groups have been targeted for destruction through the undermining of their cultural distinctiveness. While commentators like Stephen Katz limit genocide only to intentional acts of physical destruction aimed at a group (Katz believes that the Holocaust is the only world-historical event to actually satisfy this definition),[23] scholars such as Martin Shaw and Paul Boghossian argue that "a strong case can be made for saying that that concept [in international law] is deeply flawed, flaws that make its application to particular cases deeply problematic and that are hard to remedy."[24] These flaws bear on the suitability of international legal frameworks to settle the question of whether or not genocide has occurred in colonial contexts.

Genocidal Intent

For his part, French historian and editor Jean-Louis Panneé argues that reference to Lemkin's own hopes for the Genocide Convention reveals the breadth and fullness of his original conception. Panneé is especially keen to note Lemkin's concern with the systematic character of genocidal annihilation, his recognition of genocide as both a process and a political practice, and therefore as something fundamentally ideological. Writing of Lemkin's anticipation of ideas found in the work of Holocaust historian Raul Hilberg, Panneé argues that "By placing emphasis on genocide as a process, Raul Hilberg, just as Lemkin, gave it an eminently political dimension, because some individuals 'authorize themselves to kill' … in keeping with their respective Weltanschauung."[25] What marks genocide for Panneé and others is not the power it has to wreak physical destruction, but rather the qualities of mind and conduct, and along with them the structures of power, that contribute to the annihilation of a group's integrity, its capacity to renew itself, and its members' ability to flourish. This view overlaps with that of McDonnell and Moses, who put the matter thus: "Mass killing ... is not intrinsic to genocide; it can occur without executions or gassings. The proposition that scholars who think that genocide is a synonym for the Holocaust need to entertain is that Lemkin regarded the latter as a consequence of Nazi imperialism and colonialism in Europe. The Holocaust and German imperium between 1939 and 1945 was for him a continuation of the genocidal occupations that have characterized colonialism through the ages."[26] If these scholars are right, then a Lemkinian view attuned to the dynamics of history and culture might indeed be better suited to ascertaining whether or not genocide has occurred in Canada as part of Indigenous experiences of settler colonialism.

However, both in the Genocide Convention and throughout Lemkin's scholarly corpus, the "intent to destroy" is claimed to be an essential feature of genocidal processes.[27] According to Panneé, "Lemkin insisted on this dimension of genocide that, in truth, encompasses the two essential elements of this tragic story, namely the will to chase off or cause the disappearance of a specific population and recourse to extermination." He cites a passage from Lemkin's essay "What is a Genocide?" in this regard: "Would the expression 'mass murder' reflect the precise concept of this phenomenon? I think it would not, as it does not include the motive of the crime, the more so when the final aim of the crime rests on racial, national, and religious considerations."[28] For Lemkin, motive matters, and there can be no motive without intent.[29] But the issue of intent is highly problematic in the case of Canadian settler colonialism, since Canadian history offers up no evidence comparable to Adolf Hitler's autobiographical *Mein Kampf* (1924), the transcripts of the Wannsee Conference, or Heinrich Himmler's 1943 Posen speech to the SS, all of which testify to the Nazis' programmatic intention to destroy European Jews.[30] Before any argument can be marshalled that settler colonialism in Canada was genocidal, then, it is first necessary to take a closer look at what genocidal intent is. For the purposes of the analysis here, it is the international legal conception of this intent that matters most since Lemkin played a crucial role in shaping it. It speaks for his understanding of what it means to intend to destroy. It is only in the wake of such an analysis that it becomes possible to reflect more generally on the status of intent in accounts of the history of Canadian settler colonialism.

The conception of intent embodied in the Genocide Convention is relatively straightforward. It revolves around the idea of there being a "special intent" (*dolus specialis*) at work in genocides, which may be contrasted with the general intent (*dolus*) to do harm. According to criminal law professor and German judge Kai Ambos, the special and general intents comprise the two legally relevant mental elements operative during a genocide. That is, for the *genocidaire* to be legally guilty of the crime, it must be shown that he intended to do harm and understood his actions as likely to bring this harm about (the general intention); and he must be shown to intend to do harm to a particular group or groups (the special intention). Without the addition of this *dolus specialis*, even the most hideous atrocities committed as the result of only a general intention to harm would not qualify legally as genocide. For Ambos this demonstrates that genocide viewed legally is marked by a kind of surplus of intent, what he calls a "transcending internal tendency" (überschießende *Innentendenz*).[31] This surplus reflects the fact that genocides are about more than mere violence; they are acts of violence with a special purpose, namely the destruction of groups. This surplus helps to distinguish acts of genocide from those of persecution, which by definition requires the persistence of groups, albeit in states of ongoing misery.

It should be noted that the intention being privileged in this conception of the *dolus specialis* is reserved for those directing and sponsoring genocides, and not to the foot soldiers carrying genocide out on the ground. What international law cares about, and criminalizes, are the actions of those in charge of these atrocities, the "architects of doom." Abuses arranged or committed by those further down the ladder, such as mid- and lower-level bureaucrats, soldiers in the field, vigilante mobs, and so on, are considered evidence of a higher-level intent to destroy, an intention that subordinates are held to lack. Accordingly, garden-variety functionaries, militants, and bigots, those whom Daniel Goldhagen famously termed Hitler's "willing executioners," though potentially guilty of other crimes, cannot themselves be held legally responsible for genocide. This fact has the rather odd consequence of at least conceptually severing actors from their actions, since while contributing materially to the commission of a genocide (i.e., performing acts of genocide), a person would not be considered responsible for furthering genocide, either morally or in the eyes of the law. Looking at matters this way fails to take into account how the desire to eliminate a group may be present more and less explicitly in the minds and dispositions of genocidal functionaries, shaping their conduct and the institutions through which their animus is felt and operationalized. It doesn't look closely enough at who knew what and how.

Following a comprehensive survey of the relevant legal cases, Ambos argues that "the case-law approach is predicated on the understanding ... that 'intent to destroy' means a special or specific intent which, in essence, expresses the volitional element in its most intensive form and is purpose-based."[32] Dissenting from this tradition, Ambos follows Alicia Gil Gil and Otto Triffterer in exploring the possibility of reconceptualizing genocidal intention to include the *dolus eventualis*, or conditional intent. Conditional intent is what Ambos describes as "a transcending subjective element (*elemento subjetivo trascendente*) with regard to the constituent acts of the offence and the criminal result."[33] It is what philosophers of action sometimes call a "global" intention out of and against which specific "local" intentions form and become salient. It does not attach itself to specific acts, but rather coordinates them by, amongst other things, providing a conduit for rationalizations and easy access to justificatory schemes. Ambos writes that "As to these constituent acts, e.g. the killing of a member of the group in the case of genocide, *dolus eventualis* would be sufficient, combined however with intention in the sense of the unconditional will with regard to the remaining acts—i.e., the killing of other members of the group—necessary to bring about the final result of the crime, or at least knowledge of the co-perpetrators' intention to that effect, and at the same time the presumption that the realization of these acts is possible."[34] In his view it is enough to show evidence of genocidal intent when an accused is clearly responsible for acts the outcome of which might have reasonably been expected to contribute to the destruction of a group. In Alexander Greenwalt's words, "principal culpability should extend to those who may lack a specific genocidal purpose, but who commit genocidal acts while understanding the destructive consequences of their actions."[35] Since this understanding comprises the conceptual background against which the perpetrator forms intentions and acts, Ambos calls Greenwalt's a "knowledge-based approach" to the problem of genocidal intention.

Again, context matters since it is always within contexts that actions take place and intentions form; one never acts in a vacuum, or without some kind of bigger-picture understanding of one's place in the world, however broadly or narrowly conceived. Even as we want to acknowledge that genocide's foot soldiers frequently fail to act in the moment specifically with the intent to destroy, we need at the same time to recognize the ways that they understand the meaning of their actions. Accordingly it is perhaps easier to understand why sociologists, historians, and genocide scholars have expressed so much dissatisfaction with the appeal to the Genocide Convention and related international law when making determinations concerning whether or not a genocide has occurred, and also why the legal and related political establishments have been reluctant to do so. For the former, trained to prefer thick to thin descriptions and with an eye (post-Foucault) to the vagaries of Power, international law is simply far too conservative as well as reluctant to examine closely the events on which it seeks to pass judgment. For the latter, constrained by case law, a narrower conception of intent, and an inability to look beyond physical harms, genocide is only ever committed by the few who plan and clearly organize it, not by the many who carry it out.

Intent in the Canadian Case

As noted above, evidence of the intent to destroy is not totally clear-cut when it comes to making the case for Canadian settler-colonial genocide. This is not to say it is wholly absent. In one of the mostly widely quoted expressions of the Canadian government's official hostility toward Canadian Indigenous peoples, Deputy Superintendent General of Indian Affairs Duncan Campbell Scott (1862–1947), speaking for his office as well as for attitudes prevailing in Canada more generally, wrote in 1920 that "I want to get rid of the Indian problem. I do not think as a matter of fact, that the country ought to continuously protect a class of people who are able to stand alone. ... Our objective is to continue until there is not a single Indian in Canada that has not been absorbed into the body politic and there is no Indian question, and no Indian Department, that is the whole object of this Bill."[36] It is difficult to think of a more direct statement of genocidal intent, at least if one accepts the view that genocide is criminal to the extent that it results in the destruction of groups, not simply the deaths of human beings.

Andrew Woolford and other scholars of settler-colonial genocide remind us that we should not be too quick to think that Canadian Aboriginals weren't physically harmed owing to colonial policies and practices. In an important essay on genocide as "ontological destruction," Woolford observes that "while all Aboriginal groups experienced at least some degree of attempted assimilation, some also experienced high levels of physical destruction through settler violence, disease, and deadly residential-school conditions, as well as biological interference with reproductive processes."[37] His view is seconded by political scientists David MacDonald and Graham Hudson, who point out that "Many acts that constitute serious bodily and mental harm are known to have been performed by school officials and private parties during the operation of these schools. These include sexual assault, threats of death, severe beatings and assault, inhuman and degrading treatment—including systematic assaults on Aboriginal self-identity, and disfigurement and serious injuries to health as a result of the forced cohabitation of healthy children with children infected with communicable diseases."[38] Nevertheless, Woolford cautions against too easily assuming Canadian settler colonialism was genocidal. In his view there are two main difficulties confronting anyone levelling such a charge: the lack of any coordinated plan for the destruction of Canada's Indigenous peoples, and the awkward truth that many of the policies and institutions responsible for the destruction of Aboriginal life were created not to destroy Indigenous peoples but, explicitly at least, for reasons of benevolence.[39] Discussion of both of these difficulties dovetails with the preceding account of legal intent. This is because for genocide to be distinguishable from other forms of atrocious action, some kind of a distinctive intention to destroy a group must be present, whatever we understand by "intention." Benevolent intentions do not seem to qualify as genocidal in this regard, although they are certainly paternalistic, and additionally there must be evidence of coordinated action. One cannot, after all, cause a genocide either inadvertently or by oneself. Instead, one must will genocide into being and carry it out with the aid of others.

Woolford responds to these concerns by suggesting that Canadian settler colonialism gave rise to what he terms a "colonial network of destruction."[40] In explaining what this means he relies on nodal governance theory, which is concerned with charting the workings of the "outcome governing system" (OGS), or complex network of systems and structures through which a society organizes and governs itself. The OGS not only rationalizes social action, it justifies it by assigning meaning to the structures and patterns of action comprising everyday life. Woolford explains that the OGS is "a term which refers to how collective actors through both conscious and habituated actions generate collective outcomes that are perceived as 'goods' (e.g. peace, happiness, and economic well-being) or else defined as problems when things go wrong (e.g. violence, famine, and suffering)."[41]

The OGS is comprised of many "nodes," different sites "within an OGS where knowledge, capacity and resources are mobilized to manage a course of events or, in other words, to put governance into action."[42] In Canada, one such node would be the country's IRS system. Regardless of the more or less benign local intentions informing the processes and mechanisms of Aboriginal education within a specific IRS, Woolford contends that all IRSs must be seen as contributing to Canada's network of destruction. This is because all of these schools understood Aboriginal life and identity to be something in need of correction, traces of an obsolete and redundant existence out of which the country's Indigenous peoples needed to be educated. From the perspective of the IRS system and its benefactors in church and government, Indigeneity was a problem that needed to be solved. And yet, "one must acknowledge that it is only possible to claim to be providing civilizing uplift to Indigenous peoples if one misrecognizes them and treats them first as barbarous peoples. Such misrecognition allows one to bury or bracket one's intent—to act without actively admitting to the ends one seeks to achieve."[43]

Obscured in the history of Canadian settler colonialism, then, are both a prevailing conception of Indigenous life as somehow not worth living, and a corresponding global intention to eradicate it. Conception and intention echo loudly in discussions of historical genocide since they bear a striking resemblance to the Nazis' notion of "life unworthy of life," the view originally advanced by German jurist Karl Binding and psychologist Alfred Hoche in 1920, and later taken up by Hitler in *Mein Kampf*, that certain groups of people (i.e., those with mental or physical disabilities) were little more than "human ballast" in need of sterilization or euthanasia.[44] We find the idea of Indigenous non-viability and expendability historically present throughout Canada's OGS, where it can be seen underlying all of the decisions made by individuals and (governmental and non-governmental) organizations responsible for managing the country's Aboriginal affairs. That is, at its core Canadian settler colonialism developed and evolved in ways continually informed by the idea of Indigenous life as something to be overcome. Hence Woolford's observation that "Within the settler-Canadian worldview, there was little room for the continuance of Indigenous societies."[45] We can find further evidence of the eliminationist character of this worldview once again in the words of Duncan Campbell Scott, who expresses his hope for the beneficent elimination of Indigenous life thus: "The happiest future for the Indian race is absorption into the general population, and this is the object of the policy of our government. The great forces of intermarriage and education will finally overcome the lingering traces of native custom and tradition."[46]

What work by Woolford and others on Canadian settler-colonial genocide reveals is how the intent to destroy is present but unevenly distributed throughout Canada's OGS. This uneven distribution, along with the profoundly and often subtly networked character of the mechanisms and sites of colonial destruction, obliges us to rethink certain features of a genocide's causal history. Most obviously, rather than viewing genocides as coherent events organized around an overarching set of intentions to destroy a particular group—intentions held by a privileged few in power who then direct the actions of subordinates accordingly—we should instead think of them as occurring through the simultaneous operations of multiple nodes conjoined in a (dominant) cultural network seeking a group's annihilation. This network may be more or less formally justified, and insofar as its structure is concerned, it may be more or less tightly woven given the specifics of its material and historical circumstances. Any such network is genocidal to the extent that it is animated by a *dolus specialis*. This special intention has as its object the elimination of a group, but it is revealed only occasionally in the formal justifications offered to authorize specific acts. Most of the time it may be found implicit in the ideologies underpinning the logic responsible for narrowing the available choices for those making decisions about the welfare of people belonging to other groups, individuals with all levels of authority embedded in and shaped by institutions, and social structures richly permeated by eliminationism.

At least for the scholars whose work I have discussed here, this special intention more closely resembles what I have explained earlier as a *dolus eventualis*, the recognition of which requires a judgment about what a reasonable person should have known about the annihilatory consequences of his or her actions. But at times even this seems too narrow a constraint. As Woolford notes, "What this attack on ontology amounted to was an attack on habitus—a full assault upon the learned dispositions of Indigenous life that were the storehouse of the embodied practices of Indigeneity."[47] That is, the primary casualty of settler colonialism in Canada were the individuals, conditions, and structures required for a people to make sense of themselves as such. Their destruction is attributable to a diverse range of actors working in concert, not always knowingly, to achieve the end of traditional ways of being and thinking, the practice of living and not just mere physical persistence. No doubt prominent amongst these actors is Canada's IRS system, about which we are really just beginning to learn in the wake of the activities of Canada's TRC. Woolford cites Hayter Reed, a senior bureaucrat in the government department responsible for overseeing Indian affairs, who in the 1890s "instructed teachers and staff of the residential schools to employ 'every effort … against anything calculated to keep fresh in the memories of the children habits and associations which it is one of the main objects of industrial education to obliterate.' "[48]

Such clear statements of intent must, however, be read alongside less explicit expressions of moral disregard such as the dietary experiments uncovered by Ian Mosby that were conducted by the Canadian government on Aboriginal communities and residential schools between 1942 and 1952.[49] Along with Christianization, the theft of Indigenous land, the introduction of diseases, and the forcible removal and adoption of Aboriginal children (the so-called "Sixties Scoop"), these experiments may be located within a complex and evolving nodal network of destruction rationalized by the intention to destroy a form of life deemed not worth living. On this broader conception of genocidal intentionality (broader since it is a corporate intention not reducible to individual mental states), even acts of apparent benevolence may be seen as complicit in genocide to the extent that they were understood by their actors as likely to result in a group's inability to persist on its own terms. Indeed disregard of a group's *eidos*, or sense of itself—of what it regards as its history, values, and prospects—constitutes one of genocide's enduring moral harms.

Settler-Colonial Genocide in Canada: Final Thoughts

It is notable how few published works are available that specifically deny there having been a genocide committed in Canada. Denial does not seem to be an intellectually respectable position, suggesting that it is perhaps instead just a manifestation of vulgar prejudice. Certainly insofar as the community of genocide scholars is concerned, there is no real question anymore that Canadian settler colonialism was genocidal. What remains unknown is exactly how such settler colonialism functioned as a nodal network to yield ontological destruction. Unlike the Holocaust, whose history and posterity have been extensively documented and commented upon, giving it (an increasingly contested) paragonicity, the story of colonialism in Canada has not yet been comprehensively told. More importantly, perhaps, it is only just starting to be told from the perspective of Indigenous peoples themselves. To pick only two such examples, the recent production of memoirs by IRS survivors,[50] along with the testimony given before the TRC, are both in the process of revising our picture of residential schools and their workings as sites of genocide. Likewise, recent additions to the repertoire of international legal instruments such as the Declaration of the Rights of Indigenous People, which codifies "Indigenous historical grievances, contemporary challenges and socio-economic, political and cultural aspirations,"[51] have done much to introduce Indigenous perspectives on matters of history and justice, especially concerning the colonial past.

Complicating matters even more is the instability of the term "genocide" itself. As I have tried to show here, the concept has been criticized by a wide variety of scholars and activists dissatisfied with its narrow construal in international law. The "Lemkinian Turn" in genocide studies seeks to redress these perceived legal shortcomings. By reminding us of the ideological and institutional contexts within which the Genocide Convention emerged, as well as Lemkin's privileging of group destruction in his account of genocide's harms, by offering a less restrictive account of genocidal intention, and by highlighting the fact that groups may be destroyed using means other than mass murder, means often directed towards the annihilation or radical and unwanted transformation of a people's identity and culture, Lemkinian scholars are providing ample reasons to reassess judgments concerning European colonialism's legacies and history. Early results of this reassessment have thus far contributed to further cementing the conclusion that settler colonialism was generally, and in the Canadian context specifically, genocidal.

In sum, evidence continues to mount that the Genocide Convention is inadequate to the task of reliably determining when a genocide has been committed, and therefore of deciding whom to punish in its wake. Restoring the destruction of culture to the centre of our understanding of genocidal criminality is both overdue and likely to have a significant effect on how Indigenous experiences and history are generally understood. In light of this reappraisal, which requires us above all to take Indigenous perspectives seriously, it may become possible to explore new pathways towards genuine reconciliation. In MacDonald's and Hudson's words, "Changes in the UNGC to 'restore' cultural genocide, while reducing the impact of *dolens specialis* [*sic*], would have a marked impact on how Aboriginal history in Canada would be reinterpreted, both legally and morally. These changes would provide wider legal scope for reassessing the IRS system and the nature of truth and reconciliation."[52]

NOTES

1   Pete McCormack, "Genocide and the Role of the Individual: An Interview with Samantha Power," PeteMcCormack.com, http://www.petemccormack.com/interview_power_001.htm (accessed 15 February 2016).

2   Peter Burke, *Varieties of Cultural History* (Cambridge: Polity Press, 1997), 54.

3   Additional reasons included budgetary worries and a longstanding commitment by IAGS to organize an Indigenous-themed conference.

4   The TRC was originally scheduled to wind down its operations in 2014, but due to a number of factors—including the consequences of its mismanaged first year of operations under the leadership of then chairperson Justice Harry Laforme, and the late release of a trove of important government documents following a 2013 ruling by the Ontario Superior Court—the TRC's mandate was extended for an additional year. The TRC staged its closing ceremonies from 1 May to 3 June 2015, and ceased operations entirely on 18 December of that year.

5   Significantly, a 2015 survey undertaken by the Angus Reid Institute in the wake of the release of the TRC's summary report showed a large majority of Canadians agreeing with the commission that the country's residential schools perpetrated "cultural genocide" on Indigenous peoples.

6   Mary Agnes Welch, "The Genocide Test," Winnipeg Free Press, 12 July 2014, http://www.winnipegfreepress.com/breakingnews/the-genocide-test-266849891.html (accessed 2 September 2016).

7   Note that in its definition of genocide, Canada's Crimes Against Humanity and War Crimes Act (2000) defers "to customary international law or conventional international law" and "principles of law recognized by the community of nations." Available at http://laws-lois.justice.gc.ca/PDF/C-45.9.pdf.

8   Michael Melanson, "Canadian policies don't meet 'genocide test,'" *Winnipeg Free Press*, 17 July 2014, http://www.winnipegfreepress.com/ opinion/analysis/canadian--policies--dont-meet-genocide-test-267286851.html (accessed 1 September 2016).

9   Andrew Woolford, "Genocides distinct, complex," *Winnipeg Free Press*, 18 July 2014, http://www.winnipegfreepress.com/opinion/letters_to_the_editor/have-your-say-267613581.html (accessed 1 September 2016).

10   Ibid.

11   See William Korey, "Lemkin's Passion: Origin and Fulfilment," *PISM Series* 1 (2010): 75–98. Korey contends that with respect to the drafting process of the Genocide Convention, "Technical and drafting considerations had to give way, almost at the outset, to political calculation" (89).

12   Michael Ignatieff, "The Unsung Hero Who Coined the Term 'Genocide,' " *New Republic*, 21 September 2013, http://www.newrepublic.com/article/ 114424/raphael-lemkin-unsung-hero-who-coined-genocide (accessed 3 September 2016).

13   Samuel Moyn, *The Last Utopia: Human Rights in History* (Cambridge, MA: Belknap Press, 2012); Marco Duranti, "The Holocaust, The Legacy of 1789 and the Birth of International Human Rights Law: Revisiting the Foundation Myth," *Journal of Genocide Research*, 14, no. 2 (2012): 159–186.

14   Peter Balakian, "Raphael Lemkin, Cultural Destruction, and the Armenian Genocide," *Holocaust and Genocide Studies* 27, no. 1 (2013): 60.

15   Convention on the Prevention and Punishment of the Crime of Genocide. Adopted by Resolution 260 (III) A of the United Nations General Assembly on 9 December 1948, http://www.oas.org/dil/1948_Convention_on_the_Prevention_and_Punishment_of_the_Crime_of_Genocide.pdf (accessed 1 September 2016).

16   Balakian, "Raphael Lemkin, Cultural Destruction, and the Armenian Genocide," 59.

17   As cited in Balakian, "Raphael Lemkin," 60.

18   Sociologist Damien Short shows how Lemkin understood physical and cultural genocide "not as two distinct phenomena, but rather [as] one process that could be accomplished through a variety of means." See Short, "Cultural Genocide and Indigenous Peoples: A Sociological Approach," *The International Journal of Human Rights* 14, no. 6 (2010): 838.

19   See Powell and Amarasingam, "Atrocity and Proto-Genocide in Sri Lanka," in this volume.

20   Ibid.

21   Michael McDonnell and A. Dirk Moses, "Raphael Lemkin as Historian of Genocide in the Americas," *Journal of Genocide Research* 7, no. 4 (2005): 501.

22   See Ronald J. Horvath, "A Definition of Colonialism," *Current Anthropology* 13, no. 1 (1972): 45–57.

23   See Stephen Katz, *The Holocaust in Historical Context* (Oxford: Oxford University Press, 1994).

24   Paul Boghossian, "The Concept of Genocide," *Journal of Genocide Research* 12, nos. 1–2 (2010): 73. See also Martin Shaw, *What is Genocide?* (Cambridge: Polity Press, 2007).

25   Jean-Louis Panneé, "Raphael Lemkin and Raul Hilberg: About a Concept" *PISM Series* 1 (2010): 114.

26   McDonnell and Moses, "Raphael Lemkin as Historian of Genocide in the Americas," 502.

27   See David MacDonald and Graham Hudson, "The Genocide Question and Indian Residential Schools in Canada," *Canadian Journal of Political Science/Revue canadienne de science politique* 45, no. 2 (2012): 427–449; Ibid., 439.

28   In Panneé, "Raphael Lemkin and Raul Hilberg," 111.

29   Lemkin's conception of agency and causal responsibility runs contrary to that of
      Christopher Powell and Amarnath Amarasingam in their contribution to this volume.
      Powell, Amarasingam, and other structuralist/functionalist thinkers view our imme-
      diate moral and practical agency as crucially overdetermined by the various structures
      and ideologies in which we "disciplined" subjects are always already enmeshed. For
      such thinkers genocide is first and foremost "a global and systemic problem," and so
      Powell and Amarasingam feel justified in asserting that "what defines genocide is not
      so much the intentions of those engaged in its perpetration or even the moral qualities
      of the acts involved, but its distinctive qualities as a process" (See Powell and Amaras-
      ingam, "Atrocity and Proto-Genocide in Sri Lanka"). The alternative view that I am
      working to sketch here is that, per Lemkin, intentions matter to our understanding of
      what genocide is and who (or what) to hold responsible for its perpetration. However,
      I am critical of the legal conception of intention (i.e., *mens rea*), since it is far too
      crude and conspicuously disconnected from contemporary scholarly accounts of how
      people and collectivities plan and act. A more nuanced and less exclusive conception of
      intention is required to make sense of Canadian settler colonialism and other complex
      atrocities, and I've tried to provide some idea here of what one might look like although
      a thorough account exceeds (and runs in some ways parallel to) the explanatory aims of
      this chapter.

30   This is not to say that there are no relevant statements of destructive intent in the
      Canadian case, as I explain. Rather, it is difficult to connect such statements causally
      to the actual systems and structures responsible for the destruction of Canadian
      Aboriginal life. Of course this remains an issue in Holocaust scholarship too, but in
      that context intentionalism is longstanding and it has been plausibly elaborated by such
      distinguished historians as Saul Friedlander and Eberhard Jäckel, notwithstanding
      powerful functionalist critiques of the view.

31   Kai Ambos, "What Does 'Intent to Destroy' in Genocide Mean?" *International Review
      of the Red Cross* 91, no. 876 (2009): 835.

32   Ibid., 838.

33   Ibid., 840.

34   Ibid.

35   As cited in Ambos, "What Does 'Intent to Destroy' in Genocide Mean?" 840–841.

36   As cited in Brian Titley, *A Narrow Vision: Duncan Campbell Scott and the Adminis-
      tration of Indian Affairs in Canada* (Vancouver: University of British Columbia Press,
      1992): 50.

37   Andrew Woolford, "Ontological Destruction: Genocide and Canadian Aboriginal
      Peoples," *Genocide Studies and Prevention* 4, no. 1 (2009): 81.

38   MacDonald and Hudson, "The Genocide Question and Indian Residential Schools in
      Canada," 440.

39   In more recent work Woolford downplays the significance of benevolence claims, ar-
      guing that by morally justifying displacement and destruction they strategically served
      to mask an underlying and rapacious desire for land. See Woolford, *This Benevolent
      Experiment: Indigenous Boarding Schools, Genocide, and Redress in Canada and the
      United States* (Lincoln, NE: University of Nebraska Press, 2015).

40   Andrew Woolford, "Nodal Repair and Networks of Destruction: Residential Schools, Colonial Genocide, and Redress in Canada," *Settler Colonial Studies* 3, no. 1 (2013): 70.

41   Ibid.

42   Ibid.

43   Ibid., 72–73.

44   Karl Binding and Alfred Hoche, *Allowing the Destruction of Life Unworthy of Life: Its Measure and Form*, Trans. Cristina Modak (Greenwood, WI: Suzeteo Enterprises, 2012).

45   Woolford, "Nodal Repair and Networks of Destruction," 73.

46   As cited in Blanca Tovias de Paisted, "Navigating the Cultural Encounter: Blackfoot Religious Resistance in Canada (c. 1870–1930)," in *Empire, Colony, and Genocide: Conquest, Occupation, and Subaltern Resistance in World History*, ed. Dirk Moses (Oxford: Berghahn Books, 2008), 281.

47   Woolford, "Nodal Repair and Networks of Destruction," 75.

48   Ibid.

49   See Ian Mosby, "Administering Colonial Science: Nutrition Research and Human Biomedical Experimentation in Aboriginal Communities and Residential Schools, 1942–1952," *Histoire Sociale/Social History* 46, no. 91 (2013): 145–172.

50   See for example Ted Fontaine's *Broken Circle: The Dark Legacy of Indian Residential Schools* (Victoria, BC: Heritage House Publishing, 2010).

51   "Frequently Asked Questions: Declaration on the Rights of Indigenous Peoples," *United Nations Permanent Forum on Indigenous Issues*, http://www.un.org/esa/ socdev/unpfii/ documents/FAQsindigenousdeclaration.pdf (accessed 3 September 2016).

52   MacDonald and Hudson, "The Genocide Question and Indian Residential Schools in Canada," 443.

4

The Benefits and Challenges of Genocide Education: A Case Study of the Armenian Genocide

Raffi Sarkissian

Genocide education has been evolving for the past several decades. It was once commonly referred to as Holocaust education, as it primarily concentrated on the Jewish Holocaust. However, with the Armenian genocide entering our collective consciousness and the shock of contemporary genocides such as those in Cambodia, Serbia, Rwanda, and Darfur, educators have acknowledged the importance of a comparative approach to teaching about genocide. The importance of teaching from a variety of case studies, all of which carry unique qualities, has become an important component of genocide education. Thus, genocide education has now become an umbrella term that refers to the use of historical and contemporary cases of genocide to teach about social justice and human rights. The potential and urgency of genocide education has long been underestimated, as it has faced many challenges to date—for instance, the resistance displayed by some communities who deny a particular genocide and prefer the issue remain silent. For example, it was not until the 1970s that Holocaust curricula started to develop in North America, and today we see educational institutions at all levels adopting courses fully dedicated to the topic of genocide.[1]

The goal of genocide education is not solely to educate students about historical accounts of genocide, but also, I argue, to help pave the way for one of the most effective avenues to anti-racist education. Genocide is a consequence of deeply rooted societal discrimination, and it results from a series of human rights violations that render a people vulnerable to further exploitation. Racism and its dangers are therefore seen in their most visible and terrible form in genocide, making it a unique opportunity to teach and learn about these complex events. A combination of geopolitical circumstances and the manipulation of human behaviour often lead to active or indirect participation in genocide and similar crimes associated with human rights violations. Thus, genocide and human rights education creates an invaluable opportunity to explore the various choices available to all those affected by genocide, and the decisions that could have a positive impact on society even in the most difficult of times. The deep connections between individuals, the decisions we make, and the social conditions in which we live are embodied in genocide education. Genocide education also opens possibilities for empathetic forms of education to shift the barriers between societies where the concept of the Other is frequently raised and reinforced in harmful and destructive ways.

Genocide education remains a strong medium for educating students in the importance of safeguarding and understanding not just their individual human rights but also those that we share universally. According to research conducted by genocide scholar Samuel Totten, teachers strongly believe that genocide education provides opportunities for teaching about identity, moral theories, and character education.[2]

In "Holocaust Education in Ontario Schools: An Antidote to Racism?" Geoffrey Short showed that in many instances genocide education does not lead to anti-racist education unless teachers truly grasp the purpose and goals of the former. Thus, in order for genocide education to be delivered effectively, teachers require adequate professional development and continuous support. Without these conditions, it is easy for genocide education to become a survey course on genocides in history. Short goes on to cite the denial of genocide as an important concern requiring attention in the classroom: "Clearly, if the Holocaust is to function as an effective antidote to racism it is essential to counteract Holocaust denial."[3]

In *The Emergence of Holocaust Education in American Schools,* Thomas Fallace discusses the "*New York Times* debate" of the 1970s in light of the emergence of Holocaust education curricula and the New York City Board of Education's recommendation that its study be made mandatory in all its schools. Among the letters published in this debate were some denying the Holocaust and thus challenging Holocaust education. For instance, George Pape, president of the German-American Committee of Greater New York, claimed that there was no proof the Holocaust had really taken place; he also wrote that the curriculum would target innocent German Americans. Dr. M. T. Mehdi, president of an Arab-American organization, claimed the curriculum was Zionist propaganda that was going to be promulgated at the city's expense. While many non-partisan spectators also believe that teaching this curricula would disrupt the peace amongst ethnic groups and incite hatred, this view is misleading. The goals of genocide education are quite the opposite of this, and in fact are intended to dispel feelings of resentment, hatred, and discrimination that may exist between ethnic groups. This kind of false and misleading reasoning resurfaced over three decades later in the case of the Turkish government's denial of the Armenian genocide during the Toronto District School Board's implementation of genocide education.

On 13 July 2005, the Toronto District School Board (TDSB) put forward a motion that eventually led to the development of the grade eleven Genocide and Crimes Against Humanity course and, on 14 December 2005, it decided to integrate the Armenian genocide into the high school–level history curriculum. Once the inclusion of the curriculum was settled upon, and after the course had been written in 2007, the government of Turkey began an offensive to prevent proper acknowledgement and education on the issue of the Armenian genocide.

On 27 August 2008, Ottawa's *Embassy Magazine* reported on the issue in an article titled "Turkey Decries Toronto School Board Genocide Course." The author, Michelle Collins, reported that the Turkish embassy, together with the Council of Turkish Canadians (CTC), had begun lobbying against the course. Both argued, as George Pape had of the Holocaust in the 1970s, that no such thing as an Armenian genocide had ever taken place and that the TDSB's new course would expose students to racism and discrimination.

Despite the fact that a growing number of Turkish intellectuals, both in and out of Turkey, have questioned the Turkish government's position on the Armenian genocide—albeit amidst protest and death threats— the CTC aggressively denies and actively works against any effort to acknowledge, commemorate, recognize, or teach the Armenian genocide in Canada. Their website houses material denying the genocide, ranging from archived petitions to position papers in line with the Turkish government's views.[4]

One such petition is titled "Content Change for TDSB's Grade 11 Course Genocide: Historical and Contemporary Implications," published by Lale Eskicoglu on 23 November 2007. The petition claims that the course would expose Turkish-Canadian students to more racism and discrimination without presenting any documented incidents or facts to support the claim of genocide. It used multiculturalism as a pretext to exclude the Armenian genocide from the course, since it is claimed that it is unfair and unjust to impose perpetrator status on an entire nationality. The petition also includes a mention of two instances of terrorist acts against Turkish government officials in Canada, claiming these are examples of racism that could be supported by the course. It concludes by stating that many "respected historians" dispute the Armenian genocide, and it cites the supposed lack of consensus amongst historians as grounds for disqualifying the Armenian genocide from being included in the course.[5]

The TDSB provided an opportunity for individuals to present deputations to the Program and School Services Committee on 16 January 2008. Individuals were given the opportunity to either raise concerns for or express their support of the course. Deputations were made in support of the course by Leo Adler, a Toronto Criminal Lawyer, Professor Frank Chalk, Director of the Montreal Institute of Genocide Studies at Concordia University, Jim Karygiannis, MP for Scarborough-Agincourt, and David Warner, former speaker of the Ontario Assembly. Two individuals presented deputations against the course—Lale Eskicioglu, representing the CTC, and Professor Ozay Mehmet, a Turkish-Canadian academic from Carleton University. A review of the deputations provides insight into the barriers posed by genocide denial.

Lale Eskicioglu's oral deputation was a replica of the contents of the aforementioned petition, of which she was the author. She started off by targeting Barbara Coloroso's 2007 book *Extraordinary Evil: A Brief History of Genocide*, which was included in the curriculum. Eskicioglu claimed the book was used as a basis for the genocide curriculum and discredited Coloroso's work since she is not a historian. She claimed the history of the Armenian genocide is "disputed" and that the works of certain historians who held the view supported by the Turkish government were not consulted, in particular that of Justin McCarthy and Guenter Lewy. Books by

McCarthy and Lewy, known genocide deniers, were handed out to those present. She concluded by claiming that the decision for the course was one-sided and that "the claims of an Armenian Genocide are being used to justify [the] racism, hatred and prejudice our children are experiencing."[6]

The second speaker, Professor Ozay Mehmet, demanded that the TDSB re-examine the curriculum "and remove all Armenian references in this course" for the following reasons: "The Armenian component, text references and bibliographic sources are one-sided, ethnically biased, and reflecting only Armenian input and promotes ethnic hate"; the use of the term "Armenian genocide" in the course amounts to accepting forged documents as valid; the Armenian part of the course will expose Turkish children to harassment and bullying in our schools; and finally, the Canadian government's position on this matter is unclear.[7]

While the speakers opposing the course were of Turkish origin, the deputations supporting the course came from a variety of backgrounds and displayed the diverse support the inclusion of the Armenian genocide module had received. These refuted many of the concerns raised by the CTC. For example, they stressed that the course in no way equates present-day Turkish citizens with the perpetrators of genocide (i.e., the Committee of Union and Progress). Professor Frank Chalk stressed that the international scholarly consensus supports the fact that the Armenian case is rightfully classified as genocide according to the UN's genocide convention. He also suggested that the CTC would be applauded as honest and courageous if they finally confronted the history of the Armenian genocide rather than supporting the Turkish government's policy of denial. He also stressed that the Canadian government is clear on the issue of the Armenian genocide and has officially recognized it as fact.

It was apparent from the beginning that those opposed to the inclusion of the Armenian genocide had used concerns of discrimination, bullying, and terrorism, as stated in the CTC petition, merely as a guise.[8] Their position was first and foremost a defence rooted in the Turkish government's denial of the Armenian genocide.

A close look at the contents of the course would immediately dispel the CTC's fears of discrimination and racism. The course provides a thorough exploration of morals, values, prejudice, stereotyping, discrimination, and similar themes that lay the groundwork for the case studies that follow. The curriculum does not allow for any form of discriminatory sentiment or animosity between ethnic groups. It is clear in the course that *geno-cidaires* from Nazi Germany and the Ottoman Empire in no way represent the German or Turkish citizens of today—rather, the curriculum supports a movement to collectively acknowledge the wrongs of the past and build a positive future. The TDSB also addressed the concept of multiculturalism, stating that the very notion of multiculturalism supports the need for such a course:

> Given the specific multi-cultural and multi-ethnic diversity within Toronto, we feel it is essential that students born within and outside Canada have the opportunity to explore in depth the causes and consequences of genocide and the lived realities of the aggressors, targets, bystanders, and resisters to these horrific acts of violence. A study of these experiences will help foster a sense of empathy for the targets of these violent acts and hopefully encourage students to understand the connections they have to their fellow human beings.[9]

In the *New York Times* debate described above, German interest groups had presented many concerns about Holocaust education that were similar to Turkish concerns over the TDSB course. If we as a society had not disregarded these concerns as attempts at denying genocide, we might never have achieved the successes in genocide education of the past few decades. As Germany worked to come to terms with the Holocaust and use its lessons to promote positive change, this led to an inspirational and exemplary social transformation from a nation that perpetrated genocide to a pluralist society. Unfortunately, this acknowledgement of guilt, and the resulting social transformation, did not occur in Turkey, where political leaders have insisted on denying the truth and forcing a fabricated history onto its people. The CTC's defense is ultimately the product of the systematic denial of the Armenian genocide. Organizations such as the CTC and the "respected" historians mentioned in their petition ultimately perpetuate the cycle of genocide rather than one of positive social transformation. Their insistence that any mention of the Armenian genocide is a universal attack on Turks has kept generations in the dark, thus leading to the outrageous behaviour experienced by the TDSB when trying to implement curricula that is beneficial and healthy for society.

The International Association of Genocide Scholars, in a 24 January 2008 letter of support to the TDSB, addresses this claim of a "universal attack" on Turks by stating that the

> assertion that teaching the truth about the Armenian past will be demeaning to Turkish students or Turkish people in general denigrates the intelligence of Canadians of Turkish descent and strikes us as disingenuous. Education in a democracy is built on historical critique and critical evaluation. When the history of US slavery, British colonialism, German genocide of Jews and Roma, Mussolini's fascism, Stalin's purges, or Mao's human rights crimes, is taught, the descendants of the perpetrators' nationalities (Americans, British, Germans, Italians, Russians, or Chinese) are not demeaned or persecuted by anyone. On the contrary, they emerge from learning those histories better educated, with a stronger sense of how important critical analysis of the past is; and they achieve an ethical capacity crucial to good education. In dealing with the truth about their nations' histories, they develop the moral honesty crucial to the progress of human rights in a democracy. The study of genocide is not designed to impose collective guilt. It is meant to seek to understand a common human problem. Turks as a people did not commit the Armenian genocide, any more than Canadians or Americans in general committed genocide against native American populations. But some of our ancestors did commit these crimes, and it is our present responsibility to study and acknowledge them in order to prevent genocides in the future.[10]

Although German-American organizations have realized the importance and benefits of understanding and acknowledging the past as a means of creating a peaceful society, the government of Turkey has yet to do so; in the meantime, it encourages Turkish communities abroad to parrot its position.

The TDSB was not the first or only target of genocide denial on the part of the Turkish government and its affiliates. What we saw in the TDSB case study has been a common occurrence throughout North America. An earlier episode is discussed by Roger Smith, who shows how, amongst many other means of denial, the Turkish government targeted secondary schools in the United States as it grew fearful that the Armenian genocide would be discussed in classrooms. Smith notes how "a letter from the Turkish embassy in Washington was sent to secondary schools throughout the United States to dissuade them from using histories that mention the Armenian Genocide. Stronger efforts still have been made to prevent any discussion of the 1915 genocide being formally included in the social studies curriculum as part of Holocaust/genocide studies."[11]

Mark Fleming also discusses difficulties faced by the state of Massachusetts in implementing genocide education. In 1999, a guide for teaching genocide and human rights, including the Armenian genocide, was issued by the Massachusetts Board of Education. In October 2005, a group of Turkish Americans, led by the Assembly of Turkish-American Associations (ATAA), filed a lawsuit against the Board of Education claiming that the guide violated the First Amendment because it cited the Armenian case as genocide. This was a failed attempt to jeopardize the teaching of the Armenian genocide.[12]

In *Remembrance and Denial: The Case of the Armenian Genocide*, scholar Richard Hovanissian describes the significance of genocide denial:

> It has been said that denial is the final phase of genocide. Following the physical destruction of a people and their material culture, memory is all that is left and is targeted as the last victim. Complete annihilation of a people requires the banishment of recollection and the suffocation of remembrance. Falsification, deception and half-truths reduce what was to what may have been or perhaps what was not at all. ... By altering or erasing the past, a present is produced and a future is projected without concern about historical integrity. The process of annihilation is thus advanced and completed by denial.[13]

This effectively characterizes the CTC's intentions, which is part of a larger denial apparatus belonging to the Turkish government. The policies set forth by the Turkish government have had a tremendous effect on how the Armenians are viewed by those raised and educated in Turkey. The establishment of a legal framework restricting certain thoughts and encouraging others, the vilifying of the Armenian population, and genocide denial have all led to viewing Armenians as the Other, and behaviour toward them has been fashioned accordingly. Article 301 of the Turkish penal code, which criminalizes defending the existence of the Armenian genocide, has already vilified many intellectuals for their views. The assassination of the Turkish-Armenian journalist Hrant Dink, in January 2007, by an ultra-nationalist Turkish citizen in Istanbul, was a by-product of such a law. The law made Dink a criminal in the eyes of the public and thus a target for hatred and death.

Denial is an attack on the memories of survivors and their descendants. According to genocide scholar Gregory Stanton, "It is a continuing attempt to destroy the victim group psychologically and culturally, to deny its members even the memory of the murders of their relatives. That is what the Turkish government today is doing to Armenians around the world."[14] In other words, it is an attack on the collective memory of a people and their right to commemorate. Those who deny history, such as the Armenian genocide or the Holocaust, are attempting to conceal the truth. Genocide scholar Israel Charney describes deniers as individuals who "are attempting to write a final chapter to the original genocide—now by 'mass murder' of the recorded memories of human history. If being alive as human beings means some basic sense of knowing the record of history, the 'killing' of objective history is also the killing of human consciousness and evolution."[15] Denialists' motives for destroying memory are exactly the reason why we value the stories told by those who survive such mass atrocities as the Holocaust, given that a great deal of education is centred on the sharing of testimonies. If that very memory were to be denied, and the suffering trivialized, this would leave society with lessons unlearned.

While teaching about denial in the grade eleven Genocide and Crimes Against Humanity course at the ARS Armenian Private School, I shared with the class a poem written by Canadian-Armenian author and academic Alan Whitehorn. This poem, titled "How Do We Remember the Dead?" deals with the denial of the Armenian genocide. I asked the students to reflect and record their thoughts on the poem. The responses I received were expressive of the extent to which the crime of genocide had affected their lives through its denial. I saw the student responses as calls to the government of Turkey to break the cycle of genocide and, by doing so, end its assault on the conscience of the Turkish people and the memory of the Armenians who were victimized in 1915. It was a call to also set subsequent generations free from being victims in the present.

There is a parallel between the wounds caused by physical violence during the Armenian genocide, as discussed in survivor testimony, and the wounds students have on occasion described, and which are caused by denial. These are wounds inflicted in different ways, leaving different marks but caused by the same crime. Therefore, the Armenian genocide is an event, the physical and mental consequences of which are felt across generations. Moreover, its denial has had a profound effect on the identities of Armenian communities in the diaspora.

The experience of three generations of victims and survivors is commonly shared by many members of the Armenian community and is a concept worth examining. There is an absence of research on the effects of the denial of the Armenian genocide on subsequent generations. Such research would bring to light the harmful consequences of denial that are often sanctioned under the guise of freedom of speech.

2013–2014 marked the sixth academic year the TDSB's Genocide and Crimes Against Humanity course was offered. Since its implementation, the school board has also declared April Genocide Awareness Month. Over the years, the course has become popular among students, teachers, and administrators alike. Registration numbers alone show this, as they demonstrate a consistent increase in enrolment from year to year. Facing History and Ourselves, an organization involved in developing the course, provides ongoing professional development and teacher support, ensuring teachers are confident and effective, and are meeting the goals and purpose of genocide education.

In 2014, the Federation of Turkish Canadian Associations (FTCA)—an organization similar to the CTC—released a petition to request the removal of the Armenian genocide module. It also asked that a section reading "genocide of Armenians, Assyrians and Pontian Greeks" in the school board's 2013 Genocide Awareness Month statement be removed.[16] At the start of 2014, the ATAA pursued genocide denial as the California State Assembly passed a resolution on teaching the Armenian genocide.

In light of such denial campaigns, a TDSB course proposal released in 2008 rings true:

Given the specific multi-cultural and multi-ethnic diversity within Toronto, we feel it is essential that students born within and outside Canada have the opportunity to explore in depth the causes and consequences of genocide and the lived realities of the aggressors, targets, bystanders, and resisters to these horrific acts of violence. A study of these experiences will help foster a sense of empathy for the targets of these violent acts and hopefully encourage students to understand the connections they have to their fellow human beings.[17]

Here, the TDSB provides a unique opportunity for promoting multiculturalism and diversity through genocide education; conversely, the legal and educational structure of the Turkish government—the very same government attempting to negatively influence the domestic affairs of another country—has suppressed free discussion of and research into the Armenian genocide.

The inclusion of the Armenian genocide in Canadian curricula is imperative. Canada has been engaged with Armenian communities in the Ottoman Empire since 1878. Canadian fieldworkers and missionaries were present in the empire and witnessed the destruction of the Armenian population. They often communicated their experiences and concerns through letters and news reports, thus allowing Canadians to become well aware of the plight of the Armenians. A significant increase in Canadian media coverage triggered large scale and popular support for fundraising and relief efforts as early as the Hamidian Massacres of 1895–1896, during which time three hundred thousand Armenians were murdered.[18] The Armenian Relief Fund Association of Canada was formed in 1916, to better coordinate such fundraising.

> Over 15 years, it collected an impressive $1,000,000 in donations and had among its patrons Toronto's Roman Catholic archbishop and Anglican archdeacon, an Ontario Supreme Court justice, and two governors general. Its officers were mostly businessmen and clergymen. It had more than 25 chapters and worked in conjunction with the British Lord Mayor's Fund and the American Near East Relief.[19]

The teaching of the Armenian genocide, especially in the context of Canadian history, creates opportunities to learn about the positive outcome of humanitarianism, collective action, and global citizenship. It also sheds light on the positive role government officials, religious institutions, civil society, and the media can play in effecting change.

In its revised 2013 Canada and World Studies curriculum, the Ontario Ministry of Education included the topic of the Armenian genocide as a specific expectation in the mandatory grade ten Canadian History Since World War I course. Teachers can address the Armenian genocide when studying the importance of public commemoration and the acknowledgement of past human rights violations and genocide. The students are also asked to address the importance of these actions for identity and heritage in Canada. This is an important step towards incorporating this important page in Canadian history into mandatory curricula.[20]

Genocide denial is one of the biggest challenges to the implementation of genocide education. Stanton identifies denial as the last stage of the genocide process. It is a by-product of impunity and, if left unaddressed, can fuel future instances of mass violence. For this reason, genocide denial at the state level—as it is being practised by the government of Turkey today—can be dangerous. Since the establishment of the Turkish republic in 1923, successive governments have created an atmosphere of amnesia concerning Armenia and Armenians through the manipulation of geography, culture, and official history. These exercises in memory politics have then been pursued in all possible political, legal, and socio-cultural arenas and by a variety of government ministries, from education to culture. The infamous Article 301 of the Turkish penal code stands as just one example that is often cited as problematic.

Although organizations such as the CTC and the ATAA publicly deny the Armenian genocide abroad, a growing number of Turkish intellectuals in Turkey and the diaspora have called for Turkish recognition of the Armenian genocide. These include Taner Akcam, Fatma Muge Gocek, Halil Berktay, Cengiz Aktar, and Baskin Oran. In December 2008, thousands of Turks signed a petition apologizing for the Armenian genocide and calling on the Turkish government to acknowledge this history. The authors of the petition were threatened with trial under Article 301. In April 2010, on the ninety-fifth anniversary of the Armenian genocide, an unprecedented number of Turkish intellectuals signed a petition, which in part read "We call upon all peoples of Turkey who share this heartfelt pain to commemorate and pay tribute to the victims of 1915. In black, in silence. With candles and flowers."[21] A group of intellectuals also held a vigil at the prison where hundreds of Armenian intellectuals were detained prior to being executed on 24 April 1915. The following year, the number of intellectuals reached five hundred, and it has been growing ever since, despite government intimidation and the imposing fear of imprisonment and threats. Indeed, these actions were met with thousands of protesters chanting death threats and such discriminatory slogans as "Death to the Armenian Diaspora."[22]

The Turkish government's unwillingness to acknowledge the Armenian genocide and its disallowing of any mention of it under laws restricting freedom of speech have prevented Turkish society from having an opportunity to take responsibility. By maintaining the taboo on the Armenian genocide, the Turkish government has glorified the lives of the perpetrators of genocide while maintaining silence on the history of those who should have become the heroes of Turkish society, those who saved Armenian lives in 1915. Imagine a Germany where Schindler's story was silenced by the state and Hitler's was praised. Raffi Bedrosyan gives us an idea of how the glorifying of genocide perpetrators plays out in Turkey in his article "The Real Turkish Heroes of 1915":

> And yet, it is true in Turkey, where it is acceptable to name several neighborhoods, streets, and schools after Talat Pasha and other *Ittihat ve Terakki* (Committee of Union and Progress) "heroes" who not only planned and carried out the Armenian Genocide, but were responsible for the loss of the Ottoman Empire itself.
>
> At last count, there were officially 8 "Talat Pasha" neighborhoods or districts, 38 "Talat Pasha" streets or boulevards, 7 "Talat Pasha" public schools, 6 "Talat Pasha" buildings, and 2 "Talat Pasha" mosques scattered around Istanbul, Ankara, and other cities. After his assassination in 1922, Talat was originally interred in Berlin, Germany, but his remains were transferred to Istanbul in 1943 by the Nazis in an attempt to appease the Turks. He was re-buried with full military honors at the Infinite Freedom Hill Cemetery in Istanbul. The remains of the other notorious *Ittihat ve Terakki* leader, Enver Pasha, were also transferred in 1996 from Tajikistan and re-buried beside Talat, with full military honors; the ceremony was attended by Turkish President Suleyman Demirel and other dignitaries.[23]

The power of education, and genocide education specifically, resonates clearly here. Genocide denial presents itself as a great obstacle to this important form of education, a roadblock above and beyond the borders of perpetrator governments as we have seen in the case of the Turkish government.

In the absence of justice, reconciliation, and social reform, denial fuels the cycle of genocide by leading the perpetrator state from a post-genocidal society back to a pre-genocidal stage outlined in Stanton's "Ten Stages of Genocide" (i.e., classification, symbolization, discrimination, dehumanization, organization, polarization, preparation, persecution, extermination, and denial).[24] Denial allows genocide to transcend time and space, following victims and their offspring. Thus, genocide does not begin and end with physical destruction, nor do its effects remain constrained to particular borders. As mentioned above, people in California, Massachusetts, and Ontario have found themselves affected by campaigns being pursued far from the time and place of the physical violence.

The transgenerational effects of genocide fuelled by denial were common themes among the Canadian-Armenian youth interviewed by the Sara Corning Centre for Genocide Education throughout the course of the Armenian genocide's one hundredth anniversary commemorative period. Titled "100 Voices: Survival, Memory and Justice," this set of interviews was conducted with secondary-level students from grade nine to twelve at the ARS Armenian Private School in Toronto. A common concern shared by the interviewees is the fact that the Turkish republic continues to deny the Armenian genocide and this continues to cause trauma for generations subsequent to those who survived. [25]

Denial is a common issue that continues to affect victim groups of all genocides, and the need to educate about the effects of genocide denial is therefore a necessity. A letter supporting the TDSB course written by Rwandan genocide survivor Leo Kabalisa on 22 January 2008 identifies how denial continues to affect all victims of genocide, irrespective of time and place, and becomes a barrier to education and prevention. A part of his letter reads:

> Your program [the TDSB course] is being implemented at the right time because we are facing the phase of denial of the genocides. Ninety-two years after the Armenian genocide, instead of learning from the past, the current leadership of Turkey is spending

time and energy to deny the sad history of their past. In the case of the genocide of Tutsis, conferences and forums of discussion have been organized throughout Europe by Hutu extremists and their supporters to revise and deny the history of the genocide of the Tutsis. For the Holocaust, we all remember last year's conference in Teheran in which the reality of the Holocaust was questioned by scholars invited by the president of Iran. ... Those who complain about the teaching of genocide too often are simply genocide deniers. Do not yield to their attempts to influence valid curriculum.[26]

By responding to and overcoming such challenges, societies demonstrate their dedication to creating safe spaces where new generations can learn and become the change. The TDSB expressed this well in its proposal to the Ontario Ministry of Education: "Democracy, justice, and the rule of law must be understood, claimed, and defended by each generation of citizens if we are to confront this demonstration of human evil. We believe that a full-credit course will engage students and allow them to study genocide, war crimes and crimes against humanity in a systematic and thoughtful way."[27] The Genocide and Crimes Against Humanity course remains true to this rationale.

Moral philosopher Annette Baier states: "The reasons for recognizing obligations to future persons are closely connected with reasons for recognizing the rights of past persons."[28] If we cannot address the past and draw lessons from it, starting with respecting the rights of past persons, then we cannot ensure the rights of persons in the future.

NOTES

1   Thomas Fallace, *The Emergence of Holocaust Education in American Schools* (New York: Palgrave MacMillan, 2008), 25–26.

2   Samuel Totten, *Teaching About Genocide: Issues, Approaches, and Resources* (New York: Information Age Publishing, 2004).

3   G. Short, "Holocaust education in Ontario high schools: An antidote to racism?" *Cambridge Journal of Education* 30, no. 2 (2000): 302.

4   See http://www.turkishcanadians.com.

5   Lale Eskicioglu, "Content Change for TDSB's Grade 11 Course Genocide: Historical and Contemporary Implications," 2007, http://www.gopetition.com/petition/15422.html (accessed 1 August 2011).

6   Hratch Aynedjian, Program Committee Deputations (16 January 2008), DVD.

7   Ibid.

8   Lale Eskicioglu, "Content Change for TDSB's Grade 11 Course Genocide: Historical and Contemporary Implications."

9   Toronto District School Board, Ontario Ministry of Education Approved Proposal For a Locally Developed Course; Genocide and Crimes Against Humanity, Grade 11, College/University Preparation (2008).

10 International Association of Genocide Scholars, letter to the Toronto District School Board, 24 January 2008: 2.

11 Richard Hovannisian, *The Armenian Genocide: History, Politics, Ethics* (New York: St. Martin's Press, 1992), 9.

12 Mark Fleming, "Government Speech, Free Speech, and Education: The Constitutional Challenge to the Massachusetts Genocide Education Guide," *University of St. Thomas Journal of Law and Public Policy* 4, no. 2 (2010): 18–30.

13 Richard Hovannisian, *Remembrance and Denial: The Case of the Armenian Genocide*, (Detroit: Wayne State University Press, 1999), 202.

14 As cited in David Holthouse, "State of Denial: Turkey Spends Millions to Cover up Genocide," Southern Poverty Law Center, 2008, http://www.splcenter.org/intel/intelreport/article.jsp?aid=935 (accessed 1 August 2011).

15 Israel Charney, "The Psychology of Denial: A Contribution to the Psychology of Denial of Genocide," *Journal of Armenian Studies* 4, no. 1 (1992): 301.

16 Harout Sassounian, "Canadian Turks Should Condemn not Condone Genocide Denial, *Asbarez*," 7 January 2014, http://asbarez.com/118052/canadian-turks-should-condemn-not-condone-genocide-denial/ (accessed 30 January 2014).

17 Toronto District School Board, Ontario Ministry of Education Approved Proposal For a Locally Developed Course; Genocide and Crimes Against Humanity, Grade 11, College/University Preparation CHG38, 2008.

18 Aram Adjemian, Isabel Kaprielian-Churchil, Daniel Ohanian, Raffi Sarkissian, *Canada and the Armenian Genocide* (Toronto: Sara Corning Centre for Genocide Education, 2015), 4

19 Ibid., 5.

20 Ontario Ministry of Education, *Canadian and World Studies: The Ontario Curriculum Grade 9 and 10* (2013): 124, 140.

21 "Turkish Scholars Urge Countrymen to Mark Armenian Genocide in Istanbul," *Asbarez*, 21 April 2010, http://asbarez.com/79594/turkish- scholars-urge-countrymen-to-mark-armenian-genocide-in-istanbul (accessed 1 August 2011).

22 Khatchig Mouradian, "Despite Obstacles, Armenian Genocide Commemorations Held in Turkey," *The Armenian Weekly*, 24 April 2010, http://www.armenianweekly.com/2010/04/24/genocide/ (accessed 1 August 2011).

23 Raffi Bedrosyan, "The Real Turkish Heroes of 1915," *The Armenian Weekly*, 29 July 2013, http://www.armenianweekly.com/2013/07/29/the-real-turkish-heroes-of-1915/ (accessed 30 January 2014).

24 Gregory Stanton, "The Ten Stages of Genocide," *Genocide Watch*, http://www.genocidewatch.org/genocide/tenstagesofgenocide.html (accessed 1 August 2011).

25   Sara Corning Centre for Genocide Education, "100 Voices: Survival, Memory and Justice," http://www.corningcentre.org/100-voices.html (accessed 1 April 2015).

26   Leo Kabalisa, letter to the Toronto District School Board, 22 January 2008.

27   Toronto District School Board, Ontario Ministry of Education Approved Proposal For a Locally Developed Course; Genocide and Crimes Against Humanity, Grade 11, College/University Preparation CHG38, 2008.

28   Annette Baier, "The Rights of Past and Future Persons," in *Responsibilities to Future Generations*, ed. Ernest Partridge (Buffalo, NY: Prometheus, 1980), 171–183.

5

"We Charge Genocide": A Historical Petition All but Forgotten and Unknown[1]

Steven Leonard Jacobs

In 1951, three years after the United Nations ratified its Convention on the Prevention and Punishment of the Crime of Genocide (December 1948), but almost four decades *before* the United States affirmed its own participation in 1988, the (American) Civil Rights Congress (CRC), under the direction of its founder William L. Patterson, presented and later published a petition to the UN under the title *We Charge Genocide: The Crime of the Government Against the Negro People.*[2] Patterson would later publish his autobiography detailing the events leading up to this all but forgotten moment in history under the title *The Man Who Cried Genocide: An Autobiography.*[3]

This chapter is an examination of the petition itself, the charges included (in a country where many, even in 2016, argue that the so-called racial divide is growing wider), Patterson's own story and understanding of the petition and its historical context, the larger socio-economic and legal questions of reparations for all victims of genocide, and what this portends in light of the recent genocides in Rwanda, the former Yugoslavia, Sudan, and those yet to occur.

A Most Peculiar Introduction

Towards the end of *The Man Who Cried Genocide*, Patterson, the primary author of *We Charge Genocide: The Crime of the Government Against the Negro People*, criticized and severely chastised Raphael Lemkin—the motivating presence behind the 1948 UN Genocide Convention, as it has come to be known, and now increasingly acknowledged as the "father" of the academic discipline of "genocide studies" (an offshoot of the field of "Holocaust studies")—for his failure to support the petition.[4] He writes:

> A letter was also sent to a select list of prominent men and women and to a number of the country's leading law schools over my signature. The letter inquired of the addressee whether he or she believed that the UN Convention on the Prevention and Punishment of the Crime of Genocide would apply to the situation of the Negro in the United States. One letter was sent to Mrs. Eleanor Roosevelt, as head of the U.S. delegation of the UN Human Rights Commission.
>
> Replies came from all sides. Interestingly enough, they were, in the main, along the color line. A majority of the Negroes polled believed that the Genocide Convention should be invoked; a majority of the white liberals and personalities were of a contrary view. ...
>
> Without exception, faculty members at law schools were adamantly opposed to the genocide charges. Most of them were in favor of the Genocide Convention as an abstract statement of law but rejected any attempt to apply it, declaring that such an attack impeached the integrity of our nation.[5] And this was the consensus of the replies we received from white liberals in general.
>
> *Among those who replied was Professor Lemkin, "father" of the Genocide Convention. ... How an honest person viewing the American scene impartially could come to any conclusion other than that forms of genocide were being practiced in the United States was difficult for us to see.*
>
> *Professor Lemkin experienced no such difficulty.* In a considerable correspondence with me,[6] *he argued vehemently that the provisions of the Genocide Convention bore no relationship to the U.S. Government or its position vis-à-vis Black citizens.*[7] Lemkin and other law professors and practicing attorneys were evidently fearful of criticizing a government in relation to its Black citizens was a disgrace to civilized mankind.[8]

Several pages later, he continued his critique:

> Across the Atlantic, Paul Robeson and other members of the CRC who accompanied him had presented copies of the petition to the officers of the UN Secretariat. The event was reported in the *New York Times* of December 18, 1951.
>
> *The* Times *had also taken the trouble to elicit the view of Dr. Lemkin at Yale. His anti-Soviet opinions proved of more significance to the* Times *than the words he had written into the Genocide Convention. Dr. Lemkin, according to the* Times, *said: "The accusations were a maneuver to divert attention from the crimes of genocide committed against Estonians, Latvians, Lithuanians, Poles, and other Soviet-subjugated peoples." Lemkin branded Paul Robeson and me as "un-American elements serving a foreign power." This was a procedure that was to be repeated many times. Dr. Lemkin was attempting to put the shoe he held on the wrong foot.*[9]

However, after carefully examining my own extensive cataloguing of more than twenty thousand pages of Lemkin's papers, including vast numbers of copies of letters to persons all over the world, neither William L. Patterson nor the Civil Rights Congress—nor the petition *We Charge Genocide*—have yet to surface, raising serious doubts, not only about Mr. Patterson's critique of Lemkin's position, but also about his use of the phrase "considerable correspondence" with someone who literally saved copies of *every* letter written or received as well as numerous other documents.[10]

If, however, his comments are accurate with regard to his undiscovered correspondence with Lemkin, what are we to conclude? As noted below, Lemkin's reluctance to criticize his adopted country was of a piece with his desire to do everything within his power to ensure the passage and later adoption/ratification of the UN Genocide Convention by the United States. That orientation, coupled with the increasing rift between the United States and the Soviet Russia after the Second World War and the beginning of the Cold War, more than likely factored into that reluctance as well. Adding to that negativity must have been the common understanding in the American press and other venues that identified Patterson, Paul Robeson, and the CRC itself as Communists all, resulting in Lemkin's *New York Times* comments.

More germane to the topic at hand, however, four questions present themselves: who was William L. Patterson? What was contained within the *We Charge Genocide* petition directed at the United Nations? What became of the petition? And what about reparations for African-Americans?

William L. Patterson

William L. Patterson was born on 27 August 1891,[11] in San Francisco, and died on 5 March 1980 in New York City. Graduating from high school in Mill Valley, California, at age twenty, *the first African-American to do so*, he went on to study at the University of California Hastings College of Law in 1915, where he received his law degree in 1919, and afterwards joined the National Association for the Advancement of Colored People (NAACP).[12] It was during this period that he read the writings of W. E. B. Du Bois, American sociologist, historian, civil rights activist, Pan-Africanist, author, and editor, and A. Philip Randolph, a leader in the African-American civil rights movement, the American labour movement, and Socialist political parties. Though he flirted with Socialism, the result of a trip to London, he ultimately became a committed member of the Communist Party USA, largely the result of the notorious Sacco-Vanzetti case. It should also be noted that his mother, Mary Galt Patterson, born in 1850, had been a slave and spent her childhood on a plantation in Virginia, as had her mother and her grandmother. His father was James Edward Patterson, born in the British West Indies, in Kingstown (the capital of St. Vincent), who initially earned his living smuggling Chinese into the United States, and who later became a Seventh Day Adventist missionary to the island of Tahiti, abandoning his family for long periods of time. There were three additional brothers and a sister by his mother's previous marriage. It was, however, his maternal grandfather, William Galt, whose influence upon him was evident, as he writes:

> William Galt took part in other great liberation battles, prepared anti-racist conferences and conventions, helped fight civil rights cases through the state and federal courts in valiant efforts to make the Emancipation Proclamation and post-Civil War constitutional amendments instruments for freedom. It was of great political importance that California come into the Union as a free

state, and Negroes, both escaped slaves and freed Black men, participated in that fight. There was a victory but not a complete one. The democracy preached to Black men, Mexican Americans and Indians did not come with statehood, and few white Americans who fought for statehood were concerned with a fight for democracy for all the people.[13]

Moving to Harlem after returning to the United States, he opened a law office in 1923 with two friends with a primary legal focus on those who were wrongfully accused of criminal acts. It was during this period that he met and became lifelong friends with Paul Robeson, African-American singer and actor who became involved with the civil rights movement. Two of the more famous cases in which he was involved were those of the anarchists Nicola Sacco and Bartolomeo Vanzetti who were unjustly executed in 1927 for the supposed murders of two men, and for whom, in support, Patterson was himself arrested on the picket line; as well as the infamous case of the "Scottsboro (Alabama) Boys," in which nine young African-American men were falsely charged and convicted of the rape of two white women on a train in 1931 (as of 2013, all had had their convictions overturned or were granted pardons by the Alabama legislature). In the 1960s, he was also involved in the defence of black Communist activist Angela Davis, today a professor at the University of California, Santa Cruz, and the Black Panthers, a radical Socialist liberation organization founded by Huey Newton and Bobby Seale, and whose original title was the Black Panther Party for Self-Defense.

After the deaths of Sacco and Vanzetti, Patterson travelled to Soviet Russia on more than one occasion, initially enrolling in the Far East University and participating in the Sixth Comintern Congress in Moscow during his time there (1928), experiencing, according to him, no discrimination whatsoever on account of his black skin. In 1930, he also attended the World Conference against Racism and Anti-Semitism in Paris, where he again met his third wife, Louise Thompson (to whom he was first introduced in 1919 in Oakland), friend and collaborator of famed black poet Langston Hughes.

Returning to the United States, he initially resumed his law practice in New York, after a brief sojourn in Pittsburgh, before moving to Chicago in 1938 and actively working with the Communist Party USA, and later becoming the executive secretary of the International Labor Defense (ILD) and founder of the CRC, which merged the ILD and the National Federation for Constitutional Liberties in 1946, becoming its national executive secretary in 1949, and putting his legal training to good use in a number of cases, successful and unsuccessful, involving innocent black defendants. In 1951, he and ninety-two other petitioners, along with his wife Louise, presented "A Petition to the United Nations" both at the UN Secretariat in New York and the General Assembly in Paris entitled *We Charge Genocide: The Crime of the Government against the Negro People*, and in Patterson's own words "becoming the first organization in history to charge the Government of the United States with the crime of genocide."[14] In 1952, he received an award from the International Fur and Leather Workers Union "In recognition of [his] devotion to the cause of Constitutional rights and for outstanding contributions in the struggle against genocide."

In 1971, he published his autobiography, *The Man Who Cried Genocide*, with the left-leaning New York publishing house International Publishing Company, whose website today (www.intpubnyc.com) advertises "Books to Help You Understand and Change the World!" and notes especially titles by "[Karl] Marx and [Friedrich] Engels, and selected books by [Nicolai] Lenin and other Marxist scholars and activists."

Patterson remained active in civil rights causes throughout the 1960s and 1970s. He died in 1980 at age eighty-nine.

"We Charge Genocide"

In printed form (239 pages plus 5 appendices[15]), *We Charge Genocide: The Historic Petition to the United Nations for Relief from a Crime of the United States Government Against the Negro People*, opens with an undated photograph of "two young Negro men"—Dooley Morton and Bert Moore—"murdered in a brutal double lynching" in Columbus, Mississippi, and captioned on the obverse "The Face of Genocide," and with the further explanation, "Such horrifying violence is only one of the many crimes against the Negro people of the United States which together form the major crime of genocide."[16] Prior to Patterson's introduction, articles 2 and 3 of the UN Convention on the Prevention and Punishment of the Crime of Genocide are included, as well as the names and states of the more than ninety petitioners,[17] and a page entitled "New Acts of Genocide" summarizing ten additional cases.

The petition is itself divided into four parts: "The Opening Statement," "The Law and the Indictment," "The Evidence," and, obviously, the centrepiece of the Petition itself, and "Summary and Prayer."[18]

In his introduction, Patterson decries a "record of mass slayings on the basis of race," and correctly notes that the crime of genocide, as defined by the UN convention, includes a racial group as one of its four victim groups, and that the destruction *in part* of such a group constitutes genocide. He further argues that "the oppressed Negro citizens of the United States, segregated, discriminated against and long the target of violence, *suffer from genocide as a result of the consistent, conscious, unified policies of every branch of government.*"[19] Thus was the petition submitted to the UN against the United States in an attempt to charge the latter with violating both the UN Charter and the convention itself. (It should also be stressed that, at the time of the petition's submission, the United States was *not* a signatory to the Genocide Convention. That would not occur until 1988, under the presidency of Ronald Reagan.)

In defending this action, Patterson states that the CRC is "rendering a service of inestimable value to progressive mankind," a leftist phrase of the 1950s and one fully associated with the American Communist Party, of which he was an active member. Waxing somewhat eloquently, Patterson further writes that the petition "will speak with a tongue of fire loosing an unquenchable moral crusade, the universal response to which will sound the death knell of all racist theories."[20]

And thus, Patterson and the CRC "call upon the United Nations to act and to call the Government of the United States to account."[21] Going even further, and perhaps too ambitiously, he states:

> We [the CRC] believe that this program [i.e., petition] can go far toward ending the threat of a third world war. We believe it can contribute to the establishment of a people's democracy[22] on a universal scale.[23]

Part 1, "The Opening Statement," includes "a Review of the Case and an Offer of Proof, giving something of the scope and historical background of the genocide being committed against the Negro people of the United

States." What then follows is a description of the situation of blacks in the American South during the 1940s, including "Klan Terror," "Mental Harm," "Denial of the Right to Vote," "Typical Cases" resulting in death, and "Other Race Matters."

Part 2, "The Law and the Indictment," is a review of the history of the Genocide Convention, the legitimacy and applicability of the plaintiffs' petition (being neither a nation-state nor a government),[24] and the indictment itself, further detailing how the various parts of the Genocide Convention apply in the case of African-Americans.

Part 3, "The Evidence," is a 137-page record of

> Various acts of genocide against the Negro people of the United States from January 1, 1945 to June 1951, chronologically arranged under those articles and provisions of the Genocide Convention which they violate.[25]

It ends with a listing of those persons, organizations, and institutions guilty of complicity under article 3 (e) of the Genocide Convention, and includes the president, Congress, Supreme Court, attorney general, Department of Justice, eleven southern states, the KKK, "the Morgan, Rockefeller, Du Pont, and Mellon interests" (as spelled out in appendix 3), and the following individuals: James Byrnes and J. Strom Thurmond of South Carolina; Fielding L. Wright, John Rankin, and James O. Eastland of Mississippi; Herman Talmadge of Georgia; and Allen J. Ellender of Louisiana—all accused of racist white supremacist statements and incitements to violence.

For the petitioners, as expressed in the summary, there was no doubt that genocide was being practiced against fifteen million African-Americans and that this was a criminal act. Though today's scholarly community appears to be of two minds—i.e., that while *cultural* genocide was very much in evidence in the story of the Africans brought to the United States as slaves, there was little to no intention of *physical* genocide as economic interests, especially in the American South, took precedence. And while the disagreements continue, the "African-American story" does *not* appear in the contemporary literature on genocide as a central focus.[26] As regards Lemkin himself, in his (incomplete) three volume *History of Genocide*, the plight of blacks was to be as follows: part 1, "Antiquity"; part 2, "Middle Ages," chapter 8, "Genocide Against the Moors and Moriscos"; part 3,

"Modern Times," chapter 1, "Genocide against the Native Africans"; chapter 3, "Belgian Congo"; chapter 11, "Hereros"; chapter 12, "Hati"; and chapter 13, "Hottentos."[27] Unfortunately, only part 2, chapter 8, on the Moors and Moriscos, part 3, chapter 1 on the native Africans, and chapter 11 on the Hereros were completed and now published in *Lemkin on Genocide* (2012).[28] Significantly, and returning to Patterson's negative comments in the introduction, no chapter on the plight of African-Americans was part of Lemkin's outline.[29]

At the heart of *We Charge Genocide*, as presented in the summary, was the following:

> We ask that the General Assembly of the United Nations find and declare by resolution that the Government of the United States is guilty of the crime of Genocide against the Negro people of the United States and that it further demand that the government of the United States stop and prevent the crime of Genocide.
>
> We further ask that the General Assembly by resolution condemn the Government of the United States for failing to implement and observe its solemn international obligations under the Charter of the United Nations and the Genocide Convention and that the General Assembly also demand that the United States immediately take effective steps to carry out and fulfill its international obligations under the Charter and the Genocide Convention.
>
> In Part II of this petition we asked, and now ask again, for action under Article VIII of the Genocide Convention which provides that a contracting party can "call upon the competent organs of the United Nations to take action under the Charter for the prevention and suppression of acts of Genocide."[30]

Significantly—and one would think by design—no appeal was made to the UN Security Council, where the United States remains one of the five permanent members with veto power.

Further, an appeal is made that "a contracting party (i.e., a nation-state) now make our case its own," and "call upon the competent organs of the United Nations to take action."[31] None did so given the post–Second World War and Cold War realities of the time.[32]

Two additional appeals conclude the text:

In addition we asked in Part II of this petition, and now ask again, that any dispute as to the applicability of the Genocide Convention to the crime here alleged be submitted to the International Court of Justice in accordance with Article IX of the Genocide Convention. ...

We ask now, therefore, that the General Assembly take steps to assure that prevention. And we ask, finally, for whatever other measures shall be deemed proper by the General Assembly, under the Charter of the United Nations and the Genocide Convention, to assure the safety of the Negro people of the United States. In so doing it will contribute to the peace of the world.[33]

As Gerald Horne, author of *Communist Front? The Civil Rights Congress, 1946–1956*, writes:

The genocide petition whipped up the kind of necessary pressure that led to the final cracking of the spine of Old Jim Crow.

What was this book that stirred so much contention? There were two elements that made it important and attention-getting. First of all presented in the form of an "Opening Statement," "The Law and Indictment," "The Evidence," and a "Summary and Prayer," Patterson and his colleagues presented a devastating argument on the impact of U.S. policies toward Blacks.

Secondly, this argument reached an international audience in that it was presented to the United Nations. At a time when Washington was charging the USSR and its allies with all manner of human rights deprivations, Patterson's indictment hit with the force of a rifle shot between the eyes and set U.S. foreign policy back on its heels. No wonder that Patterson's passport was confiscated upon his return from Paris after having presented the petition.[34]

What Became of the Petition?

As Patterson said, the petition was presented both in New York at the UN Secretariat by a delegation headed by Paul Robeson, and, at the same time, by Patterson himself at the General Assembly meeting in Paris. Ultimately, it was scuttled, largely due to the efforts of US emissaries and none other than Eleanor Roosevelt, head of the UN Human Rights Commission who, three years earlier, had scored a major coup with the passage of the Universal Declaration of Human Rights on 10 December 1948.[35] Though very much in favour of the petition, at least initially, Mrs. Roosevelt would come to reject its going forward. One can thus only conclude that her international prestige and seeming political ability to "work the system" at the UN led to its going nowhere, and its relegation to the dustbin of history. Whatever advances the United States has made in the area of race relations in the aftermath of the turbulent 1960s, and the passage of the US Civil Rights Act of 1964, which was signed into law by President Lyndon B. Johnson on 2 July of that year, have been accomplished independent of *We Charge Genocide*. Presented a decade before the violence of the civil rights struggle, one would be hard-pressed today to find persons who suffered and endured those horrors who were even familiar with the petition.

Patterson, in his autobiography, does, however, include an excerpt from a lengthy interview given by Mrs. Roosevelt to William Rutherford[36] of the New York *Amsterdam News* and the Associated Negro Press on 12 January 1951:

> When questioned about the petition charging the United States with genocide, which the Civil Rights Congress headed by William L. Patterson has been trying to present to the United Nations, Mrs. Roosevelt commented that it was "well done as a petition … (and was) based on sound and good documentation. (It) was not presented with spurious reasoning.
>
> She went on to add: "The charge of genocide against the colored people in America is ridiculous [sic] in terms of the United Nations definition." Her reasons were (1) although the Negro death rate is high in America, so is the birth rate; (2) although sickness and diseases carry off more colored people than in other groups, a real effort is being made to overcome this.
>
> Mrs. Roosevelt thought that in spite of these objections, the petition would do some good in focusing world attention on the bad situation in America. She also expressed the fear that the petition would play into the hands of some Southerners who would like nothing better than to institute genocide against the Negro people.[37]

It is sadly ironic that the very document which she championed—the Universal Declaration of Human Rights—contains within it the following articles:

> 2: Everyone is entitled to all the rights and freedoms set forth in this Declaration, without discrimination of any kind, such as *race*, colour, sex, language, religion, political or other opinion, national or social origin, property, birth, or other status.[38]

> 4: No one shall be held in slavery or servitude; slavery and the slave trade shall be prohibited in all their forms.

> 5: No one shall be subjected to torture or to cruel, inhuman or degrading treatment or punishment.

> 16.1: Men and women of full age, without any limitation due to *race*, nationality or religion, have the right to marry and to found a family. They are entitled to equal rights as to marriage, during marriage and at its dissolution.[39]

> 26.2: Education shall be directed to the full development of the human personality and to the strengthening of respect for human rights and fundamental freedoms. It shall promote understanding, tolerance and friendship among all nations, *racial* or religious groups, and shall further the activities of the United Nations for the maintenance of peace.[40]

What about Reparations?

Nowhere in Patterson's autobiography or the petition itself does the word "reparation" appear. Nor does it appear in the index to *The Man Who Cried Genocide*. Nor does it appear in Laurence Mordecai Thomas's comparative text *Vessels of Evil: American Slavery and the Holocaust*.[41] Substituting the word "restitution" for "reparation," however, it *does* appear in Randall Robinson's at times controversial book *The Debt: What America Owes to Blacks*, specifically chapter 9, "Thoughts about Restitution."[42] (Robinson is an African-American lawyer, author, activist, and founder of TransAfrica, a think tank addressing American foreign policy as it relates to Africa and the African diaspora, which he founded in 1977, and today serves as distinguished scholar-in-residence at the Pennsylvania State University Dickinson School of Law, in Carlisle, Pennsylvania.)

Robinson begins by reminding his readers that Representative John Conyers (D-MI), himself an African-American, annually introduces legislation for a "Commission to Study Reparations Proposals for African-Americans" which, for more than a decade, continues to die within committee, never making it onto the floor of the US House of Representatives. Robinson then cites other failed instances of the case for reparations in recent American history, largely attributing it to an "out of sight, out of mind" attitude, and strenuously arguing that it remains an *unpaid debt* to the children and grandchildren of those brought to the United States as slaves and enslaved for almost three hundred years. But nowhere in his book does he cite either William Patterson or *We Charge Genocide*.

He does, however, cite the two most well-known examples of successful reparations: the case of Jews after the Holocaust and the case of Japanese-Americans after the Second World War, and he references a 1993 document of the Organization of African Unity which acknowledges both.

Canadian scholar Rhoda Howard-Hassmann, in an important article entitled "Getting to Reparations: Japanese Americans and Africans," reminds us that "framing claims for reparations requires decisions about who is the perpetrator of a wrong, who is the victim, what exactly is the wrong to be compensated, and what are the reparations desired."[43] And while acknowledging the efforts led by Robinson, weak as they are, she says, in the case of African-Americans, the situation is even more complicated than that of Japanese-Americans, and suggests that there is not one phase being addressed but three: slavery, Jim Crow (post–Civil War to the Second World War), and the post–Second World War period. Going even further, she states:

The African American claim faces two major difficulties. First, it is difficult to frame the call for reparations in a convincing manner because many of the victims are long since dead, there are too many of them, and they cannot easily be identified. Second, the causal chain between past harms and present victims is too long and too complex, with too many actors and events implicated.[44]

Returning, however, to Patterson and his petition, we do not have any insight whatsoever as to whether or not reparations was on his agenda or that of the CRC, only that the United Nations was asked to find the United States guilty for its failures to implement and observe its obligations under both the UN Charter and the Genocide Convention (again acknowledging that, at the time, the United States was *not* a signatory to the convention); to further stop and prevent genocide of its African-American people; and to ensure that the appropriate "organs of the UN" (which we assume to mean its various agencies and commissions) were to take action (again not defined) to stop the ongoing genocide. Reparations do not appear to be part of this mandate, and there is simply no evidence that Patterson the attorney was thinking in these terms

To be sure, with the "success" of the State of Israel and individual Jews and Jewish organizations (e.g. the Claims Conference) and Japanese-Americans, other victims of genocide—Armenians, Bosnians, Darfuris, Native Americans, Hereros, Rwandans— and their allies have begun to raise similar claims, but their voices are still somewhat muted and their plaints have not yet entered the international court system.

Whether or not the racist practices of the United States in bringing unwilling and captive Africans to these shores in the 1600s, enslaving them for nearly three hundred years, and continuing to disadvantage them from the Emancipation Proclamation of 1865 to the Civil Rights Act of 1964 is a clear-cut case of genocide is still open to debate, even if that debate does not occupy centre stage in the emerging field of genocide studies. What is not open to debate, however, is that, given the political climate of the 1950s, the failure of the UN to allow the petition *We Charge Genocide* to go forward accords it no honour. Just as the failure of the United States to fully address its own past in the case of both its African-American and Native American population carries with it a historical stain worthy of seeing the light of day if remedies, solutions, future preventions—and reparations—are to have any meaning whatsoever.

NOTES

1   As Charles H. Martin notes, *We Charge Genocide* was not the only petition presented to the UN charging the United States with racist genocide:

> Over the next six years [1945–1951], three American civil rights organizations—the National Negro Congress (NNC), the National Association for the Advancement of Colored People (NAACP), and the Communist-influenced Civil Rights Congress (CRC)—did in fact utilize this forum [i.e. UN]. Between 1946 and 1951 each group presented its own formal petition to the UN protesting continued discriminatory treatment of black Americans and appealing for assistance.

See Charles H. Martin, "Internationalizing 'The American Dilemma': The Civil Rights Congress and the 1951 Genocide Petition to the United Nations," *Journal of American Ethnic History* 16, no. 4 (1997): 36, 57–58n7. The actual title of the NAACP petition was *An Appeal to the World: A Statement of Denial of Human Rights to Minorities in the Case of Citizens of Negro Descent in the United States of America and an Appeal to the United Nations for Redress* (New York: NAACP, 1947).

2   *We Charge Genocide: The Crime of the Government Against the Negro People* (New York: Civil Rights Congress, 1951).

3   William L. Patterson, *The Man Who Cried Genocide: An Autobiography* (New York: International Publishers, 1971).

4   Regarding Lemkin and his work, as well as his own autobiography, see Perry S. Bechky, "Lemkin's Situation: Toward A Rhetorical Understanding of Genocide," *Brooklyn Law Review* 77, no. 2 (2012): 551–624; Agnieszka Bienczyk-Missala and Slawomir Debski, eds., *Rafal Lemkin: A Hero of Humankind* (Warsaw: Polish Institute of Foreign Affairs, 2010); Ann Curthoys, "Raphaël Lemkin's 'Tasmania': An Introduction," *Patterns of Prejudice* 39, no. 2 (2005): 162–169, 170–196; Dan Eshet, *Totally Unofficial: Raphael Lemkin and the Genocide Convention* (Brookline, MA: Facing History and Ourselves, 2007); Catherine Filloux, "Lemkin's House: A Play in Two Acts" (New York: typescript, 2006); Donna-Lee Frieze, ed., *Totally Unofficial: The Autobiography of Raphael Lemkin* (New Haven, CT: Yale University Press, 2013); Steven Leonard Jacobs, ed., *Lemkin on Genocide* (Lanham, MD: Lexington Books, 2013); Steven Leonard Jacobs, ed., *Raphael Lemkin's Thoughts on Nazi Genocide: Not Guilty?* (Jacksonville, FL: Bloch Publishing Company, 2011); William Korey, *An Epitaph for Raphael Lemkin* (New York: American Jewish Committee, 2001); Dominik J. Schaller and Jürgen Zimmerer, eds., Special Issue: "Raphael Lemkin: the 'founder of the United Nation's [sic] Genocide Convention as a historian of mass violence," *Journal of Genocide Research* 7, no. 4 (2005); Robert Skloot, *If the Whole Body Dies: Raphael Lemkin and the Treaty Against Genocide* (Madison, WI: Parallel Press; 2006). Interestingly enough, there is also a (Holocaust) denialist text, itself largely unknown, by James J. Martin, *The Man Who Invented Genocide: The Public Career and Consequences of Raphael Lemkin* (Torrance, CA: Institute for Historical Review, 1984). Martin earned his PhD in history at the University of Michigan in 1949 and taught at Northern Illinois State University, San Francisco State College, Deep Springs College in California, and was the author of *Men Against the State* (1953) *and Liberalism and World Politics, 1931–1941* (1964) before turning to Holocaust denialism and founding his own publishing house, Ralph Myles Publishers in Colorado Springs in 1978, which turned out a number of revisionist and anarchist texts.

5   On the story of the passage of the Genocide Convention and its somewhat difficult journey, see John Cooper, *Raphael Lemkin and the Struggle for the Genocide Convention* (New York: Palgrave Macmillan, 2008), and the earlier text by Lawrence J. LeBlanc, *The United States and the Genocide Convention* (Durham, NC: Duke University Press, 1991).

6   I have examined more than twenty thousand pages of Lemkin's materials and have not found *any* references to Patterson or any copies of such correspondence.

7   One possible explanation, though without substantial documentation, is that Lemkin, a *naturalized* US citizen, was concerned that committing himself to this position would seriously erode or endanger his (unsuccessful at the time of his death) attempts to secure US ratification of the Genocide Convention. However, Lemkin had no trouble criticizing the UN's attempt to pass its Universal Declaration of Human Rights at the very same time (1948), the committee chair of which was the much-respected and well-loved Eleanor Roosevelt, who later blocked Patterson's attempts to move his petition forward. As Lemkin wrote in his autobiography *Totally Unofficial*:

> I felt that the Genocide Convention and the Declaration on Human Rights project must be kept separate, and each must be treated on its own merits. The difference appeared obvious to me. The Declaration on Human Right [*sic*] is only an enunciation of general principles. It has no binding force in international law. It contains no provisions for enforcement, and being a declaration it cannot be enforced as law. It cannot be signed by representatives of governments or ratified by parliaments, because it is not a treaty of nations.
>
> On the other hand, the Genocide Convention *is* an international treaty. It can be enforced both as an international law and as a domestic law. It deals with international crime and carries with itself penalties and the higher degree of legal and moral condemnation. The Genocide Convention is a definite and precise commitment before the world not to murder people and races. Therefore it must be signed by representatives of governments and then ratified by the parliaments.
>
> *The Declaration on Human Rights is only a date, but the Genocide Convention is a marriage.*

See Frieze, *Totally Unofficial*, 172; emphasis added. A lengthy excerpt from that same text is also found in Samuel Totten and Steven Leonard Jacobs, eds., *Pioneers of Genocide Studies* (New Brunswick, NJ: Transaction Publishers, 2002), 365–399.

8   Patterson, *The Man Who Cried Genocide*, 178–179; emphases added.

9   Ibid., 191; emphases added.

10   The author remains indebted to his former undergraduate assistant, Ms. Karissa Reines, for her scrupulous re-examination of the now-complete catalogue of Lemkin's papers in the author's possession. Her own investigation was the result of the author's total inability to recall any such document whatsoever, having examined them in detail prior to cataloguing them. For an understanding of what is contained in this collection, see Steven L. Jacobs, "The papers of Raphael Lemkin: a first look," *Journal of Genocide Research* 1, no. 1 (1999): 105–114.

11   As he tells it, "Although the San Francisco earthquake and fire destroyed the official birth records, I believe my correct birthdate is August 27, 1891." Patterson, *The Man Who Cried Genocide*, 19.

12   Regarding his pre-collegiate education, Patterson would write: "I did not see fully then that the educational system was designed to develop in Black youth a feeling of inferiority, and in white youth the conviction that the world was theirs, a white world." Patterson, *The Man Who Cried Genocide*, 22.

13   Ibid., 21.

14   Ibid., 177.

15   "(1) a case history of violence and illegal acts in the State of Georgia committed from 1940 through 1950 with the specific purpose of preventing Negroes from voting; (2) a study which, with some variation, is typical of other Southern states, revealing how the charge of 'rape' was transformed into a state instrument for the oppression of the Negro people in the State of Louisiana; (3) a study of monopoly control of the South; (4) a calendar of Congressional action showing its consistent refusal to act for the protection or welfare of the Negro people; and (5) a selected bibliography" (thirty-four items listed, including Gunnar Myrdal's *An American Dilemma* [1944], and *To Secure These Rights*, The Report of the President's [Harry S. Truman] Commission on Civil Rights [1947]). See Patterson, *The Man Who Cried Genocide*, 199.

16   The graphic on the cover is that of a hand with finger pointing to the title of the petition; the back cover is a lengthy quote from Justice Robert H. Jackson from his opening address at the Nuremberg War Crimes Trial of the Nazi leadership on 21 November 1945.

17   In addition to the aforementioned Patterson and his wife Louise, Paul Robeson (and his wife Eslanda), and W. E. B. Du Bois, Jewish-American novelist Howard Fast, black Communist leader Harry Haywood, and others largely unknown to us today. Patterson does, however, further identify many of them in his autobiography, *The Man Who Cried Genocide: An Autobiography*, 180–181.

18   There is no actual prayer included in the summary, but, rather, an appeal to the very humanity and integrity of the United Nations to whom it is addressed, and an acknowledgement of the centrality of religion in the life of the African-American community at the time of the writing. It should also be stressed that among the foremost leaders of the civil rights struggle and movement in the United States during the 1950s, '60s, and '70s, black clergy played a central leadership role, including Reverend Martin Luther King, Jr., Reverend Ralph Abernathy, Reverend Fred Shuttlesworth, among many, many others.

19   Patterson, *We Charge Genocide*, xii; emphasis added.

20   Ibid.

21   Ibid., xiii.

22   The phrase "people's democracy" is an additional example of the kind of leftist rhetoric popular at that time.

23   Patterson, *We Charge Genocide*, xiii.

24   Patterson and the civil rights congress recognized this difficulty as well. The United Nations is what it says—a gathering place and forum for nation-states. Thus, only nation-states are entitled, by both charter and international law, to bring their complaints regarding the behaviours of other nation-states before the various institutions, agencies, and courts established by it. Both Patterson and the CRC in their petition also appealed to one or more nation-states to adopt and thus legally legitimize their document, and, in so doing, move it forward.

25   Patterson, *We Charge Genocide*, 55.

26   One possible exception would be the article by Seymour Drescher, "The Atlantic Slave Trade and the Holocaust: A Comparative Analysis" in *Is the Holocaust Unique? Perspectives in Comparative Genocide*, ed. Alan S. Rosenbaum (Boulder, CO: Westview Press, 2009), 103–123.

27   See Steven L. Jacobs, "The papers of Raphael Lemkin," 105–114, 113–114, for a complete list of what was to be included in his *History of Genocide*.

28   Jacobs, ed. *Lemkin on Genocide*.

29   It should also be noted that Adam Muller's important contribution in this volume, "Troubling History, Troubling Law: The Question of Indigenous Genocide in Canada" (137–162), addresses in this context the importance of cultural genocide in the destruction of First Nations, as Lemkin originally intended. As noted above, however, the destruction of the cultural heritage of African-Americans as a direct result of their slavery and transport from the African continent was *not* a dominant concern during the 1950s and 1960s in the United States, when violence and death against this same population dwarfed other concerns, and this is fully reflected in Patterson's petition.

30   Patterson, *We Charge Genocide*, 196.

31   Ibid., 197.

32   Though somewhat conjectural on my part, the reluctance of other nation-states to embrace *We Charge Genocide* in the 1950s and even a bit earlier may be a holdover and (un)intended consequence of a 1947 Committee on Un-American Activities of the House of Representatives "Report on Civil Rights Congress as a Communist Front Organization," (2 September 1947), and published by the Government Printing Office on 17 November 1947. That Report concluded:

> From the facts cited above it should be clear that the Civil Rights Congress is an organization dedicated not to the broader issues of civil liberties, but specifically to the defense of individual Communists and the Communist Party, that the organization is controlled by individuals who are either members of the Communist Party or openly loyal to it, and that in carrying out its defense aims, the organization has at the same time engaged in a campaign of vilification against the American Government (19).

That understanding, when shared with the ambassadors of other nation-states at the relatively small United Nations Assembly through the offices of the US ambassador, would no doubt have had a decidedly deleterious effect and impact upon anyone seriously considering the petition and the cause it represented.

33   Patterson, *We Charge Genocide*, 197.

34   Gerald Horne, *Communist Front? The Civil Rights Congress, 1946–1956*, (Rutherford, NJ: Fairleigh Dickinson University Press, 1988), 167.

35   Two excellent sources on the journey to fruition of the United Nations Declaration of Human Rights are Mary Ann Glendon, *A World Made New: Eleanor Roosevelt and the Universal Declaration of Human Rights*, (New York: Random House, 2002), and Johannes Morsink, *The Universal Declaration of Human Rights: Origins, Drafting, and Intent* (Philadelphia: University of Pennsylvania Press, 2000).

36   According to the biographical note introducing his papers at Emory University, Ruther-
      ford was a foreign correspondent for *Time*, *Life*, and CBS (the first African-American to
      work for CBS abroad) and living in Switzerland at the time of the interview. He would
      go on to become the executive director of the Southern Christian Leadership Confer-
      ence at the urging of Martin Luther King, Jr. from 1967 to 1968.

37   Patterson, *The Man Who Cried Genocide*, 206.

38   United Nations, "The Universal Declaration of Human Rights," United Nations, http://
      www.un.org/en/universal-declaration-human-rights (accessed 31 December 2013),
      emphasis added.

39   Emphasis added.

40   Emphasis added.

41   Lawrence Mordecai Thomas, *Vessels of Evil: American Slavery and the Holocaust*
      (Philadelphia: Temple University Press, 1993).

42   Randall Robinson, *The Debt: What America Owes to Blacks* (New York: Penguin Books,
      2000). Other texts worth examining in this context are Elazar Barkan, *The Guilt of
      Nations: Restitution and Negotiating Historical Injustices* (New York: W. W. Norton
      & Company, 2000); Boris Bittker, *The Case for Black Reparations* (Boston: Beacon
      Press, 2003); Roy L. Brooks, *When Sorry Isn't Enough: The Controversy Over Apologies
      and Reparations for Human Injustice* (New York: New York University Press, 1999);
      Alfred L. Brophy, *Reparations Pro and Con* (New York: Oxford University Press, 2006);
      Angelo Corlett, *Race, Racism, and Reparations* (Ithaca, NY: Cornell University Press,
      2003); Angelo Corlett, *Heirs of Oppression: Racism and Reparations* (Lanham, MD:
      Rowman and Littlefield, 2010); Joe R. Feagin, *Racist America: Roots, Current Realities,
      and Future Reparations* (London: Routledge, 2014); Carla Ferstman, Mariana Goetz,
      and Alan Stephens, eds., *Reparations for Victims of Genocide, War Crimes Against
      Humanity: Systems in Place and Systems in the Making* (Leiden, NL: Brill, 2009); Rhoda
      E. Howard-Hassmann, *Reparations to Africa* (Philadelphia: University of Pennsylvania
      Press, 2011); Regula Ludi, *Reparations for Nazi Victims in Postwar Europe* (Cambridge:
      Cambridge University Press, 2012); Michael R. Maurrus, *Some Measure of Justice: The
      Holocaust Era Restitution Campaign of the 1990s* (Madison, WI: University of Wiscon-
      sin Press, 2009); Michael T. Martin and Marilyn Yaquinto, eds., *Redress for Injustices in
      the United States: On Reparations for Slavery, Jim Crow, and Their Legacies* (Durham,
      NC: Duke University Press, 2007); Christian Pross, *Paying for the Past: The Struggle
      over Reparations for Surviving Victims of Nazi Terror*, trans. Belinda Cooper (Baltimore,
      MD: Johns Hopkins University Press, 1998); Winbush Raymond, ed., *Should America
      Pay? Slavery and the Raging Debate on Reparations* (New York: Amstad/HarperCollins,
      2003); Nan Sagi, *German Reparations: A History of the Negotiations* (Jerusalem: The
      Magnes Press, 1980); Jeremy Sarkin, *Colonial Genocide and Reparations Claims in the
      21st Century: The Socio-Legal Context of Claims under International Law by the Herero
      against Germany for Genocide in Namibia, 1904–1908* (Westport, CT: Praeger, 2008);
      Nora Wittmann, *Slavery Reparations Time is Now: Exposing Lies, Claiming Justice for
      Global Survival—An International Legal Assessment* (Vienna: Power of the Trinity
      Publishers, 2013).

43   Rhoda Howard-Hassmann, "Getting to Reparations: Japanese Americans and African
      Americans," *Social Forces* 83, no. 2 (2004): 2.

44   Ibid., 13.

6

"A Tragedy to be Sure": Heteropatriarchy, Historical Amnesia, and Housing Crises in Northern Ontario

Travis Hay, Kristin Burnett, and Lori Chambers

Introduction

In October of 2012, the Grand Chief of the Mushkegowuk Council (a regional chief's council representing seven First Nations located in the western James Bay and Hudson Bay region) signed an official Declaration of Emergency in response to housing crises in the communities of Kashechewan, Attawapiskat, and Fort Albany. During the ensuing media frenzy, conservative news outlets such as the *National Post* and Sun Media focused almost exclusively on Attawapiskat and its Chief, Theresa Spence.[1] Among Canadian settler society, Kashechewan and Fort Albany disappeared from the public view, and what was going on (or not going on) at Attawapiskat took centre stage. This chapter interrogates the complex social and political meanings ascribed to the housing crisis in Attawapiskat in the dominant Canadian media; specifically, we situate the structural history of the housing crises on northern First Nations reserves alongside an ideological or discursive history of settler-colonial disavowal.[2]

Our examination of media coverage in this chapter does not represent the breadth and the heterogeneity of news reporting across Canada during this period; rather, it focuses on the backlash to Theresa Spence's protest as a means of illuminating certain structures of feeling and logic that inform settler colonialism at its worst.[3] Thus, while we briefly critique the institutional policies and material conditions that produced the housing crises in northern First Nations communities, we think it is equally important to understand the ideological conditions that made the state of emergency possible. As Taiaike Alfred writes, "colonialism is, more than anything else … a way of thinking about something fundamental to who we are as a society: the relationship between the past and the present, between the newcomers and the original people of this land."[4] On that basis, we argue that the sexist and racist discourse that framed these events emerged from a particular constellation of masculinist and settler-colonialist heteropatriarchal thought that has been well theorized by Indigenous feminists such as Lee Maracle, Paula Gunn Allen, and Janice Acoose.[5]

The scope of our conversation is limited to the realm of representation and the meaning-making processes that depoliticized the genocidal violence experienced by these three northern First Nations. As settlers we are deeply embedded in the systems of violence and discourses of disavowal that we are critiquing in this chapter. Indeed, we are the system's intended beneficiaries. Accordingly, we cannot communicate how the people of the Attawapiskat First Nation or other northern Cree communities experienced or felt about these events. We acknowledge that Indigenous peoples' perspectives and reactions to Chief Spence were diverse—many people supported her, some did not, and many others fell somewhere in between. For the majority of the Canadian population removed from the reality of Attawapiskat both literally and conceptually, media representations—informed by settler discourse and white supremacy—fashioned the colonial grammars through which Canadians came to know and understand current events and the history of the community.[6]

As the housing crisis began to loom large in national and international media coverage, we saw in action how media discourses were "critical in determining who exercise[d] authority and who accept[ed] it."[7] In this instance, the state transformed the "raw historical event" into a "communicative event,"[8] and created a story that was palatable for the dominant society and which resonated with pre-existing narratives about poverty in First Nations communities. Media discourses with regard to Attawapiskat placed the "problem" of Indigenous governance and corruption on the public agenda, thereby erasing the long colonial history that had created the poverty and housing crisis by offering an image of Chief Spence that embodied many of the most pernicious and colonialist stereotypes of Indigenous women and political leaders. In so doing, many Canadian media outlets failed to situate the housing crisis within the larger genocidal history of settler colonialism in Canada; they preferred instead to blame Indigenous peoples for this historical and deeply political violence. Thus, when the media drew on historical examples, they did so in a manner that reiterated the myth that Canada is a benevolent nation that has always treated Indigenous peoples in a just and righteous manner. Such a myth disguises the fact that as settler Canadians we live on lands stolen from Indigenous peoples and we continue to benefit from settler-colonial systems of apartheid, marginalization, and genocide. In denaturalizing the dominant narrative, then, we seek to outline the contours, nature, and structure of Canadian settler-colonial ideologies, and critically discuss how the media not only denied the deeper historical meanings and particularities behind Spence's hunger strike, but also obscured how her actions were symbolic of a larger Indigenous struggle against Canadian settler colonialism.

The scorn that was directed at Chief Spence revealed the deep pathological denial of colonialism and genocide that has prevented and continues to prevent a more accurate representation and deeper understanding of Canada's national history. The words of one journalist reveal the utter failure of Canadian settler society to see how the past shapes and informs the present. According to Lorne Gunter of the *National Post*, although the situation in Attawapiskat was "a tragedy to be sure ... political correctness is the root cause. It has paralyzed our political and bureaucratic establishments against taking the bold action necessary to give aboriginal-Canadians a fresh start."[9] Thus, instead of genocidal relations and colonial violence, what settlers saw, and indeed expected, were clichéd racist and gendered stereotypes that confirmed the innocence of settler Canadians.[10] As our discursive analysis of Canadian news media reveals, the constructions of Chief Spence and her actions can be read contrapuntally to show the deep connections between colonialism and patriarchy. Representations of the protest followed a deeply racialized and gendered logic that constructed Chief Spence as the stereotypically corrupt band council chief *as well as* the stereotypical "Indian" woman. As Audra Simpson notes, "when you are an Indigenous woman, your flesh is received differently."[11]

Canadian-settler exercises of governance have as their condition of historical emergence a long intellectual history of understanding Indigenous peoples as less than human (or at least as less than white settlers). These ways of knowing are *destructive* of what Sherene Razack called "suppressed knowledges," which is based on an "experience of the world that is not admitted into dominant knowledge paradigms." However, they are also *constructive* of ideas about Indigenous difference.[12] As Joyce Green writes, settler colonialism is "legitimized not only through racist construction but through creation of language celebrating colonial identities while constructing the colonized as the antithesis of human decency and development."[13] Such rhetorical strategies—what Emma LaRocque calls "discourses of dehumanization"[14]—are as central to the maintenance of the Canadian settler-colonial project as the more physical and institutional manifestations of Indian policy. Thus, while we review the material history of colonialism and the structures of band funding in Canada to dispel some of the more popular myths and rumours circulated about Chief Spence, we also seek to make visible those colonial grammars that efface, obscure, elide, and disregard the genocidal policies that have created repeated crises and emergencies in Attawapiskat and other northern Indigenous communities. As we shall see (and as numerous Indigenous feminist scholars have explained at length), the racial grammars and logics of settler-colonial genocide reveal themselves as profoundly gendered, masculinist, and heteropatriarchal.

A Note on the Conceptual Limits of "Hunger Strike"

The term "hunger strike," widely used by the media to describe Chief Spence's protest, operates as a sign or placeholder in a semiotic system of the Canadian media. In our schema, the term refers not to the reality of Spence's protest, but to the representation of that event within the settler imaginary. In this respect, we draw on the knowledge and words of Anishnaabeg scholar, writer, and storyteller Leanne Betasamosake Simpson, who reminded readers in the midst of Chief Spence's protest of the deep symbolic importance that fish broth holds for many Indigenous peoples living in the geographical area now called Canada. Chief Spence's decision to subsist mainly on fish broth prompted more journalists than can be counted to claim confidently that this was not a "real" or "true" hunger strike. However, as Simpson explains,

> [fish broth] symbolizes hardship and sacrifice. It symbolizes the strength of our ancestors. It means survival. Fish broth sustained us through the hardest of circumstances, with the parallel understanding that it can't sustain one forever. We exist today because of fish broth. It connects us to the water and to the fish who gave up its life so we could sustain ourselves.[15]

Thus, "Chief Spence [ate] fish broth because, metaphorically, colonialism has kept Indigenous Peoples on a fish broth diet for generations upon generations."[16] A "hunger strike" is a conceptual category deeply embedded within a Western historicity that is productive of the same power relations challenged by Chief Spence's protest; it is an outside predicate foisted onto the event that carries with it a kind of discursive baggage or historical excess that has done more to cover up the reality of Chief Spence's leadership than to illuminate it.[17] Acknowledging the historical specificity of Chief Spence's protest, we use the term "hunger strike" only when it is employed by journalists or when making direct reference to their comments and constructions of the events in question. Our usage of the term is meant to mark the difference between representation and reality.

Defining Genocide and Atrocity in the Canadian Context

In this chapter, we treat the housing crises in Cree communities in northern Ontario as a manifestation of the continued genocidal project of Canadian settler colonialism. However, we want to begin by suggesting that the persistence of definitional debates surrounding the concept of "genocide" is counterproductive and indeed destructive to the formulation of an effective resistance to the ongoing colonial violence against Indigenous peoples on Turtle Island. Such debates serve only to reify and legitimize the profound denial in which non-Indigenous settlers live. Admitting and owning the benefits accrued from centuries of colonialism and genocidal policies would destroy the comfort zone of many settlers. To better illustrate our perspective we employ storytelling.

The genesis of this volume was a conference held at Mount Royal University in February of 2014 entitled "Understanding Atrocities." During the conference, attendees were privileged to have the opportunity to hear from a Residential School Survivor about his experiences. Speaking on a panel with genocide scholars, the Elder shared his story of survivance and resistance that, while ultimately life-affirming and triumphant, also spoke of trauma and brutality. During the question period that followed, an individual, whom we will not identify, raised his hand to caution the room against the naming of the Indian Residential School system as an act of genocide. According to this individual, residential schools were not real "death camps" like those that existed in Nazi-occupied Europe during World War Two because, he argued, it was not the primary purpose of residential schools to bring about the physical or biological destruction of Indigenous peoples. Putting aside for the moment how offensive and inappropriate it is for someone to advise a Residential School Survivor how they should know and feel about their experiences, this incident also spoke to the frequent and insidious ways in which exclusive definitional debates characterize the professional and popular discourses of settler-colonial genocide in the Canadian context. These comments compelled us to wonder: What motivated this person to tell a Residential School Survivor how he should understand his experiences? In thinking through these and other questions, we found resonance in the following words from Israel Charney:

> For me, the passion to exclude this or that mass killing from the universe of genocide, as well as the intense competition to establish the exclusive "superiority" or unique form of any one genocide, ends up creating a fetishistic atmosphere in which the masses of bodies that are not to be qualified for the definition of genocide are dumped into a conceptual black hole, where they are forgotten.[18]

In a later conversation, the individual mentioned in the story above acknowledged his exclusivist tendencies, questioned his own motivations for evicting residential schooling from what Charney called "the universe of genocide," and admitted that the Elder's experience was certainly a story of having survived a genocide. While such an admission has no bearing on the ongoing nature of Canadian settler-colonial projects of Indigenous elimination (some of which we discuss in this chapter), the point we are trying to make is that participating in such debates regarding the definitional difficulties of the crime of genocide are the privileged practices of a scholarly community far removed from such realities and experiences. As academics, we need to acknowledge the privilege of being able to participate in such debates at a safe distance, as well as recognize the epistemological violence that we risk creating and perpetuating in doing so.

The Historical Context of the Housing Crises

The Attawapiskat First Nation is located at the mouth of the Attawapiskat River in northern Ontario, on the western shores of James Bay.[19] It is a signatory of Treaty 9. The First Nation's traditional territory extends out from the present-day reserve up the coast of Hudson Bay and stretches hundreds of kilometres inland.[20] Year-round settlement did not take place until the late 1960s, and many families delayed settling permanently on the reserve because they did not want to send their children to the infamous St. Anne's Residential School (located in Fort Albany).[21] A school—the J. R. Nakogee Elementary School—was finally built in Attawapiskat in 1976.[22] The history of the J. R. Nakogee Elementary School embodies the long history of neglect and indifference the First Nation has received from the federal government. In 1979, an industrial oil pipeline malfunctioned, leaking over 30,000 tons of diesel fuel directly under the school.[23] Neither the federal and provincial governments nor the pipeline's owners undertook cleanup or restorative measures, although Health Canada ordered residences provided for the teachers to be torn down due to contamination.[24] The school was not closed until May 2001, despite growing evidence of health concerns (many parents had long stopped sending their children to the school due to the prevalence of noxious fumes).[25] Currently, classes are held in seven portables, which reside on top of the former school's playground. The portables are in deplorable condition: the doors do not close and the heating systems are broken, forcing students to wear their coats in the classrooms.

A similar situation in Attawapiskat exists in regards to housing, and has unfortunately existed for so long that it has become normalized.[26]

Conditions of substandard housing, overcrowding, and homelessness are allowed to persist in northern First Nations because of commonly held, but patently false, beliefs that First Nations people get free housing on reserves.[27] This assumption holds that market-based housing and home ownership is non-existent on reserves and that Indigenous peoples get special treatment from the government that amounts to "free housing." While home ownership is certainly lower on reserve than off, it is still common (31 percent on reserve versus 69 percent off).[28] Still further, the federal funding that subsidizes poor and under-housed peoples on reserve comes from the Canadian Mortgage and Housing Corporation, which is the same institution that funds low-income housing off reserve. Thus, the state does not offer different or special treatment to Indigenous peoples on reserve, but enacts social welfare measures that attempt (so far extremely unsuccessfully) to mediate the severe poverty that characterizes life in many remote reserves. For example, the average on-reserve annual income is $16,160, and the cost of living in the North is substantively higher than in southern Canada.[29] This information is key to understanding the reasons why recent studies found that 41 percent of on-reserve housing stock in Ontario was inadequate or in need of major repair, with a further 5 percent needing to be replaced entirely, or that 12 percent of on-reserve housing is not "serviced by any type of sewage disposal system, roughly eight percent have no electrical servicing, and about half of the on-reserve communities have either no solid waste disposal services or those services that are provided are inadequate."[30] These are examples of what Adam Barker calls "the contemporary reality of Canadian imperialism."[31]

We also need to consider the discrepancies that exist in regards to how much federal and provincial money is spent on ensuring the well-being of settler Canadians and the existence of effective infrastructure in urban and reserve spaces. For example, federal, provincial, and municipal budgets allocated $24,000 per citizen to provide programs and infrastructure to Torontonians. In contrast, Attawapiskat First Nation received money from just one source—Aboriginal Affairs and Northern Development Canada (AANDC)—that amounted to $11,355 per person.[32] Moreover, AANDC has also placed a cap on all core program expenditure increases at 2 percent a year.[33] When combined with low annual incomes, high rates of poverty and unemployment, extraordinarily high costs of living, and long-term government neglect, it is not surprising that the Attawapiskat First Nation declared a crisis in housing conditions in 2011.

Seven years earlier, in 2004, the United Nations special rapporteur, Radolfo Staghaven, visited Attawapiskat and expressed his concerns over the housing crisis in the community; he noted a prevalence of poverty, toxic living conditions, and government underfunding.[34] This was followed in November 2007 by Miloon Kothari, United Nations special rapporteur on adequate housing, who also commented on the conditions of overcrowding, inadequate housing, and the lack of basic services like water and sanitation.[35] These two reports were not the first time the federal government had been made aware of inadequate housing in First Nations communities, and northern First Nations especially. Reports by academics, health-care professionals, and non-governmental organizations have repeatedly called on the federal government to address First Nation's housing needs and by extension Indigenous poverty.[36] In 1996 the Royal Commission on Aboriginal Peoples described on-reserve housing as "in a bad state," and other studies have drawn clear connections between health, well-being, and housing.[37] For instance, poor housing contributes to the spread of contagious diseases such as measles, intestinal, skin, and middle ear infections, as well as respiratory diseases such as tuberculosis, to name but a few.[38]

In October 2009, Chief Theresa Hall made public her concerns over the lack of federal support for the recent sewage flood in Attawapiskat, and in November, an Elder from the community embarked upon a protest walk of over 100 kilometres to raise awareness for the housing crisis (with two artificial knees, no less).[39] Taking office as Chief in August 2010, Theresa Spence was from the outset very vocal about her concerns regarding the lack of federal response to the previous two states of emergency. However, it was her decision on 28 October 2012 to declare a third state of emergency that brought her to the attention of the national media.

Initially, this state of emergency garnered almost no media attention, and Ottawa, the provincial government, and aid agencies did not step forward to offer any assistance to the communities in crisis. It was not until 21 November 2012, when Charles Angus, member of Parliament for Timmins-James Bay, published an article and posted a video on YouTube showing a mother and her small children living in a shed in frigid temperatures, that housing conditions in Attawapiskat made headline news.

Otherwise, it was business as usual in Canada. On 23 November 2012, the Red Cross announced that it would be sending a team to conduct a needs assessment in the community. The federal government responded by placing Attawapiskat under third-party management on 1 December 2013. John Duncan, minister of aboriginal affairs, explained that Ottawa was taking this step to "ensure the funding provided to [the] community [was] being spent effectively," suggesting that the community's problems stemmed from mismanagement instead of underfunding.[40] Later that August, a federal court ruled that the decision to place the First Nation under third-party management "did not respond in a reasonable way to the root of the problems at Attawapiskat."[41] The court ordered Ottawa to repay Attawapiskat for all costs accrued by the third-party manager.

From the very beginning, the federal government maintained that they were totally ignorant of living conditions in Attawapiskat. Duncan claimed to have been unaware of the extent of the housing crisis—even after two United Nations reports, two states of emergency, and the efforts of Shannen Koostachin, who had met with Duncan just that summer in regards to the need for a new school building in her community. Such assertions of ignorance are difficult to believe, given that pursuant to section 61 of the Indian Act, the minister of aboriginal affairs is responsible for approving all funding allocations. The media, however, accepted such disavowals of responsibility and its coverage of Chief Spence's efforts blamed her administration and its alleged mismanagement of funds for the community-housing crisis.[42] On 12 December 2012, Spence announced her intention to stop eating solid food until Prime Minister Stephen Harper and the governor general, the representative of the British Crown in Canada, agreed to a nation-to-nation meeting.

The Corrupt Chief, or "The Crooked Indian"

Despite the very real problems faced by the community of Attawapiskat, journalistic responses were on the whole racist, dismissive, and stained by the well-worn assumptions that characterize settler discourses of dehumanization. Of course, none of the stereotypes trotted out and perpetuated by the mainstream media were new. The first and perhaps most common trope used by the media and promoted enthusiastically by the federal government to discredit Spence and distract non-Indigenous people from the real problem was the stereotype of the corrupt band council, which suggests that all First Nations leaders are dishonest, nepotistic, and unable to manage themselves.[43] Pam Palmater recently described this cliché in a piece titled "Stephen Harper and the Myth of the Crooked Indian":

> This racist stereotype is recycled again and again when Harper is pressed to account for the fourth world conditions in some First Nations. The response always seems to be: "Well, we gave them x million dollars, where did all the money go?" What Harper never tells Canadians is that in giving First Nations x million dollars, he has given them half of what is needed to provide the specific program or service. Without all the facts, this propaganda serves to distance Canadians from First Nations.[44]

Essentially, the "crooked Indian" or "corrupt band council" stereotype implies that Indigenous leaders steal money from honest white taxpayers to purchase luxury vehicles or million-dollar homes while their communities suffer.[45] This stereotype suggests that Indigenous people are exclusively responsible for the poverty in their communities and that they lack real political leadership.

Operating in concert with this stereotype are discussions of accountability and the lack thereof amongst First Nations politicians. This stereotype flourishes in mainstream Canadian discourse despite the fact that First Nations are overburdened by federal regulations that require constant reporting. Indeed, Sheila Fraser, Canada's auditor general, criticized the federal government for this excessive requirement, which amounted to ninety-five reports per First Nation every year, or one report every three days.[46] Even so, journalists eagerly recited an orthodox racism that called Indigenous leaders irresponsible, unaccountable, and always asking for more than their fair share. Instead of government negligence, indifference, and settler colonialism being discussed as the root causes of poverty in the Canadian North, Chief Spence came to embody and signify all Indigenous politicians: she was constructed as solely responsible for conditions in Attawapiskat (conditions that were almost a century in the making). A piece published in early January 2013 by Lorne Gunter of the *National Post* was emblematic of this oft-repeated falsehood when it described Chief Spence as failing to take ownership of her actions and accept responsibility for living conditions in Attawapiskat. Gunter, who also gave the present chapter its titular quotation, suggested that "there [was] no recognition that much of the plight of Canada's aboriginals is self-inflicted. In [Spence's] mind and Idle minds, everything is the fault of government and non-aboriginals."[47] According to this journalist, childlike avoidance is a central feature of Indigenous peoples who have failed to take responsibility for the last five hundred years of colonialism and genocide. Or, as Kelly McParland of the *National Post* ignorantly penned, the reasons behind First Nations' grievances are "difficult to comprehend, the origins lost in time."[48] McParland's comments operate on several levels: they suggest that Indigenous peoples are unreasonable in their continued efforts to achieve justice and equality. The comments also draw on the oft-repeated notion that Indigenous peoples should just "get over it." In this manner, settlers are rewriting and retelling history so that the dispossession of Indigenous peoples is erased and can therefore go comfortably unacknowledged and conveniently forgotten.[49] The tacit approval of a false history serves to strengthen the state of white supremacy in North America. To borrow from Thomas King's recent work, *The Inconvenient Indian*, which stressed the importance of historical meaning-making, it is essential to remember that while "most of us think that history is the past. It's not. History is the stories we tell about our past … [and] they're not chosen by chance."[50] Thus, when other people get to tell your stories, in "effect what they're doing is defining to the world who you are, what you are, and what they think you are and what they think you should be."[51]

The Gendered and Sexualized Logics of Settler-Colonial Genocide

The construct of the corrupt and irresponsible band chief is also a highly gendered one and was employed together with the well-worn constructions of Indigenous womanhood as that which is licentious, dusky, and deviant. Numerous historians have shown that such racist and sexist representations of Indigenous women have been central to the socio-economic formation of a settler society that "has no place for Indigenous women."[52] Significantly, these scholars highlight how Indigenous women's bodies are often used as the "mechanisms of oppression against whole communities."[53]

Journalists focused on Chief Spence's personal relationships, physical appearance, and the insistence that she was not undertaking a "real" hunger strike. In this last respect, she was routinely and unfavourably compared to famous male political figures such as Gandhi and Bobby Sands. Larry Miller—the Conservative MP who tastelessly compared the long gun registry in Canada to the legal regime of Adolf Hitler's Nazi Party—offers us one example of how the corrupt band council stereotype operates in the settler-colonial imaginary.[54] Miller told the *Toronto Sun* that Chief Spence's hunger strike was "nothing but another project of hers to divert attention away from what she and maybe some other officials in her band have done"; Miller claimed that Spence's "people suffered because of some of the things she did. It isn't from a lack of money from the federal government, the provincial government or even the mine that's in that part of the country."[55] Echoing Miller, Iain Hunter of the aptly named *Times-Colonist* (Victoria, BC) argued that the media's coverage of Attawapiskat served as a useful reminder for Canadians because it drew "our attention to the fact that Spence lives in a 'well-heated' house on her reserve, drives a substantial vehicle, has stayed in a hotel, not a tent, while in Ottawa, and her 'boyfriend' has been making $850 a day as band manager."[56] This quotation neatly reproduces not only the stereotype of the corrupt band council chief who starves her own people at the expense of Canadian taxpayers, but also the gendered logic of settler-colonial racism and its complicity with patriarchy. The special emphasis Hunter places on the word "boyfriend" signifies a symbolic order of North American colonial racism wherein the Indigenous woman is a degenerate figure who is sexualized, corruptible, and corrupting.

Christie Blatchford, well known for her anti-Indigenous op-ed pieces, went so far as to call Chief Spence a terrorist.[57] Highly critical of the fact that Chief Spence's partner, Clayton Kennedy, was allowed to hold an administrative position with the band, Blatchford reported that, at the beginning of Chief Spence's administration, the two "were already common-law partners, or life partners as they prefer, and presumably sleeping together. But no one was aware that could be thought to be a conflict of interest?"[58] Originally published in the *Regina Leader-Post*, Blatchford's article was so well received that it was republished in the *Edmonton Journal*, the *Montreal Gazette*, the *Vancouver Sun*, and the *Star-Phoenix* in Saskatoon (a good example of how one author's work gets picked up and published by numerous Canadian newspapers). In her opinion piece (we refuse to call it journalism), Blatchford made connections between what she characterized as the inevitable and sneaky underhandedness of Indigenous womanhood and the failure of band governance. She wrote that "the revelation that the purportedly professional financial co-manager who was appointed by the Attawapiskat council … is none other than Chief Theresa Spence's boyfriend is a revelation of the order that the sun will rise in the east tomorrow."[59] Apparently, according to Blatchford and her audience, the "fact" that Indigenous female leaders are political and sexual deviants is as certain as the existence of gravity.

Underscoring the gendered and sexually violent ideology of Canadian settler colonialism were the oft-repeated comments of conservative politicians and media commentators regarding Chief Spence's body. For example, Ezra Levant of the Sun News Network (easily the most inflammatory and unapologetically racist media source during Spence's protest) felt the need to comment sarcastically that "there is a lot of her to love," and he also referred to her as having a "trademark double chin."[60] More famously, Senator Patrick Brazeau and Conservative MP Royal Galipeau made what can only under the most generous of interpretations be described as "fat jokes" at a fundraiser for the Conservative Party.[61] As feminist scholar Susie Orbach writes, the identification of a woman as fat serves to immediately isolate and invalidate her: "almost inevitably, the explanations offered for fatness point a finger at the failure of women to control their weight, control their appetite, and control their impulses."[62] These comments on Chief Spence's body thus revealed a blatant misogyny, but also a specific kind of settler-colonial masculinity that saw Chief Spence's body as open to public censure and as a physical manifestation of the alleged weakness of her moral character or propensity to self-destructive indulgence. What is interesting outside the immediate context of our discussion here is the way in which fatphobia revealed itself in Brazeau's comments to be a complex component of a broader ideological structure that upholds settler-colonial regimes of racialized, gendered, sexualized, and body-based forms of oppression. Brazeau—an Indigenous man—recruited misogyny as a means of establishing an internal solidarity within the larger, white-dominated Conservative Party of which, at the time, he was a member. In calling attention to her body as a site of poor self-control, these politicians and media figures enacted an implicit denial of Chief Spence's leadership and legitimacy that was both colonial and patriarchal, and she was invalidated to the extent that masculinism, fatphobia, and lateral violence (read: Brazeau's comments) constituted a settler-colonial configuration that sought to destroy and discredit the image of Chief Spence by any means necessary. This is why coverage during the end of her protest also claimed that, "prior to going on her fast on Dec. 11, Spence didn't look like she'd missed many meals in her life."[63] Borrowing Sherene Razack's words, these fatphobic and misogynist statements served to construct the Indigenous body "as the space of the greatest disorder" and thus reaffirmed the settler-colonial desire for further control of Indigenous peoples by constructing Chief Spence in particular—and Indigenous peoples in general—as unhealthy, out of control, and in need of outside help (which arrived in the form of third-party management). Of course, these continual comments about the physical body of Chief Spence also served the purpose of denying the authenticity of her protest.

The objectification of Chief Spence's body went hand-in-hand with the purported failure of Chief Spence to carry out what the media saw as a legitimate "hunger strike." The media latched onto the information that Chief Spence would continue to ingest liquids and fish broth with shocking vigour. For example, Ezra Levant wrote that

> Gandhi never lasted more than 21 days on his hunger strikes. The IRA hunger strikers looked like skeletons by 26 days, and started dying weeks later. Not Spence—she's still positively Rubenesque.[64]

Not to be outdone, the *Toronto Sun* claimed that there was an obvious "irony in Spence's hunger strike … hers is not an ideological gesture like those IRA hunger strikers who died for their cause, but a blackmail attempt to force Harper to pay attention to her."[65] The important issue to note in these passages is the accusation of mimicry and the construction of a "real" hunger strike in relation to Chief Spence's protest. In this misogynist representation, Chief Spence is said to desire attention from the male gaze. What is more, constant comparisons to men such as Gandhi or Sands deny Chief Spence's political actions any rational, critical, or independent thought. Simultaneously, her protest is effectively removed from the broader historical context of Indigenous traditions. What is accomplished in these passages, then, is the complete removal of a sign from its cultural context, and an elision of the historical specificity of Indigenous fasting as a mode of embodied resistance (as discussed by Simpson above). By suggesting Chief Spence's actions are a "failed diet," the symbolic importance and historical context of drinking fish broth is made invisible under the settler-colonial gaze, and the image of Chief Spence on a hunger strike became nothing more than a sign that reinforces the original structural relationships and common-sense racisms of the settler-colonial project.

Levant continually linked Chief Spence with the sexual and the indulgent. Not only did he refer to her body as sexually provocative and voluptuous when he described her as "Rubenesque"; in a tirade aired on Sun News Levant argued that "Idle No More is just an Aboriginal reboot of Occupy Wall Street. It has the same vague demands, summarized as 'give us more free stuff.' It has the same low-level criminality—Occupy illegally squatted in parks and was heavy into drug use and public sex."[66] This passage not only collapses Chief Spence's protest into the Idle No More and Occupy movements, but also enacts an erasure of all non-conservative, contrapuntal politics. To Levant, all of these social rights movements signify the same fundamental alterity to law, order, progress, civilization, bodily integrity, and respectability.

Together these specious opinion pieces construct Chief Spence as a lewd and licentious terrorist; they also reveal that there was a broad cross-section of the Canadian media that depicted Chief Spence as a kind of ultimate Other precisely because she was a political leader who was both Indigenous *and* a woman. The strength, determination, and righteousness with which she pursued her protest was, in the settler-colonial imaginary, an unsettling symbolic provocation that had to be reconstructed. In order to make these events understandable and palatable to settlers, deeply racist and sexist stereotypes had to be employed in order to avoid the events in Attawapiskat being seen for what they really are: genocide.

Conclusion

As we see through reviewing these various passages, well-worn and deeply racist stereotypes and colonial constructions of corrupt band councils, Indigenous womanhood, and inauthenticity worked to produce a network of meaning that Canadian settler society could attach to the protest in order to understand Indigenous peoples as plagued by selfishness, indulgence, corruption, and bodily irresponsibility rather than as survivors of an ongoing genocide wherein the resilience of Indigeneity threatens the legitimacy of Canadian settler society. The Canadian media served as the vehicle through which settler Canadians conveniently rewrote the public record of the housing crises in the Canadian North. Indeed, the rewriting that took place in this instance was part of the larger pattern of conscious historical reimagining that has enabled settlers to avoid the uncomfortable admission that land theft, broken treaties, the Indian Act, and other federal policies have been primarily responsible for impoverishing Indigenous communities, destroying matrilineal systems of governance, and replacing them with so-called democratic band council systems that are always set up to fail. What we see in this recycling of unoriginal colonial stereotypes is an attempt to protect the image of Canada as a neoliberal, multicultural paradise by dehumanizing Indigenous peoples. The fact that this dehumanizing discourse was obviously articulated through the language of patriarchy and women-hating reveals the connections between patriarchy and colonialism theorized by Indigenous feminists who articulate sexual violence as the very logic of genocide.

Indigenous feminist frameworks help to explain the otherwise curious conflation of band council stereotypes, constructions of Indigenous womanhood, and accusations of inauthenticity or mimicry in the dominant discourse of the hunger strike. In this event specifically, we can also see how discourses about women's bodies and access to nutrition continue to be bound up within colonial power relations. This example of fatphobia's intersection with settler colonialism—along with the fact that Spence was also routinely infantilized and called "childish"—orients us towards critiquing different discourses of domination (such as body shaming) as situated within the settler-colonial social order. As readers will see in this collection's final chapter, the signification of racial violence "between the spectacular and the embodied" may play a deeper role in the interpretative frameworks of genocides far outside a Canadian context.[67] The coverage of Chief Spence's protest, then, was not only the *destruction* of any public discourse about Kashechewan and Fort Albany, but also a *construction* of a new discourse or way of understanding the housing crisis in a single community as representing all First Nations communities. Media coverage consistently denied the fact that the source of the problem lies not with Indigenous peoples, but rather with the gendered racism of social and structural white supremacy that remains foundational to the Canadian settler state and society. This coverage remakes and elides the history of genocidal policies towards Indigenous peoples in Canada and "whitewashes" the colonial stains from our national history.[68]

NOTES

1   Within this paper, we have drawn upon a representative, not exhaustive, set of Canadian newspaper articles. This method was selected over and against a method that compared the regional differences between the *Vancouver Sun* and the *Montreal Gazette* or the ideological differences between the *Globe and Mail* and the *National Post*. We did this for two reasons: primarily, because mainstream Canadian media coverage of the event showed more glaring similarities than interesting differences; secondly, because the Canadian newspaper industry is itself much less heterogeneous than we believe. For example, a front-page article in the *Ottawa Citizen* might be reprinted in later issues of the *Montreal Gazette*, the *Toronto Star*, the *Vancouver Sun,* or the *Calgary Herald.* The database used for many of the sources in this paper was the Canadian Newstand Major Dailies database, which uses the ProQuest website interface, see http://www.proquest. com/products-services/canadian_newsstand.html (accessed 14 February 2016).

2   Lorenzo Veracini, "Settler Collective, Founding Violence and Disavowal: The Settler Colonial Situation," *Journal of Intercultural Studies* 29, no. 4 (November 2008): 363–379.

3   For a more theoretically rigorous and analytically exhaustive critique of the reception of Chief Theresa Spence, see Audra Simpson, "The Chiefs Two Bodies: Theresa Spence and the Gender of Settler Sovereignty", Keynote Address at R.A.C.E. Network's 14th Annual Critical Race and Anticolonial Studies Conference: "Unsettling Conversations: Unmaking Racisms and Colonialisms," University of Alberta, October 2014, https://vimeo.com/110948627 (accessed 21 January 2016). Importantly, Simpson's address wields a critique of what she calls the "ahistorical multicultural liberal handbook" alongside her theorizing of "the chief's two bodies." In this talk, Simpson includes references from sources such as the *Huffington Post.*

4   Taiaiake Alfred, "Warrior Scholarship: Seeing the University as a Ground of Contention" in *Indigenizing the Academy: Transforming Scholarship and Empowering Communities*, eds. Devon Abbot Mihesuah and Angela Cavendar Wilson (Lincoln: University of Nebraska Press, 2004), 82.

5   See Paula Gunn Allen, *The Sacred Hoop* (Boston: Beacon Press, 1986); Lee Maracle, *I Am Women: A Native Perspective On Sociology and Feminism* (New York: Global Professional Publishing, 1996); Janice Pelletier Acoose, *Iskwewak Kah' Ki Yaw Ni Wahkomakanak: Neither Indian Princess Nor Easy Squaws* (Toronto: Women's Press, 1995); and Andrea Smith, *Conquest: Sexual Violence and American Indian Genocide* (Brooklyn, NY: South End Press, 2005).

6   See Stuart Hall's *Representations: Cultural Representations and Signifying Practices* (London: Sage Publishing, 1997).

7   Murray Edelman, *Constructing the Political Spectacle* (Chicago: University of Chicago Press, 1988), 12.

8   Stuart Hall, "Encoding/Decoding" in *Stuart Hall*, ed. James Procter (London: Routledge, 2004), 64. It is useful to recall, moreover, Hall's claim "that representation

doesn't occur after the event; representation is constitutive of the event. It enters into the constitution of the object that we are talking about. It is part of the object itself; it is constitutive of it. It is one of its conditions of existence, and therefore representation is not outside the event, not after the event, but within the event itself; it is constitutive of it." For a transcript of the lecture containing this passage, see Media Education Foundation, "Stuart Hall: Representation and the Media," 1997, http://www.mediaed.org/assets/products/409/transcript_409.pdf (accessed 12 February 2015).

9   Lorne Gunter, "Conditions in Attawapiskat can be blamed on political correctness," *National Post* (Toronto), 2 December 2011. The use of capitalization and terminology in this passage should not go unnoticed; as Janice Acoose argues, "What a culture deems important or significant according to its dominant ideological framework is signified by using capital letters." See her *Iskwewak Kah' Ki Yaw Ni Wahkomakanak*, 34.

10 Boyd Cothran has written extensively and powerfully on the cultural production of "American innocence" within the context of settler colonialism. See his *Remembering the Modoc War: Redemptive Violence and the Making of American Innocence* (Chapel Hill: University of North Carolina Press, 2014).

11 Audra Simpson, "The Chiefs Two Bodies."

12 Sherene Razack, *Looking White People in the Eye: Gender Race, Class and Culture in Courtrooms and Classrooms* (Toronto: University of Toronto Press, 1998), 36.

13 Green quoted in Emma LaRoque, *When the Other Is Me: Native Resistance Discourse, 1850–1990* (Winnipeg: University of Manitoba Press, 2010), 37.

14 LaRoque, *When the Other Is Me*, 37–58.

15 Leanne Simpson, "Think Chief Spence is on a 'Liquid Diet'? I Think You're Ignorant," *Huffington Post,* 20 January 2013, http://www.huffingtonpost.ca/leanne-simpson/fish-broth-chief-spence_b_2517450.html (accessed 12 December 2013).

16 Ibid.

17 Dennis McPherson, "Indian on the Lawn: How are Research Partnerships with Aboriginal Peoples Possible?" *APA Newsletter* 5, no. 2 (Spring 2006): 3–24.

18 Quoted in Ward Churchill, *Kill the Indian, Save the Man: The Genocidal Impact of Indian Residential Schools* (San Francisco: City Lights Books, 2004), 7.

19 Some scholars and community members claim that "Kattawapiskak," and not Attawapiskat, is the proper place name for the Mushkegowuk Cree who live in this First Nation. We use the latter in this paper for the purpose of consistency.

20 Attawapiskat First Nation Education Authority, *Important Dates in the History of Attawapiskat*, 2008, http://www.afnea.com/about.html (accessed 12 December 2013). Also, see Jacqueline Hookimaw-Witt, "Keenebonanoh Keemoshominook Kaeshe Peemishikhik Odaskiwakh (We Stand on the Graves of Our Ancestors): Native Interpretations of Treaty No. 9 with Attawapiskat Elders," PhD diss., Trent University, Peterborough, 1997.

21 St. Anne's Residential School is the site of a federal cover-up operation in which evidence of systemic sexual abuse and the use of electric chairs to torture of children was actively suppressed. For an account of this, see: http://www.ndp.ca/news/feds-suppressed-evidence-abuse-st-annes-residential-school (accessed 12 December 2013); see also Colin Perkel, "Ottawa thwarting residential school compensation claims from 'electric chair' victims, advocates say," *National Post* (Toronto), 11 July 2013, http://

news.nationalpost.com/2013/07/11/ottawa-thwarting-residential-school-compensa-tion-claims-from-electric-chair-victims-advocates-say/ (accessed 12 December 2012).

22   Attawapiskat First Nation Education Authority, *Important Dates in the History of Attawapiskat.*

23   For a journalistic account of this affair, see Kelly McParland, "The answer to Attawa-piskat is … well, we'll get back to you," *National Post* (Toronto), 12 January 2011, http://fullcomment.nationalpost.com/2011/12/01/the-answer-to-attawapiskat-is-well-well-get-back-to-you/ (accessed 12 December 2013).

24   Karl Reimer, "What Other Canadian Kids Have: The Fight for a New School in Attawa-piskat," *Native Studies Review* 19, no. 1 (2010): 126.

25   Aboriginal Affairs and Northern Development Canada, "Attawapiskat First Nation Elementary School—Chronology of Events," 4 November 2013, http://www.aadnc-aan-dc.gc.ca/eng/1100100016328/1100100016329 (accessed 12 December 2013).

26   Ryan Lux, "Hundred Homeless in Attawapiskat," *Daily Press* (Timmins, ON), 9 November 2011, http://www.timminspress.com/2011/11/09/hundreds-homeless-in-at-tawapiskat (accessed 12 February 2015).

27   Chelsea Vowel, "The Free Housing for Natives Myth," *âpihtawikosisân, Law, Language, Life: A Plains Cree Speaking Metis Woman in Montreal,* http://apihtawikosisan.com/2012/08/the-free-housing-for-natives-myth/ (accessed 12 February 2015).

28   CMHC, "Preconditions Leading to Market Housing On Reserve," *Research Highlight* (March 2009): 1.

29   Nathan Compton, "Dispossession under the First Nations Property Ownership Act," 31 January 2014, http://rabble.ca/blogs/bloggers/mainlander/2013/01/dispossession-un-der-first-nations-property-ownership-act (accessed 12 February 2015). Also, see Daniel Wilson and David MacDonald, "The Income Gap between Aboriginal Peoples and the rest of Canada" (Ottawa: The Canadian Centre for Policy Alternatives, 2010), http://ywcacanada.ca/data/research_docs/00000121.pdf (accessed 15 February 2015).

30   Robert Robson, "Suffering an Excess Burden: Housing as a Health Determinant in the First Nations Community of Northern Ontario," *Canadian Journal of Native Studies* 28, no. 1 (2008): 72.

31   See Adam Barker, "The Contemporary Reality of Canadian Imperialism: Settler Colo-nialism and the Hybrid Colonial State," *American Indian Quarterly* 33, no. 3 (Summer 2009): 325–351.

32   Lorraine Land, "Taking a Second Look at those Attawapiskat Numbers," 13 December 2012, http://www.oktlaw.com/blog/taking-a-second-look-at-those-attawapiskat-num-bers/ (accessed 15 February 2015).

33   Kristen Jacklin and Wayne Warry, "The Indian Health Transfer Policy in Canada: To-ward Self-Determination or Cost Containment," in *Unhealthy Health Policy: A Critical Anthropological Approach,* eds. Arachu Castro and Merrill Singer (New York: Altamira Press, 2004), 222–223.

34   Radolfo Staghaven, United Nations Education, Scientific, and Cultural Organization, "Human Rights and Indigenous Issues: Report of the Special Rapporteur on the Situa-tion of Human Rights and Fundamental Freedoms of Indigenous People," 12 December 2004, http://repository.un.org/handle/11176/247309 (accessed 18 September 2016).

35   Miloon Kothari, "Report of the Special Rapporteur on Adequate Housing as Component of the Right to an Adequate Standard of Living, and on the Right to Non-Discrimination in this Context," Mission to Canada, 9–22 October 2007, https://documents-dds-ny.un.org/doc/UNDOC/GEN/G15/294/52/PDF/G1529452.pdf?OpenElement (accessed 18 September 2016).

36   Pamela Palmater, "Stretched Beyond Human Limits: Death by Poverty in First Nations," *Canadian Review of Social Policy* no. 65/66 (2011): 112–127.

37   Robson, "Suffering an Excess Burden," 72.

38   Ibid., 73.

39   See *Wawatay News*, "Attawapiskat Elder Completes 110km Trek," 10 December 2009, https://issuu.com/wawatay/docs/10dec2009 (accessed 12 December 2013).

40   See Aboriginal and Northern Affairs Canada, *Update on Government of Canada's Response to Attawapiskat: Statement from Minister Duncan*, 5 December 2011, http://news.gc.ca/web/article-en.do?nid=963989 (accessed 18 September 2016).

41   Tristan Hopper, "Attawapiskat officials kick out third-party manager sent to control reserve's finances," *National Post* (Toronto), 5 December 2011, http://news.nationalpost.com/2011/12/05/attawapiskat-officials-kick-third-party-manager-off-reserve/ (accessed 12 December 2013).

42   See Indian Act, section 61 (1), which reads "the Governor in Council may determine whether any purpose for which Indian moneys are used or are to be used is for the use and benefit of the band."

43   Hugh Shewell, *Enough to Keep Them Alive: Indian Welfare in Canada, 1873–1965* (Toronto: University of Toronto Press, 1994), 60–64.

44   Pam Palmater, "Stephen Harper and the Myth of the Crooked Indian," blog entry, 26 November 2014, http://rabble.ca/blogs/bloggers/pamela-palmater/2014/11/stephen-harper-and-myth-crooked-indian (accessed 12 February 2015).

45   For examples see Ezra Levant, "The Scandals of Chief Theresa Spence and Attawapiskat," Sun News, 3 January 2013, http://www.ottawasun.com/videos/featured/featured-ott/1213592866001/the-scandals-of-chief-theresa-spence-and-attawapiskat/2070970263001#.UkuH2FM_xFU.gmail (accessed 10 August 2014); Christie Blatchford, "Attawapiskat Audit Reveals Reserve Finances in Complete Disarray," *National Post* (Toronto), 8 January 2013, http://fullcomment.nationalpost.com/2013/01/08/christie-blatchford-attawapiskat-audit-reveals-reserve-finances-in-complete-disarray/ (accessed 27 August 2014); Anonymous, "Crisis of Management: Attawapiskat Reserve Plunged into Despair While $34 Million Is Squandered," *Toronto Sun*, 3 December 2011, http://www.torontosun.com/2011/12/02/crisis-of-management (accessed 27 August 2014); and Kent Driscoll, "Chief Spence meets the spin cycle," *APTN National News*, 4 January 2013, http://aptn.ca/news/2013/01/04/chief-spence-meets-the-spin-cycle/ (accessed 27 August 2014).

46   Pam Palmater, "Stephen Harper and the Myth of the Crooked Indian."

47   Lorne Gunter, "Theresa Spence Shows No Interest in Taking Ownership of Issues," Sun News, 9 January 2013, http://www.sunnewsnetwork.ca/sunnews/straighttalk/archives/2013/01/20130109-080205.html#.UkuDz8oZ-m8.gmail (accessed 27 August 2014).

48   Kelly McParland, "Theresa Spence's Carefully Woven Cause Starts to Unravel," *National Post* (Toronto), 9 January 2013.

49 LaRoque, *When the Other Is Me*, 37-58.

50 Thomas King, *The Inconvenient Indian: A Curious Account of Native People in North America* (Toronto: Anchor Canada, 20102), 3.

51 Lenore Keeshig-Tobias cited in Karen Coody Cooper, *Spirited Encounters: American Indians Protest Museum Policies and Practices* (Lanham, MD: Altamira, 2008), 1.

52 See Sarah Carter, *Capturing Women: The Manipulation of Cultural Imagery in Canada's Prairie West* (London: McGill University Press, 1997); also, see Sarah Carter, *The Importance of Being Monogamous: Marriage and Nation Building in Western Canada to 1915* (Edmonton: University of Alberta Press, 2008), 283. Further, see Sylvia Van Kirk, *Many Tender Ties: Women in Fur-Trade Society, 1670–1870* (Oklahoma: University of Oklahoma Press, 1983), 5. Also, see Cecily Devereux, "New Woman, New World: Maternal Feminism and the New Imperialism in the White Settler Colonies," *Women's Studies International Forum* 22, no. 2 (1999): 175–184. Finally, see Adele Perry, *On the Edge of Empire: Gender, Race, and the Making of British Columbia, 1849–1871* (Toronto: University of Toronto Press, 2001).

53 Barbara Gurr, *Reproductive Justice: The Politics of Health Care for Native American Women* (New Brunswick, NJ: Rutgers University Press, 2015), 26.

54 Videos of this speech by Larry Miller are widely available online. See http://www.youtube.com/watch?v=1YmLKKho2P4 (accessed 9 February 2014).

55 Kristy Kirkup, "Conservative MP slams Theresa Spence's appeal to UN on racial discrimination," *Toronto Sun*, 26 February 2013, http://www.torontosun.com/2013/02/26/conservative-mp-slams-theresa-spences-appeal-to-un-on-racial-discrimination (accessed 9 February 2014).

56 Iain Hunter, "Spence has Government Knees Jerking," *Times-Colonist* (Victoria, BC), 13 January 2013.

57 Christie Blatchford, "Inevitable puffery surrounds Theresa Spence hunger strike while real problems forgotten," *National Post* (Toronto), 27 December 2012.

58 Christie Blatchford, "Audit Says Attawapiskat had no Budget," *Leader-Post* (Regina) 9 January 2013.

59 Christie Blatchford, "It's a Disgrace, Not a Surprise," *National Post* (Toronto), 3 December 2011.

60 Ezra Levant, "Chief Spence Knew What She Was Doing Pulling Her Dieting Stunt in Ottawa," *Rebel Media*, 6 January 2013, http://www.ezralevant.com/chief_spence_knew_what_she_was/ (accessed 12 December 2013).

61 "Sen. Brazeau mocks Chief Spence, Idle No More movement," *CTV News*, 31 January 2013, http://www.ctvnews.ca/canada/sen-brazeau-mocks-chief-spence-idle-no-more-movement-1.1138545 (accessed 27 August 2014).

62 Susie Orbach, *Fat is a Feminist Issue* (New York: Berkley Books, 1978), 4.

63 Peter Worthington "Theresa Spence Hunger Strike Not Ideological Gesture But Blackmail," Sun News, 5 January 2013, http://www.sunnewsnetwork.ca/sunnews/straighttalk/archives/2013/01/20130105-073522.html#.UkuEA_S8occ.gmail (accessed 27 August 2014).

64 Ezra Levant, "Chief Spence Knew What She Was Doing."

65 Peter Worthington, "Chief Spence's Hunger Strike not Ideological."

66 Ezra Levant, "Chief Spence Knew What She Was Doing."

67 Our language here is borrowed from Patrick Anderson and Jisha Menon, eds., *Violence Performed: Local Roots and Global Routes of Conflict* (New York: Palgrave, 2008), 5. Readers can find a fuller and more exhaustive theoretical treatment of the relationship between the body and the spectacle in Donia Mounsef's chapter in this collection, "Atrocity, Banality, and *Jouissance* in Performance."

68 See Taiaiake Alfred, *Wasáse: Indigenous Pathways to Action and Freedom* (Peterborough, ON: Broadview Press, 2005); specifically, see chapter 2, "Colonial Stains on Our Existence," 101–178. Also, see Taiaiake Alfred, "Colonial Stains on our Existence" in *Racism, Colonialism, and Indigeneity in Canada*, eds. Martin Cannon and Lina Sunseri (Toronto: Oxford University Press, 2011), 3–10.

7

Remembering Them All: Including and Excluding Atrocity Crime Victims

Andrew R. Basso

This chapter offers a critical genocide studies perspective on the construction of narratives and memories of victimization in atrocities.[1] It deconstructs exclusive memory constructions and offers critiques that challenge prevalent narratives regarding the Ottoman destruction of Christian minorities (Armenians, Greeks, and Assyrians) from 1912 to 1925 and the victimization of Tutsis, Hutus, and Twa in the Rwandan genocide of 1994.[2] Traditional studies of these two crimes have focused on the two main victim groups involved—Armenians and Tutsis—and have typically failed to consider and analyze the experiences of all other victim groups involved, as well as the implications of these exclusions. Exclusionary memory campaigns, as will be demonstrated, can lead to incomplete, inaccurate, and isolated histories that are devoid of their larger contexts. Exclusionary memory campaigns can also contribute to current and future exploitations of isolated histories to undermine democratic governance.

Future scholarship must be critically aware of the problems with exclusionary histories and remedy them by utilizing a comparative-inclusive approach to atrocity studies on "other" victim groups. Inclusive approaches are a moral imperative, a necessity for holistic historical accuracy, and a tool for combatting attempts to politicize remembrance.[3] By identifying and remembering all victims of atrocity, it is possible to create rich historical narratives that recognize all victimization and give some semblance of equal justice to victims.

The comparative-inclusive approach presented in this chapter will demonstrate that privileging one victim group over others excludes important historical memories that can otherwise be used to construct insightful narratives, and allows for deliberate distortions of memories for personal political gain. In short, inclusive approaches avoid relegating lesser-known victim groups to oblivion, where they remain forever in the shadow of larger victim groups that can "claim a monopoly on public attention, ensuring that others will remain shrouded in obscurity."[4]

The Ottoman Genocide of Christian Minorities: Victim Memory Exclusion

During the last great caliph, the Ottoman Empire undertook a devastating project of social restructuring and almost rid itself of its Christian minority populations *in toto*. Three main victim groups—Armenians, Greeks, and Assyrians—were killed in succession by two different regimes in two different time periods: the Young Turks (1912–1918) and the Kemalists (1919–1925),[5] led by the first president of modern-day Turkey, Mustafa Kemal Atatürk. When analyzed together, the campaigns of destruction against Armenians, Greeks, and Assyrians are connected in that the genocides represent a concerted effort to rid the Ottoman Empire of its Christian populations, thereby eliminating Christian influence from the Holy Land. While these crimes were framed as a battle of religions, there were many other factors that caused the Young Turks to conclude that genocide was the appropriate response for solving the empire's problems.

Victimization of Christian Minorities: Shared Pathways to Destruction

Christians' socio-economic and political roles in the empire have been emphasized as key exacerbating factors contributing to their destruction.[6] Due to the intersection of international and domestic politics, as well as religious and ethnic differences over centuries, the imperial, authoritarian, and democratic leaders of the Ottoman Empire (later Turkey) blamed the empire's problems on Christian minorities, who were framed as fifth columnists and separatists who could be scapegoated for all that was wrong with the declining empire.[7] But while religious difference can offer face-value reasoning for why Christians were killed, this was at most an underlying factor, and as such is an insufficient explanation of the type of destruction Christian minorities faced. Christian minorities were collectively persecuted in large part due to the multitude of perceived injustices that Christians had inflicted upon the crumbling Ottoman Empire. Existing literatures offer varying contextual justifications for the destruction of the Armenians, Greeks, and Assyrians by the Ottoman/Turkish perpetrators, but macro anti-Christian sentiments that link these individual accounts can offer more powerful explanations for why Christians were targeted for similar reasons and exterminated using similar methods. German historian Tessa Hofmann argues that the genocide of Aegean, Thracian, Pontic, and other Anatolian Greeks should be considered a "cumulative" genocide. Cumulative is utilized here in the sense that the genocide was perpetrated over the course of a decade and victims were killed in varying geographical locations depending on exogenous and endogenous socio-political factors.[8] The notion of a cumulative genocide offers a rich conceptual starting point for analyses of this genocide and is a propitious label to apply to the shared pathways of destruction Christian minorities experienced as a whole.

Before the genocide, Christians were marginalized as slaves or semi-freed peoples in the period leading up to the Young Turk Revolution of 1908. Christian women were sold into harems, men and women forced into labour, and, for comparison's sake, sometimes treated worse than Russian serfs. The non-slave, "freer" Christians were ostracized from many facets of the Ottoman socio-economic system, most notably the traditional agrarian sector. Christians did, however, find some affluence and capitalized on trade, small-business ownership, and banking, areas that were ultimately perceived by other Ottomans as contributing to the demise of the once-great empire.[9]

The empire's economic decline had everything to do with previous poor planning choices, and the sultan's answers to these problems. The Ottoman Empire was the "sick man of Europe" and the sultan knew that in order to compete with other European economies, the empire had to modernize and westernize its economy.[10] However, the modernization effort had unintended consequences, most notably the creation of tensions between the traditional Ottoman ways of life and the "modern" ways of Western Europe. The sultan called upon Western advisers to instruct the

Ottoman state on how to construct its new economy around the sectors that, coincidentally, Christians were forced into and dominated. This was wrongly interpreted by Ottoman citizens as Christians helping Christians, and intentionally excluding Muslims, in order to bring about the empire's downfall and its colonization by European powers.[11] This misinterpretation simultaneously ostracized the majority of Ottoman Muslims who held chauvinistic beliefs in the traditional Ottoman economy—the very policies that brought the empire to crisis—and led to widespread distrust in the modernization process.[12] Ironically, some Christian minorities prospered in the socio-economic roles to which they had been segregated with the new modern, Western economy.[13]

To fund these modernization projects, the Ottoman state went into debt with the very nations that sent advisors—Western Christian nations. This debt resulted in Western countries, most notably Britain and France, controlling over 90 percent of the Ottoman banking system, handicapping the Ottoman state's ability to spend on social institutions that could ease the negative repercussions of economic decline, and address problems with individual citizens' financial endeavours.[14] The high level of economic control and the resulting stagnation of the Ottoman economy, and specifically Christian control over the crumbling empire, eventually became an emphasis of the Young Turks in creating the discriminatory and toxic conditions necessary for the blanket victimization of Christian minorities.[15]

Christian wars of independence in the Balkans reinforced and solidified the Ottoman belief that Christians were the underlying cause of the empire's demise. Four Balkan states—Bulgaria, Greece, Montenegro, and Serbia—achieved independence from the empire between 1912 and 1913. The loss of these territories was not only detrimental to Ottoman prestige, but also meant that the empire had effectively lost all of its European holdings in the span of just two years. This fuelled the belief that Christian minorities within the empire could not be trusted as these subversive elements would seek independence from within.[16] The Ottoman fear that the great European powers desired to carve up the empire came true after the Great War (1914–1918), meaning that once again Christians were perceived as responsible for the dissolution of the empire.[17]

Compounding these issues was Christian minorities' protracted struggle for equal rights in the empire. As a caliphate, the empire systematically repressed non-Muslim minorities, and the *Tanzimat*, or reforms, of 1839 and 1876 were intended to overhaul Ottoman society so it could modernize and establish at least a semi-equality. The reforms, on paper, gave Christians rights and freedoms equal to Muslim citizens in an attempt to shift the empire away from an officially discriminatory religious state to a secular one that allowed free religious expression and practice. However, Christian rights were never fully realized, nor were the modern visions of the sultanate's and empire's advisers. The lack of policy implementation, enforcement, and societal acceptance ultimately doomed the *Tanzimat* and caused great social strife, again leading to a scapegoating of Christians as a problem group. Russia's involvement in securing the *Tanzimat* was particularly troubling for increasingly disaffected Ottoman citizens.[18]

These issues, coupled with the overall decline of the empire, gave Ottomans a feeling of helplessness and loss, and they sought a scapegoat that could be blamed for initiating these disastrous programs. The Young Turks' successful revolution of 1908 ushered in four years of relative peace, but an internal coup d'état spearheaded by Mehmed Talaat, Ismail Enver, and Ahmed Djemal led to a new ruling regime that embraced the anti-Christian dogmas of the İttihat ve Terakki Cemiyeti (Committee of Union and Progress—henceforth referred to as the Young Turks regime).[19] Rather than solely blaming the sultan for the empire's problems, the Young Turks then shifted all blame towards Christian minorities and turned their back on their own cosmopolitan ideals. Christians were then persecuted along religious lines due to devolving political and socio-economic circumstances.[20] Religious and ethnic difference alone, it should be noted, are insufficient variables for explaining this destruction; there has to be *more* than simple religious and ethnic difference in order to make war and atrocity possible.[21]

Even though Christians had participated in the Young Turks revolution from its inception to its end, when the Young Turks regime took power, Christians were targeted when the "Three Pashas" (Talaat, Enver, and Djemal) began ruling the empire with genocidal aims. The three men consolidated power amongst themselves and turned their backs on the cosmopolitan ideals of the previous Young Turks ideology.[22] They exploited religious difference and the socio-economic and political factors outlined above to collectively target and punish Christians in the empire as a whole for the demise of the once-great Ottoman Empire. The majority of Christian victims had absolutely no connection to the ostensible causes of their persecution by the power-consolidating and scapegoating Young Turks regime. Rather, Christians were targeted because of historical and contemporary political and cultural anti-Christianism that exploited and skewed existing religious divisions based on the scapegoating of Christians as the primary cause of the decline of the empire. These actions culminated in an empire-wide jihad against Christians in November 1914.[23] Perception dominates and is the element most revealed when examining the shared victimization of Christians in the empire against the vitriolic and destructive Turkish nationalism of the Young Turks and Kemalist regimes.

The ideals of Pan-Ottomanism were transformed into Pan-Turkism, specifically the exclusion of Christians from this new vision for the empire, and the Young Turks' new propaganda machine organized itself around the discriminatory and dehumanizing anti-Christian messages of Ziya Gökalp and other ultra-nationalists and provocateurs.[24] Genocidal goals were developed and called for the expulsion or killing of Christians in the empire's borders to make the Ottoman Empire a region for Turks only. The Young Turks, and later Kemalists, worked according to a 5-to-10-percent principle which dictated that non-Muslims could only comprise between 5 and 10 percent of a locality's population; all non-Muslim groups exceeding this number had to either be destroyed or transferred to a different part of the empire.[25] This resulted in the killing of approximately 2.5 million Christians (1.5 million Armenians; 750,000 Greeks; and 250,000 Assyrians).[26] Christians were collectively punished for exogenous and endogenous political, economic, and socio-cultural pressures felt by Ottoman citizens. Despite the allure of blaming the killing on mere religious difference, this narrative is false.

Linking Narratives: Towards Macro Perspectives on Memories of Genocide

A problematic element of the memories of genocide against Christian minorities is that studies of the Armenian genocide have almost exclusively claimed the history of persecution and genocide. While these studies are certainly correct in arguing that Armenians were victimized on a wide scale, a focus on Armenian victimization excludes the larger context which saw anti-Christian sentiments and actions directed against *all* of the empire's Christians, not one group specifically. Little attention is paid to Greek and Assyrian victims in these literatures and these groups have not had penetrating studies of their experiences conducted on a systematic scale comparable to English-language scholarship on the Armenian genocide.[27] Perhaps most important is the recognition that the victimization process applies to all of these persecuted groups, and that isolated individualized pathologies of destruction fall short of cumulative understandings of genocide and memory. A cumulative comparative-inclusive perspective offers holistic and macro understandings of victimization processes better than isolated narratives. The dominant political and cultural shifts to targeting Christian minorities for extermination were the main driving factors in the genocidal efforts of the Young Turks regime. These shifts were later carried on by the Kemalist regime, which once again initiated and expanded anti-Christian violence.[28]

Comparative-inclusive, macro analyses of the victim groups provide insight into geopolitical effects on shared victimization and genocidal processes. Generally (when all Christian minority groups are included), the genocide can be said to have taken place from 1912 to 1925. The peculiarities of perpetration as a whole, however, reveal that the Young Turks and Kemalist regimes were cognizant of and calculating towards potential and real national enemies in both the Great War and the Turkish War of Independence (1919–1923), and this deeply affected the time periods and areas in which Christians were killed. More Assyrians were killed in 1925 by the Turks and Kurds following Kurdish independence revolts and subsequent Turkish repression and control.[29]

Kurds were treated with Janus-faced Ottoman policies during this time. Predominantly Muslim, Kurds were simultaneously perpetrators of genocide against Christian minorities and victims of displacements and massacres at the hands of the Young Turks and Kemalists. Over 700,000 Kurds were forcibly displaced during the Great War, and approximately 350,000 were killed via direct and indirect methods that were also utilized against Christian minorities.[30] Kurds as victims and perpetrators at the same time is an important historical challenge to be examined in future scholarship and may have profound implications for understanding the roles of individuals and groups in atrocities as a whole.

A cumulative look at the genocide of Christian minorities, though, reveals that Aegean Greeks, residing along the littoral western coast of the empire, were the first victims of genocidal processes between 1912 and 1916, and again from 1919 to 1923. Assyrians, living in the heartland of the empire, were victimized from 1914 to 1918 and 1919 to 1925; Armenians, living primarily in major cities and heartland areas, from 1915 to 1923; and the Pontic Greeks, residing along the Black Sea coastline, from 1916 to 1918 and 1919 to1923.[31] One of the striking elements of the genocide of Christian minorities is that there was no continuous killing of individual victim groups throughout the years 1912 and 1925. Instead, the killing occurred in waves, a genocide progressing from the Aegean coastline to the interior and back again with different groups killed at different times in different places by many types of perpetrators—be they special death squads, brigands, or military personnel.[32] When the Young Turks and Kemalist regimes' policies and victims are analyzed cumulatively, two things become clear: the intended extermination and displacement of all Christian minorities, and the fact that these groups were killed in distinct intervals and not all at the same time.

By the time genocidal policies were fully implemented in the Ottoman Empire, the *genocidaires* had considerable experience in implementing extreme solutions against Christians and other minority populations, fuelling their campaign of destruction.[33] The genocide against Christians did not fully start until approximately 1912, when Greeks along the Aegean littoral areas were deported either to Greece and Southern Europe, or were sent to the interior of the empire, where they were killed by indirect methods. Indirect killing methods included, but were not limited to, starvation, dehydration, death by exhaustion, disease, and exposure.[34] These are highly cost-effective forms of killing and require few resources to perpetrate, and constitute elements of what Helen Fein has called "genocide by attrition."[35] The destruction of Christian populations by displacement and indirect killing methods would constitute a "displacement atrocity."[36]

One geopolitical factor concerning the Greeks as a whole was the varying intensity of violence utilized by perpetrators. The political pressures that the forced displacement of Aegean Greeks placed on Greece was no doubt the impetus for German encouragement of the Turks to stop the displacements, with which the Turks complied.[37] The political and military ties between Germany and the Ottomans during the Great War certainly necessitated keeping Greece neutral. If Greece entered the war against the Central Powers, a new battlefront would have opened up and would have undermined the efforts of the alliance on the western and eastern fronts, as well as destabilize the Ottoman Empire's relative security from attack due to its geographic location. It was because of the war that the genocidal policies of the Young Turks and later Kemalist regimes were tailored to distinct geopolitical situations and implemented cumulatively.[38] In the early genocidal period, the military position of the Central Powers was far from consolidated and the war was far from decided.[39] It was only later in the war and during the postwar period that the Aegean Greeks suffered massive casualties, far beyond the displacement of the early years, perhaps as it became more viable, militarily and politically, to kill them. In this way, stopping the violence against Aegean Greeks can be considered a military decision, demonstrating that genocidal policies often have military strategy intertwined with perpetration beyond the use of soldiers as killers. That said, the later Kemalist regime reinitiated the violence to the same degree as the Armenian and Pontic Greek deportations.

The Assyrian genocide began in 1914 and lasted until 1925, after which survivors of the death marches languished in refugee camps, a stateless people whose plight was internationally known.[40] Approximately 50 percent of the population was killed by indirect and direct means. Like other Christian groups, the final intent of Ottoman/Turkish policies was death or assimilation into primarily Turkic habitations.[41] The years and geographic location of persecution coincided with war. While this correlation does not prove causation, the unique varying regional presence or threat of war in all cases of destruction of Christian minorities does signal a link between war and the presence of genocide in geographical regions within the empire. Assyrians were targeted during the Great War, the British Mesopotamian campaign, and the Russian incursion into Turkey, presumably in part to clear potential combat zones of Christians who might sympathize with the British or Russian causes.[42] After the war, Assyrians were left to die in refugee camps or were killed by Turkish forces, both regular and irregular, into the 1920s, when the Turks began focusing on the eastern and western fronts against Greece.[43] While the Assyrians did offer military resistance, their geographical location, like that of the Armenians, meant that no outside force could aid them, save for the British and Russians. The correlation between Ottoman killing campaigns and the British in Mesopotamia and Gallipoli and the Russians in Pontus and the Caucuses may have been more significant factors in deciding when to kill the Assyrians at the local and national levels than has been recognized previously.

After halting campaigns against the Aegean Greeks, the Ottomans shifted the machinery of death towards the Anatolian Armenians who could not be saved by foreign powers due to their physical isolation. The official Armenian commemoration of the beginning of the genocide is 24 April 1915, when leading Armenian intellectuals and community leaders were arrested and killed in Constantinople. However, as early as 25 February 1915, Armenian men were being drafted into the *amele taburları*, the brutal Ottoman forced-labour battalions where death rates were typically over 90 percent.[44] Even in 1914, Aegean and Pontic Greeks were drafted into the *amele taburları* and were being killed using various indirect methods: exposure, exhaustion, starvation, dehydration, and disease.[45] The recruitment of Armenians was the next step for the *genocidaires* and, in addition to indirect deaths, the members of the *amele taburları* were subjected to torture, mutilations, and murder. The *genocidaires* again tailored their plans to geopolitics, utilizing forced labour to carry supplies for the military, freeing Muslim Ottomans to fight.[46] This simultaneously allowed the perpetrating regimes to continue to situate and justify the killing and poor treatment of Christians in terms of an "us" versus "them" mentality (i.e., Muslims versus Christians). War, therefore, galvanized internal Ottoman beliefs about Christians attempting to impose themselves on the empire.

The *amele taburları* were but one element of the genocide. The primary means of perpetration were the deportation caravans of Christian victims from all over the empire. The caravans were comprised of Christians who were forced to march while being systematically deprived of water, food, clothing, shelter, and medical care by the perpetrators. Deportation was utilized to facilitate faster deaths among victims with little cost to the perpetrators, either in terms of bullets or the psychological strain of directly killing individuals.[47] The remaining populations were sent from their place of residence to Der Zor in the Syrian Desert, and the death rate for these columns typically ranged from 80 to 90 percent.[48] The columns were escorted by the Teşkilât-ı Mahsusa (Special Organization) and Çetes (mostly organized brigands), and individual victims were often assaulted during deportation, including physical mutilation, psychological torture, and rape.[49] Women and girls were sometimes sold into harems, used as personal sexual slaves, or assimilated into Muslim households. Some of the most outrageous and degrading actions were inflicted upon Armenians during these deportations.[50]

The majority of the killing of Armenians occurred between 1915 and 1916, while violence and forced assimilations continued until 1923.[51] In 1916, however, the perpetrators turned their focus to the Pontic Greeks. Former American ambassador to the Ottoman Empire, Henry Morgenthau, noted that any documented cases of violence against the Armenians could just as easily have been written about what was done to the Pontic Greeks.[52] The Pontic Greeks were forced to march over 800 kilometres from the Black Sea to Der Zor, and were subjected to the same kinds of brutality as the Armenians, which is one of the lost stories of this genocide. Pontians, and other groups, were sometimes taken onto the Black Sea in maritime craft and drowned en masse.[53] Pontians were killed from 1916 until 1918, the end of the Great War, and again from 1919 to 1923, during the Kemalist regime and the Greco-Turkish War (1919–1922). The second phase of killing can be understood as a structural legacy of the Young Turks regime; it was carried on by Kemal's uniquely Turkic and anti-Christian nationalism, which ignited genocide once again in Pontus. Pontic Greek collaboration with Russian forces during the Great War was used as a justification to collectively punish the group, as was the case with other Christian collaborators.[54] The initial deportations were stopped by the end of the First World War, at which point all states wanted to avoid future conflicts with others, but were again initiated when the empire's improved politico-military situation made it possible (i.e., the Greco-Turkish War). Perhaps this is one reason why the killing of Greeks stopped in 1918–1919, but Armenians, who did not have a nation-state of their own to threaten the Ottoman Empire (and with diminished Russian political and military support after the Bolshevik Revolution of 1917), continued to be killed along with Assyrians.

While Kemal denounced the crimes of the Young Turks regime, and the empire participated in the Turkish courts-martial (1919–1920) to punish leading perpetrators, the underlying hatred of Christian minorities was fanned again under Kemal.[55] The courts-martial turned into a political and legal blunder, and perpetrators avoided facing justice for their actions.[56] Ironically, Kemal, who denounced the Young Turks' crimes, instituted the exact same policies against Christian minorities, such as labour battalions, forced marches, violent brutality, and sexual slavery, all of which climaxed with the Great Fire of Smyrna (1922). The Turkish-Greek population transfers of 1923 rid the empire of most of its

Christians while the continued violence against Assyrians completed over fourteen years of genocide.[57]

Beyond Isolated Victimization; Towards Collective Narratives

Alexander Hinton notes that the Armenian genocide, the Holocaust, and the Rwandan genocide form the initial triad and first generation of genocide studies, while the Greek and Assyrian cases lay on the periphery as a fourth generation.[58] One contribution of this chapter is to link these generations of genocide studies to form more holistic accounts of similar cases. Beyond these links, three key historical patterns are striking when all groups are analyzed together. First, Christians were targeted when exogenous factors like war made it either necessary or more politically feasible to commit atrocities against them, most notably coinciding with the Great War as well as the Turkish War of Independence (specifically the Greco-Turkish War). Second, despite the realpolitik of Kemal's regime, which paid lip service to liberal cosmopolitan values, the regime had every intention of finishing the killing that the Young Turks had begun. Endogenous political forces also affected the genocidal policy of both the Young Turks and Kemal regimes. Finally, the cumulative character of the Ottoman's genocide of Christian minorities demonstrates once again that genocide can at times be an ever-unfolding process, rather than a single cataclysmic event in one designated year.[59]

While all the decisions for the killing practices may not have been planned from the beginning, the perpetrators followed a methodical and systematic blueprint for the destruction of Christian communities. Victims were starved to death in the desert, killed via exhaustion in labour battalions, and some were sold into slavery—tactics that are clear evidence of genocide against Christian minorities. The genocide took years to decimate the Ottoman Christian population but the results were cumulative—fourteen years of displacement and death leading to a near complete extermination of Christians and their influence in the empire. The correlation of genocidal processes with war in the Ottoman Empire is also an important research question that requires further scholarship to establish a solid link. A comparative-inclusive, macro lens cannot replace memories of the individual victim groups. It can, however, augment current knowledge and offer a more comprehensive collection of narratives of the genocidal processes involved. A macro lens can both reveal the complexities involved in genocides that target multiple victim groups and also create holistic narratives that take all experiences into account for the linking of memories so victims do not experience a second genocide—that of the memory of their victimization.

The Rwandan Genocide: Omitting Victims for Political Gains

The story of the Rwandan genocide represents a move from an inclusive to an exclusive memory construction. Rwandan president Paul Kagame is an enigma: a democratic leader, yet with shades of authoritarianism in his political repertoire. He saved hundreds of thousands of lives when the Rwandan Patriotic Front (RPF) swept into Rwanda in mid-1994 and stopped the Hutu extremist–perpetrated Rwandan genocide—one hundred days of slaughter of primarily Tutsis. Approximately 800,000 Rwandans were killed by thousands of their fellow citizens, while another 250,000 were raped; 4 million were left internally displaced, and 2.3 million became refugees.[60] However, more than twenty years after the genocide, the Rwandan government is in the process of shifting the memory from the "Rwandan genocide" to the "Rwandan genocide *against the Tutsi*," which excludes other victim groups and suggests that the memory of atrocity is being obfuscated for contemporary political purposes.

One Hundred Days

The genocide began on the night of 6 April 1994, when President Juvénal Habyarimana's aircraft was shot down while on the final approach to Kigali. This triggered a frenzied and patterned response from the Presidential Guard and Hutu extremists, who established roadblocks and checkpoints around the capital to search for Tutsis, assassinated critical moderate political and civic actors and voices in Rwanda, and began an orgy of violence that eventually killed approximately 30 percent of the Rwandan Twa population, between ten and one hundred thousand Hutus, and the vast majority of Rwandan Tutsis.[61] The variation in the number of Hutu victims ranges so greatly because of a lack of credible and unbiased accounts. Studies of this sort are politically untenable in Rwanda at present. The variation is also indicative of the limited state of research on Hutu and Twa genocide victims. Tutsis were immediately either killed, raped, or tortured in the most barbaric ways. Hutus who had the physical appearance of a stereotypical Tutsi, a contrived caricature spread by Hutu hate propaganda, were also killed, as were moderate Hutus who worked with or were allies of the so-called *inyenzi* ("cockroaches," an extremist slur for Tutsis).[62]

The violence spread from Kigali to the countryside, and the Hutu extremist *Interahamwe* ("those who fight together") and *Impuzamugambi* ("those who have the same goal") paramilitaries incited and perpetrated genocide nationwide.[63] The extremists' vulgarisms were spread by radio organizations and graphic cartoons in order to dehumanize their victim groups.[64] There are scores of massacre sites in Rwanda, but some of the most disturbing are in churches, where Tutsis and others sought refuge from their Hutu extremist killers but found only destruction.[65] Tutsis were hunted down in papyrus marshes and cities by roving bands of predominantly Hutu killers. Many Tutsis were raped, mutilated, and tortured before being killed or left to bleed out on the emerald green hills of Rwanda.[66] The victims of this genocide were primarily Tutsis—but Hutu moderates and Twa were murdered en masse using similarly ferocious and brutally direct killing methods.[67]

The killing was eventually stopped by the RPF, led by Kagame, who is sometimes referred to as the "Napoleon of Africa" for his tactical and strategic prowess as a military and political commander.[68] There is no doubt that Kagame ended the genocide with his invasion from Uganda. However, while the RPF's victory in Rwanda stopped the genocide, it also simultaneously compelled many Hutus to flee over the border to Zaire (now the Democratic Republic of the Congo, or DRC), which further destabilized that already unstable country, renewing the brutal civil war and leading to international armed conflict. Kagame's orders and actions in the 1996–1997 Rwandan invasion of the DRC are the subject of particularly pointed criticism, especially the mass murder of approximately two hundred thousand Hutu refugees. While the Rwandan government claims those killed were only Hutu extremists and *genocidaires*, less biased sources argue that many were civilians—a serious breach of the laws of armed conflict.[69] In Rwanda, a new democratic government was installed with Pasteur Bizimungu serving as president from 1994 to 2000, a period in which Kagame was nonetheless the *de facto* ruler. In 2000, Kagame was elected president and has twice been re-elected due to his unrivalled popularity.[70]

Rwanda engaged in a sweeping program of transitional justice, employing traditional Gacaca courts to place over a million alleged perpetrators on trial; it has also readily participated in the International Criminal Tribunal for Rwanda (ICTR), allowing for some sixty prominent leaders of the genocide to be tried in Arusha, Tanzania. Beyond this, a national Rwandan ethnic unity program has been launched that seeks to break down ethnic differences between Hutus, Tutsis, and Twa, and in their place promote a single Rwandan identity.[71]

Exclusive Memory Construction

The Rwandan government's insistence on adding the words "against the Tutsi" to "Rwandan genocide" may, in the long run, undermine the reconciliatory efforts fostered by Rwandans and international organizations. Internationally, "against the Tutsi" was not mentioned regularly until the early 2010s, and it is entirely absent from most international documents and resolutions. The ICTR's mandate and many United Nations Security Council (UNSC) resolutions refer to "genocide in Rwanda" or the "Rwandan genocide" without specifying ethnicity. The ethnic modifier was promoted by the Rwandan government for years and was first formally mentioned in UNSC Resolution 2136 on 30 January 2014. The text of the resolution reads, "genocide against the Tutsi in Rwanda, during which Hutu and others who opposed the genocide were also killed."[72] The Rwandan government has accentuated "against the Tutsi" and lauded its inclusion, willfully ignoring the other victims mentioned in the resolution. Strangely, the resolution itself did not specifically focus on Rwanda—it was a renewal of an arms embargo in the DRC, and "against the Tutsi" was only mentioned once. Official international documentation includes the other victim groups and there is a legitimacy issue beyond problems of historical accuracy. Clearly, all victims of atrocity deserve historical recognition. As for legitimacy, the Rwandan government is towing a thin ethos by claiming international recognition of "against the Tutsi," even though the ethnic modifier was only tangentially mentioned in an arms embargo resolution, *not even pertaining to Rwanda*. Without question, the genocide was perpetrated in large part against the Tutsi. More troublesome is how the memory of moderate Hutu and Twa victims is either being distorted or eliminated by the government.

Known for his rich and penetrating studies on the Rwandan genocide, Scott Straus notes that killing Tutsis at first required the elimination of political and social opponents of the Hutu Power movement.[73] The first days of the genocide were clearly planned and many moderate Hutus, including the progressive and moderate Hutu prime minister Agathe Uwilingiyimana, were systematically hunted down and slaughtered by the extremists.[74] The extremists required a mass fear campaign to silence opposition voices; the task of killing Tutsis was significantly streamlined as virtually no Hutu opponents to the killing still lived or were willing to risk death by expressing opposition. Pacifying internal ethnic resistance to killing Tutsis was a critical linchpin of the genocidal plan in Rwanda.[75] Like Tutsis, these moderate Hutus had to be killed—there was no room for opposition in the Hutu Power ideology as opposition would undermine toxified and hateful messages of ethnic homogeneity and togetherness in killing operations. All Hutus were commanded to undertake their duties as Hutus and enact their roles as killers of the *inyenzi* in order to secure Rwanda as a place for Hutus. Dissident voices, especially among the Hutu, were not tolerated.

Perpetrators of the Rwandan genocide acted for many different reasons, ranging from personal gain to personality type, particularly the true believers identified by Eric Hoffer.[76] But not all Hutus were killers, nor did all of them support the killing. Many moderate Hutus were resisters, saviours, victims, and perhaps sometimes, forced killers.[77] Hutu involvement in the genocide is deeply complex, understudied, and requires research that is difficult to conduct given the current political situation in Rwanda. There were a variety of roles these individuals played and simply reducing the memory of the genocide to Tutsi victim and Hutu perpetrator, as the title "against the Tutsi" suggests, belies Hutus' complex memories and narratives as both individuals and an ethnic group.

The Twa are another largely forgotten victim group. The *genocidaires* often killed the indigenous Twa because of a legacy of discrimination dating from the colonial period, and because of the generalized hostility of Hutu Power to non-Hutus.[78] Hutu extremists committed numerous village massacres of the Twa throughout Rwanda.[79] While some did join the extremists, Twa were almost exclusively victims. They were "saved" by the RPF invasion, but the RPF, like the extremists, also committed individual and village massacres of the Twa.[80] Approximately one-third of the Twa fled during the genocide, one-third were killed, and one-third remained in Rwanda, where they continue to experience socio-economic and political marginalization. The Twa have been almost wholly excluded from the memory of the Rwandan genocide.[81] Their socio-political exclusion in Rwanda continues to be a stain on national and international reconstruction and rehabilitation efforts, and serves as an indictment of the divisive politics of the post-genocide regime that has refused to remedy this situation.

The Rwandan genocide was a national experience and all individual Rwandans participated in varying roles, be they victims, perpetrators, bystanders, or, perhaps, a combination of multiple roles. Many Rwandan groups were killed during the genocide—Tutsi, Hutu, and Twa alike. Narrowing the memory to solely Tutsi victims is selective history and also supports troubling changes in Rwanda's political culture and its attitudes toward the memory of the genocide. The memory the Rwandan government wants to construct is that of Tutsi victim and Hutu perpetrator, while at the same time spearheading a national program de-ethnicizing the population. Amidst this backdrop, "against the Tutsi" can be viewed as a deliberate obfuscation of memory for domestic political purposes.

Kagame's Rwanda: An Emerging Semi-Authoritarian Democracy

Marina Ottaway's concept of semi-authoritarianism is best applied to the current situation in Rwanda. Ottaway argued that there are many regimes in the world that have democratic institutions, but which engage in authoritarian practices intended to maintain the appearance of a democracy without exposing elite actors to the risks posed by free democratic elections. Regimes insulate themselves by tampering with voter rolls, engaging in clientelism, proscribing political candidates, monopolizing media outputs and public opinion, subtly harassing opposition, exploiting asymmetric power structures, and exercising control over state agencies and patronage networks to create undemocratic electoral fields.[82] Rwanda, to its credit, has engaged in democratizing activities, but underlying authoritarian principles are still at work among the most elite actors in Rwanda, most notably President Kagame.

Kagame's exclusion of Hutu and Twa victims from the memory of the Rwandan genocide manifests itself in three ways: in the Gacaca court system, through the persecution of dissidents, and through the development of a Kagame personality cult. The refusal to include all victims has profound political consequences in each of these areas—all of which benefit the Kagame administration. The administration's control over many facets of Rwandan life has troubling implications for the future of Rwanda's democracy, the prospects for peace, and also for the historical record and memory of all victims of atrocity.

The Gacaca court system has tried tens of thousands of cases in connection with the Rwandan genocide, but there has been a staged quality to these efforts at reconciliation. Instead of operating as unifying institutions, the Gacaca courts have been silently crystallizing ethnic differences in Rwanda by enforcing ethnically proscribed roles. Recent research indicates that the courts are imposing the Kagame administration's memory—"Hutus are perpetrators" and "Tutsis are survivors"—despite the supposed plans for an ethnically homogenous Rwanda.[83] While Rwandans are supposed to move forward together, Gacaca may act as an anchor and prevent reconciliation, in essence creating a Rwanda for Tutsis and a Rwanda for Hutus that is separate and unequal (and definitely excludes the Twa). Gacaca courts were originally voluntary to attend, but the Kagame administration soon made attendance "obligatory—if not by law, then in practice."[84] Research on the satisfaction of participants in Gacaca courts suggests that they have serious flaws. Rwanda is split along ethnic lines and simply commanding difference away from the top down will not attain lasting reconciliation. At the same time, this approach instructs Rwandans to endorse ethnic difference. Gacaca's entrenching of ethnicity can be seen as an extension of the "against the Tutsi" modification and the ideas behind the modifier are implemented by local officials in the Gacaca system.

A strong criticism levelled against Gacaca is that the hearings are more like a theatrical production.[85] Typically, there is a Hutu perpetrator on trial, with Tutsi survivors, and other Hutus, testifying against them. A sentence is levelled against the Hutu on trial, and reconciliation between perpetrator and victim occurs, whether it is genuine, forced, or insincere.[86] This is a scripted judicial hearing that occurs repeatedly. Ultimately, Gacaca's effectiveness is questionable and far from fully reliable. It has definitely prosecuted thousands of perpetrators—those who incited, supported, and executed genocide—but Gacaca may not be providing genuine reconciliation nor actual legal justice. The "against the Tutsi" modifier manifests itself in the idea of a "Hutu perpetrator" and the fact that only Hutu crimes are prosecuted; RPF crimes against Hutus and Twa are left unpunished and undiscussed, leaving reconciliation in the aftermath of genocide and its immediate consequences incomplete.[87] Gacaca has also been criticized from a legal perspective with regards to a person's right to due process and legal counsel, and from a human rights perspective for being an illegitimate representation of justice.[88] If Gacaca is just theatre, and Rwandans are either directly or indirectly forced to attend this form of reconciliation, what then is its purpose if not to solidify governmental ideas while offering limited justice and reconciliation? Gacaca, it should be noted, has been vigorously implemented by the Kagame regime.

Forced reconciliation may prosecute inordinate numbers of perpetrators. Perpetrator accounts note that individual killers admit to killing many Tutsis, Hutus, and/or Twa in 1994.[89] There were approximately 800,000 victims in 1994, and there have been approximately 361,590 perpetrators found guilty in the Gacaca system. This number, however, may not be mathematically sound because individual killers have admitted to killing more Rwandans than they can count, signalling that Gacaca courts have espoused an inaccurate victim-to-killer ratio.[90] In this case there may not be enough victims for the number of killers prosecuted, and so this problem requires more research. The Gacaca system may be wrongly prosecuting Hutus because they are conceptualized as "Hutu perpetrators," as is the implied rhetoric under Kagame. Straus's original estimation of 150,000 hardline perpetrators conducting most of the killing may be accurate, but the constructed memory of all Hutus as perpetrators is false. The "against the Tutsi" aspect of memory surfaces in the Gacaca system as Hutus are assumed to be guilty, tried and judged, and are commanded to be subservient to the governmental memory *du jour*. Justice in Rwanda is highly politicized and does not necessarily deliver truth. Instead, it delivers verdicts. The government's rhetoric that *all Hutus are perpetrators*, and therefore share a collective ethnic guilt for genocide, is a simplistic memory formation that undermines the government's ethnic unity campaign and has the potential to reinforce ethnic fault lines and the divisions undermining future peace.

There are also legitimate and serious questions about the ability of Rwandan citizens to express themselves freely, and about the government's receptivity to dissenting points of view.[91] Kagame's administration has a tenebrous history of silencing critics and opponents of the regime, and of causing them to disappear, similar to former Latin American military juntas.[92] While Rwanda is often hailed by other African states and the international community as having made a successful transition from a genocidal to a democratic state, there are questions regarding whether this transformation is authentic.

Physical and psychological attacks on political opponents in both Rwanda and other countries are one mechanism the Rwandan government utilizes to silence dissent. Exiled general Faustin Kayumba Nyamwasa, who publicly objected to Kagame's dictatorial tendencies, was recently the target of a failed assassination attempt in South Africa.[93] Mounting evidence suggests that the Kagame administration is running an assassination program against dissenters and critics and is willing to do so both at home and abroad.[94] Theogene Rudasingwa, the former Rwandan ambassador to the United States, and now exiled to that country, claimed that, "if you differ strongly with Kagame and make your views known from the inside, you will be made to pay the price, and very often that price is your life."[95] Augustine Iyamuremye was publically denounced for voicing modest criticism of Gacaca and faced being stripped of his role as a senator because of it.[96] Paul Rusesabagina, the hotel manager at the Hôtel des Mille Collines in Kigali who saved over twelve hundred Tutsis and Hutus, has also been exiled for his criticisms of the Rwandan government. Kagame iconoclastically claimed that Rusesabagina was "a manufactured hero" made in the West, and that real heroes are made domestically.[97] Rusesabagina is planning on running for president of Rwanda in response to Kagame's semi-authoritarianism.[98] For non-Rwandans, the Kagame government is just as much a threat to freedom of expression, research, and journalism. Kagame's administration has been criticized for its crackdown on dissenting points of view and the government apparatus that controls foreign researchers in Rwanda has the power to reject proposals it deems unfit.[99] The state of research on Hutu moderates and Twa is underdeveloped and needs to be extended for historical accuracy and to preserve the memories of all Rwandans—though it will take the Rwandan government to approve research projects dealing with Hutu and Twa experiences during and after the genocide to make these studies possible.

Domestic censorship also manifests itself in Rwandan election results. Post-genocide Rwanda has consistent voter turnout numbers upwards of 96 percent, and Paul Kagame won 95.05 percent and 93.08 percent of the vote in 2003 and 2010, respectively.[100] These numbers seem unrealistic for any competitive democracy with multiple parties; they resemble instead those of authoritarian countries.[101] They suggest political interference, and both of Kagame's elections were marred by systemic voter harassment and electoral gerrymandering.[102] Beyond these issues, recently Kagame has almost singlehandedly rewritten the Rwandan Constitution to extend the number of terms a president may run for office. Due to these changes, as of 2016 it is possible for Kagame to remain president (if he wins all elections) until the year 2034, hardly the hallmark of a successful liberal-democratic transition.[103] While the constitutional change has upset Western donors, most notably the United States, the coming years will tell if this change disrupts international donations to Rwanda.

None of the political repression in Rwanda, however, would be palatable if it were not for the modifier "against the Tutsi" and Kagame's cult of personality. The following logic flow poses serious threats to peace in Rwanda: if it is solely the Rwandan genocide *against the Tutsi*, then the Tutsis are the only "true" victims afforded space in this memory. If the Tutsi are the only victims, then the entity that stopped the genocide (the RPF) must be the saviour of the Tutsis, with Kagame as the embodiment of this achievement. Kagame, then, is the saviour of the Tutsi and can utilize this newfound socio-political capital to gain goodwill, both domestically and internationally. If Kagame is considered the saviour of the Tutsi, then his policies and actions are legitimized by the skewed memory of the genocide. This, then, allows for the increasingly messianic Kagame to insulate himself and institute policies he deems necessary to his administration's survival, bypassing the democratic process without being questioned because he is perceived as always doing right by Rwanda.[104] This assumption is percolating through many levels of government and society, deeply affecting policy and its outcomes. Speaking against the saviour of the Tutsi is illegitimate, leading to a silencing of voices in addition to the other repressions Kagame has instituted.

The subtle change in memory to make the Tutsi an exclusive victim group, while neglecting the Hutu and Twa as victims, appears to be a deliberate strategy of the Kagame government to solidify its mythology and expand domestic and external political power. The government's memory policies solidify ethnic difference, despite the national unity program. Kagame's semi-authoritarian tendencies are troubling as he is creating intransigent memory roles for Tutsis, Hutus, and Twa that only serve to harden ethnic differences. Abusing this memory is a form of revisionist history and may undermine reconciliation. The exclusive memories reveal the fragility of victim remembrance and how elite actors can emphasize some historical truths and omit others. These memories also highlight the fact that this process is subtle, manifests itself in many small cultural fissures, and has profound impacts on policy and policy outcomes as the selective use of history changes the political-cultural lens through which events, ideas, and policies are viewed and understood.

The difference between freedom and repression can be slight. Freedom is the ability to speak and express oneself openly. Repression is the ability to speak and express oneself *only after engaging in self-censorship for fear of repercussions.* While the modifier "against the Tutsi" did not create the political issues discussed in this section, it is a tool by which the Kagame administration exercises its will to dominate Rwandan politics. Rwanda is an emerging example of how victim groups can be exclusive with memories, and how elite political actors from a victim group can deliberately distort memories for their own semi-authoritarian political gains.

Inclusive and Exclusive Memories of Atrocity Victims

The two cases examined offer perspectives on how a comparative-inclusive approach to memory can move towards more grounded macro conclusions. These conclusions can also be a tool to combat exclusive memorialization campaigns. The most important contributions are the stories of the "other" victim groups and how these experiences can augment existing or developing narratives about atrocities. When all victim groups are analyzed together, more holistic and accurate understandings of atrocities themselves are made possible. All of the various groups' experiences add to our knowledge about the planning and perpetration of crimes. Beyond this, accuracy and inclusivity in historical studies may aid in preventing the formation of a collective memory that is intentionally confusing, and used for political ends.

Innocent or intended structural denial or exclusive constructions of memory can lead to the establishment of political institutions that reinforce these problems. These exclusive institutions may lead to individualized and isolated histories, and possibly to discrimination and structural violence against omitted victims. For Christian minorities, the severe lack of memory coordination is troubling and perhaps undermines efforts calling for Turkish recognition of past crimes, though Armenia recently recognized the victimization of Greeks and Assyrians, which may bring memories of shared victimization processes to the fore.[105] Coordinated memories from multiple groups calling for the recognition of a single memory using a macro perspective—the genocide of Christian minorities as a whole—may carry deeper political clout than individual recognition efforts from isolated victim groups. In Rwanda, it is clear that Kagame intends to construct memories that only have room for Tutsis, and this action most certainly lays the groundwork for discrimination and isolation of Hutus and Twa. Despite Kagame's efforts to create stability and to consolidate and centralize his power, he may, ironically, destabilize Rwanda's fragile ethnic peace. This would undermine democratizing efforts in the near future and threaten the country's future stability.

The two cases discussed in this chapter are representative of the in-depth and holistic analyses that a comparative-inclusive approach can offer genocide scholars. An inclusive lens for studying atrocity can lead to macro conclusions that accentuate shared victimization experiences. It can also aid in undermining deliberate distortions of collective memory. Comparative-inclusive studies augment the case studies of individual victim groups and the conclusions they offer. Comparative studies can and will produce complex and layered narratives that include all victim groups in analyses rather than privileging one group over the others. As atrocity scholars, we owe it to all victim groups to research, understand, and share these experiences so the memories of rights violations do not die; comparative research will aid us in remembering them all. Scholars should be wary of exclusive writings by asking who they include, how these studies combine to affect memories of atrocity, and the impacts of our constructed memories on historical narratives and contemporary issues. By challenging and understanding the boundaries of genocide studies, and asking what the implications of research are, we engage in a timely and critical move forward within the field.

NOTES

1   Alexander L. Hinton, "Critical Genocide Studies," in *Genocide Matters: Ongoing Issues and Emerging Perspectives*, eds. Joyce Apsel and Ernesto Verdeja (New York: Routledge, 2013).

2   Taner Akçam, *A Shameful Act: The Armenian Genocide and the Question of Turkish Responsibility* (New York: Henry Holt and Company, 2006); Tessa Hofmann, "Cumulative Genocide: The Massacres and Deportations of the Greek Population of the Ottoman Empire (1912–1923)," in *The Genocide of the Ottoman Greeks: Studies on the State-Sponsored Campaign of Extermination of the Christians of Asia Minor (1912–1922) and Its Aftermath: History, Law, Memory*, eds. Tessa Hofmann, et al. (Scarsdale, NY: Melissa International, 2011); Allison Des Forges, "Leave None to Tell the Story," *Human Rights Watch*, March 1999, http://addisvoice.com/Ethiopia%20under%20Meles/Rwanda.pdf (accessed 20 March 2015).

3   Israel W. Charny, "The Integrity and Courage to Recognize All the Victims of a Genocide," in *The Genocide of the Ottoman Greeks: Studies on the State-Sponsored Campaign of Extermination of the Christians of Asia Minor (1912–1922) and Its Aftermath: History, Law, Memory*, eds. Tessa Hofmann, et al. (Scarsdale, NY: Melissa International, 2011).

4   René Lemarchand, "Introduction," in *Forgotten Genocides: Oblivion, Denial, and Memory* (Philadelphia: University of Pennsylvania Press, 2011), 10–11.

5   Hannibal Travis, " 'Native Christians Massacred': The Ottoman Genocide of the Assyrians During World War I," *Genocide Studies and Prevention* 1, no. 3 (December 2006): 334; Raymond Kévorkian, *The Armenian Genocide: A Complete History* (New York: I. B. Tauris & Co., 2011), 120–126 and 195; Adam Jones, *Genocide: A Comprehensive Introduction* (New York: Routledge, 2011), 149–172; Donald Bloxham, "The Armenian Genocide of 1915–1916: Cumulative Radicalization and the Development of a Destructive Policy," *Past & Present* no.181 (November 2003), 141–146.

6   Akçam, *A Shameful Act*, 109–204; Peter Balakian, *The Burning Tigris: The Armenian Genocide and America's Response* (New York: HarperCollins, 2003), 35–62 and 103–196.

7   Norman M. Naimark, *Fires of Hatred: Ethnic Cleansing in Twentieth-Century Europe* (Cambridge, MA: Harvard University Press, 2002), 24–27; Erik J. Zücher, *The Young Turks Legacy and Nation Building: From the Ottoman Empire to Atatürk's Turkey* (New York: I. B. Tauris & Co., 2010), 79–83; Akçam, *A Shameful Act*, 32; Ronald Grigor Suny, "Writing Genocide: The Fate of the Ottoman Armenians," in *A Question of Genocide: Armenians and Turks at the End of the Ottoman Empire*, eds. Ronald Grigor Suny, et al. (New York: Oxford University Press, 2011), 33.

8   Hofmann, "Cumulative Genocide," 39; Matthias Bjørnlund, "The Persecution of Greeks and Armenians in Smyrna, 1914–1916: A Special Case in the Course of the Late Ottoman Genocides," in *The Asia Minor Catastrophe and the Ottoman Greek Genocide*, ed. George Shirinian (Bloomingdale, IL: The Asia Minor and Pontos Hellenic Research Centre, 2012).

9   Rouben Paul Adalian, "The Armenian Genocide," in *Century of Genocide: Critical Essays and Eyewitness Accounts,* Third Edition, eds. Samuel Totten and William S. Parsons (New York: Routledge, 2009), 55; Taner Akçam, *The Young Turks' Crimes Against Humanity: The Armenian Genocide and Ethnic Cleansing in the Ottoman Empire* (Princeton: Princeton University Press, 2012), xvi–xvii.

10   Halil İnalcık, Suraiya Faroqhi, and Donald Quataert, *An Economic and Social History of the Ottoman Empire,* Vol. 2 (New York: Cambridge University Press, 1997), 761.

11   Ibid.

12   Walter F. Weiker, "The Ottoman Bureaucracy: Modernization and Reform," *Administrative Science Quarterly* 13, no.3 (December 1968): 452, 469–470; Donald Quataert, "Labor History and the Ottoman Empire, c. 1700–1922," *International Labor and Working-Class History* 60 (Fall 2001): 98–105.

13   Erik J. Zürcher, *Turkey: A Modern History* (London: I. B. Tauris & Co., 2004), 85; Hans-Lukas Kieser, *Nearest East: American Millennialism and Mission to the Middle East* (Philadelphia: Temple University Press, 2010), 76–77.

14   Balakian, *The Burning Tigris,* 35–36; Akçam, *A Shameful Act,* 19–27, 100.

15   Rhiannon S. Neilsen, " 'Toxification' as a More Precise Early Warning Sign for Genocide Than Dehumanization? An Emerging Research Agenda," *Genocide Studies and Prevention* 9, no. 1 (2015): 83–95.

16   John Mourelos, "The Persecutions in Thrace and Ionia in 1914 and the First Attempt at an Exchange of Minorities between Greece and Turkey," in *The Genocide of the Ottoman Greeks: Studies on the State-Sponsored Campaign of Extermination of the Christians of Asia Minor (1912–1922) and Its Aftermath: History, Law, Memory,* eds. Tessa Hofmann, et al., (Scarsdale, NY: Melissa International, 2011), 114.

17   Travis, " 'Native Christians Massacred'," 327–328.

18   Ariel Salzmann, "Citizens in Search of a State: The Limits of Political Participation in the Late Ottoman Empire," in *Extending Citizenship, Reconfiguring States,* eds. Michael Hanagan and Charles Tilly (Oxford: Rowman & Littlefield, 1999), 39; Halil İnalcık, "Application of the Tanzimat and its Social Effects," *Archivum Ottomanicum* 5 (1973): 111; Ronald Grigor Suny, "Eastern Armenians Under Tsarist Rule," in *The Armenian People from Ancient to Modern Times,* ed. Richard G. Hovannisian (New York: St. Martin's Press, 1997), 113; Vahakn N. Dadrian, *Warrant for Genocide: Key Elements of Turko-Armenian Conflict* (New Brunswick, NJ: Transaction Publishers, 2003), 39–46.

19   Jones, *Genocide,* 153; Donald Bloxham, "The Armenian Genocide of 1915–1916: Cumulative Radicalization and the Development of a Destructive Policy," *Past & Present* no. 181 (November 2003): 141–146; Zücher, *The Young Turk Legacy and Nation Building.*

20   Akçam, *A Shameful Act,* 32; Ronald Grigor Suny, "Writing Genocide," 33.

21   James Fearon and David Laitin, "Explaining Interethnic Cooperation," *American Political Science Review* 90, no.4 (December 1996): 715–735; James Fearon and David Laitin, "Ethnicity, Insurgency, and Civil War," *American Political Science Review* 97, no.1 (February 2003): 75–90.

22   Jones, *Genocide,* 153; Bloxham, "The Armenian Genocide of 1915–1916," 141–146; Christos Papoutsy, *Ships of Mercy: The True Story of the Rescue of the Greeks: Smyrna, September 1922* (Portsmouth, NH: Peter E. Randall, 2008), x–xi.

23   Donald Bloxham, *The Great Game of Genocide: Imperialism, Nationalism, and the Destruction of the Ottoman Armenians* (New York: Oxford University Press, 2007), 70–72.

24   Kévorkian, *The Armenian Genocide,* 120–126.

25   Akçam, *The Young Turks' Crime Against Humanity,* xvi.

26   Jones, *Genocide*, 150–151.

27   Matthias Bjørnlund, Tessa Hofmann, and Vasileois Meichanetsidis, "Introduction," in *The Genocide of the Ottoman Greeks: Studies on the State-Sponsored Campaign of Extermination of the Christians of Asia Minor (1912–1922) and Its Aftermath: History, Law, Memory*, eds. Tessa Hofmann, et al. (Scarsdale, NY: Melissa International, 2011), 1.

28   Travis, " 'Native Christians Massacred'," 290; George Horton, *The Blight of Asia: An Account of the Systematic Extermination of Christian Populations by Mohammedans and of the Culpability of Certain Great Powers; with the True Story of the Burning of Smyrna* (Indianapolis, IN: Bobbs-Merrill Company, 1926); Henry Morgenthau, *Ambassador Morgenthau's Story* (Garden City, NY: Doubleday, Page & Co., 1918).

29   Travis, " 'Native Christians Massacred'," 333–335.

30   Dominik J. Schaller and Jürgen Zimmerer, "Introduction," in *Late Ottoman Genocides: The Dissolution of the Ottoman Empire and Young Turkish Population and Extermination Policies*, eds. Dominik J. Schaller and Jürgen Zimmerer (New York: Routledge, 2009).

31   Hofmann, "Cumulative Genocide," 109, Travis, " 'Native Christians Massacred'," 334, Kévorkian, *The Armenian Genocide*, 123,195; Jones, *Genocide*, 149–172.

32   Akçam, *The Young Turks' Crimes Against Humanity*, xvi–xvii; Thea Halo, *Not Even My Name: A True Story* (New York: Picador, 2001).

33   George Shirinian, "The 'Great Catastrophe': The Genocide of the Greeks of Asia Minor, Pontos, and Eastern Thrace, 1912–1923," *Genocide Prevention Now*, http://www.genocidepreventionnow.org/Portals/0/docs/Great_Catastrophe.pdf (accessed 10 February 2015).

34   Helen Fein, "Genocide by Attrition 1939–1993: The Warsaw Ghetto, Cambodia, and Sudan: Links Between Human Rights, Health, and Mass Death," *Health and Human Rights* 2, no.2 (1997): 10–13.

35   Ibid.

36   Andrew R. Basso, "Towards a Theory of Displacement Atrocities: The Cherokee Trail of Tears, the Herero Genocide, and the Pontic Greek Genocide," *Genocide Studies and Prevention* 10, no. 1 (June 2016): 5–29.

37   Taner Akçam, *The Young Turks' Crime Against Humanity*, xvi–xvii.

38   Jay Winter, "Under the Cover of War: the Armenian Genocide in the Context of Total War," in *America and the Armenian Genocide of 1915*, ed. Jay Winter (New York: Cambridge University Press, 2003), 37–51.

39   G. J. Meyer, *A World Undone: The Story of the Great War 1914 to 1918* (New York: Bantam Dell, 2006), 103–356.

40   David Gaunt, "The Ottoman Treatment of the Assyrians," in *A Question of Genocide: Armenians and Turks at the End of the Ottoman Empire*, eds. Ronald Grigor Suny, et al. (New York: Oxford University Press, 2011), 244–247.

41   Ibid., 244–255.

42   Akçam, *A Shameful Act*, 246–250; Travis, "Native Christians Massacred," 329–334.

43   Bloxham, *The Great Game of Genocide*, 159–169.

44   Hofmann, "Cumulative Genocide," 57, 102; Akçam, *A Shameful Act*, 182–196; Morgenthau, *Ambassador Morgenthau's Story*, 324–325.

45   Hannibal Travis, *Genocide in the Middle East: The Ottoman Empire, Iraq, and Sudan* (Durham, NC: Carolina Academic Press, 2010), 289–291; Hofmann, "Cumulative Genocide," 64.

46   Erik J. Zürcher, "Ottoman Labour Battalions in World War I," in *The Armenian Genocide and the Shoah*, eds. Hans-Lukas Kieser and Dominik J. Schaller (Zürich: Chronos-Verlag, 2002), 187–194.

47   Ibid.; Basso, "Towards a Theory of Displacement Atrocities," 2016.

48   Hofmann, "Cumulative Genocide," 64.

49   Akçam, *The Young Turks' Crimes Against Humanity*, xvi–xvii.

50   Bloxham, *The Great Game of Genocide*, 2–26; Vahakn N. Dadrian, *The History of the Armenian Genocide: Ethnic Conflict from the Balkans to Anatolia to the Caucasus* (New York: Berghahn, 1995); Akçam, *The Young Turks' Crimes Against Humanity*.

51   Bloxham, *The Great Game of Genocide*, 2.

52   Morgenthau, *Ambassador Morgenthau's Story*, 324–325.

53   Nikolaos Hlamides, "The Greek Relief Committee: America's Response to the Greek Genocide," *Genocide Studies and Prevention* 3, no.3 (December 2008): 376–378.

54   Michael A. Reynolds, *Shattering Empires: The Clash and Collapse of the Ottoman and Russian Empires1908–1918* (New York: Cambridge University Press, 2011), 107–139; David Gaunt, *Massacres, Resistance, Protectors: Muslim-Christian Relations in Eastern Anatolia during World War I* (Piscataway, NJ: Gorgias Press, 2006), 135, 315.

55   Vahakn N. Dadrian and Taner Akçam, *Judgment at Istanbul: The Armenian Genocide Trials* (New York: Berghahn, 2011).

56   Ibid.

57   Raoul Blanchard, "The Exchange of Populations Between Greece and Turkey," *Geographical Review* 15, no. 3 (July 1925): 449–456.

58   Hinton, "Critical Genocide Studies," 54.

59   Sheri Rosenberg, "Genocide is a Process, Not an Event," *Genocide Studies and Prevention* 7, no.1 (Spring 2012): 16–23.

60   Roméo Dallaire, *Shake Hands with the Devil: The Failure of Humanity in Rwanda* (Cambridge, MA: Da Capo Press, 2005), xxii–7; Jared Cohen, *One Hundred Days of Silence: America and the Rwanda Genocide* (Lanham, MD: Rowman & Littlefield Publishers, 2007), 1.

61   Unrepresented Nations and Peoples Organization, "Batwa: Final Report 1994," http://unpo.org/images/reports/batwa%20report%201994.pdf (accessed 10 January 2015); Alan J. Kuperman, "Rwanda in Retrospect," *Foreign Affairs* 79, no.1 (January–February 2000), 101; Jerome Lewis and Judy Knight, *The Twa of Rwanda: Assessment of the Situation of the Twa and Promotion of Twa Rights in Post-War Rwanda* (World Rainforest Movement and International Work Group for Indigenous Affairs, 1995).

62   Jean Hatzfeld, *Machete Season: The Killers in Rwanda Speak* (New York: Picador, 2003), 129–134; Philip Gourevitch, *We Wish to Inform You That Tomorrow We Will Be Killed With Our Families: Stories From Rwanda* (New York: Picador, 1998); Des Forges, "Leave None to Tell the Story," 62 and 192.

63   Dallaire, *Shake Hands with the Devil*, 129, 420, 464; Fiona Terry, *Condemned to Repeat? The Paradox of Humanitarian Action* (Ithaca, NY: Cornell University Press, 2002), 159;

Hatzfeld, *Machete Season*, 10–47 and 66–77; Jean Hatzfeld, *Life Laid Bare: The Survivors in Rwanda Speak* (New York: Other Press, 2006), 35–57.

64   Dallaire, *Shake Hands with the Devil*, 261; Elizabeth Baisley, "Genocide and Constructions of Hutu and Tutsi in Radio Propaganda," *Race & Class* 55, no. 3 (January/March 2014): 38–59; Des Forges, "Leave None to Tell the Story," 31–34, 366.

65   Timothy Longman, "Church Politics and the Genocide in Rwanda," *Journal of Religion in Africa* 31, no. 2 (May 2001): 163–170; Jean Hatzfeld, *The Antelope's Strategy: Living in Rwanda after the Genocide* (New York: Picador, 2009), 40.

66   Dallaire, *Shake Hands with the Devil*, 279–314 and 439; Gourevitch, *We Wish to Inform You That Tomorrow We Will Be Killed With Our Families*.

67   Unrepresented Nations and Peoples Organization, " 'Batwa: Final Report 1994',"; Des Forges, "Leave None to Tell the Story," 32–33.

68   Dallaire, *Shake Hands with the Devil*, 67.

69   Filip Reyntjens and René Lemarchand, "Mass Murder in Eastern Congo, 1996–1997," in *Forgotten Genocides: Oblivion, Denial, and Memory* (Philadelphia: University of Pennsylvania Press, 2011), 20–36.

70   Stephen Kinzer, *A Thousand Hills: Rwanda's Rebirth and the Man Who Dreamed It* (Hoboken, NJ: John Wiley & Sons, 2008), 220–225.

71   Susan Thompson and Rosemary Nagy, "Law, Power and Justice: What Legalism Fails to Address in the Functioning of Rwanda's *Gacaca* Courts," *The International Journal of Transitional Justice* 5 (March 2011): 16; Danielle Beswick, "Democracy, Identity and the Politics of Exclusion in Post-Genocide Rwanda: the Case of the Batwa," *Democratization* 18, no. 2 (April 2011): 490.

72   Security Council Resolution 2136 (2014), Resolution 2136, S/RES/2136 (30 January 2014), http://www.un.org/en/ga/search/view_doc.asp?symbol=S/RES/2136(2014) (accessed 1 April 2015).

73   Scott Straus, *The Order of Genocide: Race, Power, and War in Rwanda* (Ithaca, NY: Cornell University Press, 2006), 46–49.

74   Ibid.

75   Ibid.; Ben Kiernan, *Blood and Soil: A World History of Genocide and Extermination from Sparta to Darfur* (New Haven, CT: Yale University Press, 2007), 559.

76   Cyanne E. Loyle, "Why Men Participate: A Review of Perpetrator Research on the Rwandan Genocide," *Journal of African Conflicts and Peace Studies* 1, no. 2 (2009): 26–42; Omar Shahabudin McDoom, "Antisocial Capital: A profile of Rwandan Genocide Perpetrators' Social Networks," *Journal of Conflict Resolution* 58, no. 5 (2014): 865–893; Nicole Hogg, "Women's Participation in the Rwandan Genocide: Mothers or Monsters?" *International Review of the Red Cross* 92, no. 877 (March 2010): 69–102; Eric Hoffer, *The True Believer: Thoughts on the Nature of Mass Movements* (New York: Harper Perennial, 2010).

77   Kuperman, "Rwanda in Retrospect," 108, 114; Straus, *The Order of Genocide*, 122–152.

78   Beswick, "Democracy, Identity and the Politics of Exclusion in Post-Genocide Rwanda," 495; Unrepresented Nations and Peoples Organization, "Batwa: Final Report 1994."

79   Ibid.

80   Ibid.

81   Ibid.; Beswick, "Democracy, Identity and the Politics of Exclusion in Post-Genocide Rwanda," 492–504; Unrepresented Nations and Peoples Organization, "Batwa: Final Report 1994."

82   Marina Ottaway, *Democracy Challenged: The Rise of Semi-Authoritarianism* (Washington, DC: Carnegie Endowment for International Peace, 2003).

83   Thompson and Nagy, "Law, Power and Justice," 23; Max Rettig, "Gacaca: Truth, Justice, and Reconciliation in Postconflict Rwanda?" *African Studies Review* 51, no. 3 (December 2008): 25–50.

84   Rettig, "Gacaca," 32.

85   Ibid., 13, 22–23; Laura Eramian, "Representing Suffering: Testimony at Rwanda's Gacaca Courts," *In Tensions* 1 (Spring 2008): 2–6.

86   Thompson and Nagy, "Law, Power and Justice."

87   Ibid., 23–28; Human Rights Watch, "Justice Compromised: The Legacy of Rwanda's Community-Based Gacaca Courts—Summary" (2011), 2, http://www.hrw.org/node/99177/section/2 (accessed 5 January 2015).

88   Phil Clark, *The Gacaca Courts, Post-Genocide Justice and Reconciliation in Rwanda: Justice Without Lawyers* (New York: Cambridge University Press, 2010), 85–97.

89   Hatzfeld, *Machete Season*.

90   Hollie Nyseth Brehm, et al., "Genocide, Justice, and Rwanda's Gacaca Courts," *Journal of Contemporary Criminal Justice* 30 (August 2014): 340.

91   Yash Ghai, "Rwanda's Application for Membership of the Commonwealth," *Commonwealth Human Rights Initiative*, August 2009, 27–54.

92   Ibid.; Jeffrey Gettleman, "The Global Elite's Favorite Strongman," *New York Times*, 4 September 2013.

93   "Rwandan Nyamwasa murder plot: Four guilty in South Africa," *BBC*, 29 August 2014.

94   Ian Birrell, "Assassins Linked to Kagame Regime," *Independent* (London) 29 August 2014.

95   Howard W. French, "The Case Against Rwanda's President Paul Kagame," *Newsweek*, 25 January 2013.

96   James Munyaneza, "Senator Augustine Iyamuremye Under Probe," *New Times* (Kigali) 12 July 12 2006.

97   Terry George, "Smearing a Hero," *Washington Post*, 10 May 2006.

98   Bill Lambrecht, "Africa Hero, Now Living in S.A., Will Run for Rwanda Presidency," *San Antonio Express-News*, 28 January 2016.

99   Ministry of Education, "Application for Authority to conduct Research in Rwanda," http://www.mineduc.gov.rw/IMG/pdf/Research_Authority_Aplication_Form.pdf (accessed 10 November 2014); Ministry of Education, "Rules and Regulations for Research Activities in Rwanda," http://www.mineduc.gov.rw/IMG/pdf/Research_Rules_and_Regulations.pdf (accessed 10 November 2014).

100   Rwandan National Electoral Commission, "Amatora ya Perezida 2010," http://www.nec.gov.rw/details/?tx_ttnews%5Btt_news%5D=49&cHash=7990f6c09f43eeeafb70dc-b38a2dbd56 (accessed 15 November 2014); Ingrid Samset and Orrvar Dalby, "Rwanda: Presidential and Parliamentary Elections 2003," *NORDEM*, Report 12/2003, http://www.cmi.no/publications/2003/rwandaelections2003.pdf, 40 (accessed 15 November 2014).

101   Ottaway, *Democracy Challenged*, 2003.

102   "Divisionists Beware: Progress and Repression in Rwanda," *Economist*, 6 March 2010;
       "Rwanda: Silence Dissent Ahead of Elections," *Human Rights Watch*, 2 August 2010,
       http://www.hrw.org/news/2010/08/02/rwanda-attacks-freedom-expression-free-
       dom-association-and-freedom-assembly-run-presi (accessed 1 November 2014); David
       E Kiwuwa, *Ethnic Politics and Democratic Transition in Rwanda* (New York: Routledge,
       2012); Danielle Beswick, "Managing Dissent in a Post-genocide Environment: The
       Challenge of Political Space in Rwanda," *Development and Change* 41, no. 2 (April
       2010): 233–236.

103   Clement Uwiringiymana, "Rwandans vote on constitution change to extend rule,"
       Reuters 18 December 2015; Reuters, "Rwandan president Paul Kagame to run for third
       term in 2017," *Guardian* (London), 1 January 2016.

104   Joann Weiner, "Does Rwanda's Economic Prosperity Justify President Kagame's
       Political Repression?" *Washington Post*, 13 August 2014.

105   National Assembly of the Republic of Armenia, "National Assembly Continues the
       Work of the Four-day Sittings," http://www.parliament.am/news.php?cat_id=2&News-
       ID=7338&year=2015&month=03&day=24&lang=eng (accessed 30 March 2015).

Helping Children Understand Atrocities: Developing and Implementing an Undergraduate Course Titled War and Genocide in Children's Literature

Sarah Minslow

In fall 2012, I taught War and Genocide in Children's Literature for the first time. The course was offered as a third year cross-listed course at the University of North Carolina at Charlotte, a large public university with majors in English, history, and international studies, and minors in children's literature and childhood studies, and the Holocaust, genocide, and human rights. Part of UNC Charlotte's mission is to "prepare students to become active citizens of the world," and this is a mission that underpins most of my pedagogy. While the desire I have for my students to become active citizens of the world is multifaceted, the population I focus most of my energy on is children in times and areas of conflict. More than a million children were murdered during the Holocaust. Today, one in every two displaced people is a person under the age of eighteen. According to Human Rights Watch, during the Rwandan genocide "countless thousands of children were slaughtered. ... [A]t a mass grave in Kibuye province, some 44% [of the bodies] were of children under the age of fifteen."[1] Despite the glaring fact that children are heavily involved in and affected by war and genocide, people do not tend to combine war and genocide with children's literature. Partly, this is because when some people outside of literary circles hear the term "children's literature," they tend to think of books that are happy, simple, apolitical, and unsophisticated. Rarely do they think about books that may broach the subjects of atrocity, genocide, death, destruction, or war. Whereas Romantic notions of childhood would have adults protect children from the unjust and often brutal aspects of life, many twenty-first-century authors of children's literature have found interesting ways to represent atrocities to children without traumatizing readers in the process of educating and socializing them. While Mavis Reimer states that "it is the literature of the last half of the nineteenth century that has set many of the narrative paradigms and practices of what we continue to recognize as children's texts,"[2] Zohar Shavit acknowledges shifts that have occurred in the past twenty years, writing in 2005 that "More than a decade ago, children's literature in the West was opened up to a number of subjects that had formerly been taboo and presented them in all their hardness—showing no mercy to young readers—in the belief that this is the pedagogically and psychologically correct way to prepare children to cope with the world."[3]

Children's "literature of atrocity" does "prepare children to cope with the world" when authors demonstrate great care and concern for their intended audiences.[4] They do not keep the darker realities of being a human in our world from child readers, but they present darker aspects of humanity in ways that allow child readers to gradually understand some reasons why conflict occurs—and most offer hope that the world can be a more peaceful place. In fact, children's literature has a long history of representing the darker sides of societies, often as a way to encourage children to change those societies. Kimberly Reynolds sees representations of social issues in writing for young people as potentially radical and transformative; she writes that "childhood is certainly a time for learning to negotiate and find a place in society, but it is also about developing individual potential suited to a future in which societies could be different in some significant ways."[5] This chapter is an examination of the classroom as a space for collectively arriving at criteria for children's "literature of atrocity" and understanding how social power can be wielded to change societies in significant ways. It is also an examination of strategies employed to move students from a misconception of children's literature as unsophisticated and apolitical to see its potential for changing attitudes, behaviours, and (potentially) the world.

In War and Genocide in Children's Literature, students read a variety of books intended for children and young adults that represent conflict, war, and genocide.[6] Texts include fiction, poetry, non-fiction, testimonies, textbooks, and memoirs. The books selected for the course are written by twenty-first-century authors from English-speaking countries, including Australia, the United Kingdom, and the United States. In addition, the books chosen have won awards and are popular, widely available, and, thanks to high sales, still in print. Choosing books most students have not previously read allows the process of discovery to be mutual. This fosters a more cohesive sense of community and equality in the classroom, which is essential for an effective collaborative learning environment. The intended audiences of these texts range from roughly seven to seventeen years old.

The course begins with a discussion about how we will approach the books, and I model how to read for layers of ideological interpretations. This begins with the following questions: What is ideology? How do we identify ideologies in texts? And which ideologies are being challenged and which are being reinforced? Peter Hollindale describes the three main ways in which ideologies are represented in children's books: as either "surface ideology," the explicit and didactic purpose of the text; "passive ideology," the implicit beliefs of the author or narrator; or "underlying climate of belief," the surrounding social and cultural influences that give meaning to a word, action, label, or belief. He writes, "The first and most traceable is made up of the explicit social, political or moral beliefs of the individual writer, and his wish to recommend them to children through the story … its presence is conscious, deliberate, and in some measure 'pointed'. … It is at this level of intended surface ideology that fiction carries new ideas, non-conformist or revolutionary attitudes."[7] Passive ideology, Hollindale's second category, embraces those broader cultural attitudes, beliefs, and values that shape a text. The third level of ideology includes invisible (or underlying) ideologies: "the private, unrepeatable configurations which writers make at a subconscious level from the common stock of their experiences." Insofar as invisible ideologies often lead to "huge commonalities of an age," Hollindale argues that "a large part of any book is written not by its author but by the world its author lives in."[8] To elucidate the passive and underlying ideologies represented in a text, we need an approach to reading children's literature that ensures we remain attuned to multiple levels of ideological representation. Students are asked to consider how authors represent the atrocities associated with war and genocide to a young audience and how these books may be used to socialize and educate children. Students also analyze the texts to determine whether they encourage positive or negative attitudes towards difference, war, and violence. They also consider how literature can function as a tool for promoting social change. The course addresses how these texts help child readers construct concepts of themselves as global citizens. However, at least half of the students are not English majors, and even those who are are not always used to close reading and critical engagement with children's literature. Borrowing from the disciplines of history, psychology, and political science, I begin by modelling how to read children's literature of atrocity while keeping in mind the multiple layers of ideology presented therein.[9] Modeling literary analysis gives students a better understanding of the expectations for future assignments and is a strategy for scaffolding their learning so that they are able to independently analyze texts through close reading. I also try to make them more aware of the thought processes involved in interpreting picture books. We review different elements of images, starting with a painting, and students discuss the body language, facial expressions, positioning, juxtaposition, colours, shadows and tones, and use of white space. These practice sessions prepare students to be more aware of the details in images in picture books they read for class.

By the end of this course, students are expected to be able to define the terms associated with genocide and xenophobia and thoughtfully discuss reasons for and the effects of xenophobia in society; discuss the circumstances of several different wars and genocides that have occurred (including who, what, where, and aspects of how), and how their effects have resonated in contemporary society; and analyze children's literature about war and genocide from critical positions in reference to concepts of the "child" and "childhood," and how those texts may shape children's attitudes.

Arguments regarding whether or not literature of atrocity should be written for young audiences are, unsurprisingly, numerous, and most students are unsure how "war and genocide" marries with "children's literature." So on the first day of class, students are asked to reconsider what a "child" is. In the first reading I assign, Susan Honeyman explains that "adults construct childhood based on biases that are personal, constantly changing, and often contradictory. There is no irrefutable or universal meaning of 'child.' "[10] To proceed, students must understand not only how Western societies have constructed concepts of the child as innocent, apolitical, asexual, helpless, and dependent, but also how far this conception is from the realities of childhood for most real children. While it's true that there are millions of children who live in conflict zones and witness atrocities on a daily basis (the United Nations Children's Fund reported that 2014 was "a devastating year for children" because "as many as 15 million young people are caught in conflicts in the Central African Republic, Iraq, South Sudan, the Palestinian territories, Syria and Ukraine"), there are also many children who are much more resilient, hopeful, and capable of dealing with reality than adults often give them credit for.[11] Honeyman argues that "the obviousnesses of childhood have been: children are helpless; children should be protected; and if children do wrong, it is because they do not know any better. … [W]e view them as not having agency or consequence in ideology."[12] Yet this conception of childhood contradicts the evidence of memoirs from people who were children during times of war and genocide, such as Alfons Heck's *A Child of Hitler: Germany in the Days When God Wore a Swastika* or Dith Pran's *Children of Cambodia's Killing Fields: Memoirs by Survivors*. What students begin to realize is that children are powerful agents who continually reconfigure their identities in an attempt to survive within highly political, often traumatic contexts. What the students, in turn, begin to realize is that the Western conception of childhood is overgeneralized, essentialist, and ignores versions of childhood vastly different from middle-class, white, heterosexual ones.

Honeyman's concerns about essentializing the child have been expressed in various ways by multiple scholars of children's literature, since definitions of "children" influence which texts are labelled "children's literature." John Stephens writes that "writing for children is usually purposeful."[13] However, Perry Nodelman believes that "the differences [between adult literature and children's literature] are less significant than the similarities, that the pleasures of children's literature are essentially the pleasures of all literature."[14] For me, two of the most important "pleasures" of literature are its ability to offer alternative perspectives and inspire empathy. As reported in *Scientific American*, "Researchers at The New School in New York City have found evidence that literary fiction improves a reader's capacity to understand what others are thinking and feeling."[15] In the chapter "Benefits and Challenges of Genocide Education," Raffi Sarkissian argues that genocide education "opens possibilities for empathetic forms of education to shift the barriers between societies where the concept of the Other is frequently raised and reinforced in harmful and destructive ways." As part of genocide education, children's literature also has the power to inspire social change. As Lindsay Myers writes, "If they are made with the right care and attention, books can be powerful agents of social change. Teaching children about war, however, is not so much about explaining the past as it is about inciting questions. ... By actively involving the young reader in the history-making process, they convey in a very tangible way the importance of love, responsibility, peace, and truth."[16] So how do I get students from a simple awareness of children's literature of atrocity to the point where they are confident in their abilities to determine if a particular children's book about war or genocide is "good" or "bad"?

After defining the key terms for the course—including genocide, xenophobia, and war—and complicating students' conceptions of the "child" and "children's literature," we delve into categorizing people according to their action (or inaction) during genocide. Students are asked to consider specific conflicts from the perspectives of perpetrators, victims, bystanders, rescuers, and beneficiaries—terms discussed by Steven Baum and Christopher Browning. These categories function as a way to begin literary discussions about character, morality, ethics, idealism versus realism, and empathy. For instance, when reading Katherine Patterson's *The Day of the Pelican*, about a family from Kosovo that is forced to flee during the Bosnian genocide, readers are positioned to sympathize with the family, especially the narrator's older brother, Mehmet, who is kidnapped and beaten by Serbs. Later in the novel, when Mehmet expresses his hatred for Serbs and his pleasure in their destruction—"NATO is going to begin bombing the Serbs!"—readers are positioned to empathize with his feelings. However, in the next paragraph, Meli, the narrator, states "How could Mehmet be so happy. ... Bombs don't know, when they fall, if you are a Serbian soldier or a Kosovar child. Bombs don't ask if you are guilty or innocent. They just fall, and if you are below, they kill you."[17] Forty pages later, Meli states that Baba took the family to America because it "was far from the threat of those Mehmet had learned so well how to hate. Hatred and the ancient thirst for revenge: that was what Baba feared most."[18] There is a general consensus among scholars of children's literature that literature of atrocity should always adopt an ethical position against war. Here,

The Day of the Pelican complicates the seeming simplicity of that ethical position because the book at once encourages empathy for someone who hates the people who have targeted him and his family for persecution, while simultaneously reinforcing the ideology that war is never victimless and that hate is dangerous and a learned behaviour. Most readers will understand why Mehmet is angry and has revenge fantasies against the Serbs, yet through the thoughts of Meli and Baba, readers are not allowed to ignore the damaging effects of war on humanity if Mehmet is to react with violence. Readers of *The Day of the Pelican* are positioned to consider whether Mehmet can have justice without risking the death of innocent civilians, and if not, what takes priority.

These ethical dilemmas provide space for young readers to consider the complexities of war. Even though writing literature of atrocity for children is complicated, "the subject cannot simply be avoided" because there is "a moral obligation upon adults to tell children what happened."[19] Claiming that literature of atrocity for young audiences "sets out to inform a new generation of readers about the horrors" of the past, Ruth Gilbert agrees: the reasons children need to be informed are to encourage empathy, to prevent future atrocities, and to prepare children for the real, often unjust, world.[20] Reynolds has acknowledged a more recent shift after the "issue" books of the 1960's became popular and portrayals of children shifted noticeably from those of the "innocent" child to those of the "knowing" child. Trying to protect children from history and reality is a form of censorship and while many people's knee-jerk reaction is to discourage an awareness of war and violence among young people, there are those who agree with Honeyman that "Denying any young person access to certain types of knowledge … is an infringement, not protection—it is robbing another person of their rightful agency—but we have morally twisted the imperative of protecting the innocence of childhood to the point that we usually fail to see it clearly, and even more rarely do we feel comfortable questioning it, lest we be accused of harshness toward those we should protect."[21] Therefore, the first hurdle to overcome for some students is understanding why children's literature of atrocity is important. To explain why, students respond to a few simple questions by raising their hands. The questions include: How many of you were taught in school that what settlers did to Native Americans was genocide? How many of you saw images in textbooks of the destruction caused in Japan by the dropping of the atomic bombs? By revealing to students their own gaps in knowledge based on selective education and then showing them that there are children's books that fill these gaps, most students begin to wonder why they were not taught certain aspects of history as young people. One student said that a big part of becoming an adult is realizing you have been lied to most of your life.

Yet, the literature of atrocity must also provide special consideration for young people who at once need to be encouraged to learn history, prevent future wars, and feel some sense of control over or power to respond to or prevent atrocity. "Educating without overwhelming" requires a delicate balance.[22] At the beginning of the course, we do quite a lot of reading to develop a shared vocabulary with which to talk respectfully about genocide without creating hierarchies of suffering or victimization. Students have to read the first two chapters of Doris Bergen's *War and Genocide* to get a better understanding of the background to the Holocaust and other genocides in general. Students are asked to compose a list of criteria they may use to evaluate children's literature of atrocity before they read any scholarly articles. This list becomes a working document. After reading several critical articles, such as Lydia Williams's "We're All in the Dumps with Bakhtin: Humor and the Holocaust," Sarah Jordan's "Educating without Overwhelming," Elizabeth Baer's "A New Algorithm in Evil: Children's Literature in a Post-Holocaust World," and Ruth Gilbert's "Grasping the Unimaginable: Recent Holocaust Novels for Children by Morris Gleitzman and John Boyne," the students evaluate their individual lists based on the arguments they have read. Then, as a class, they defend their final list until we devise a list of criteria they see as essential do's and don'ts when writing literature of atrocity for young audiences, and as a way to begin establishing a method of evaluating the literature. This process demonstrates how they can use their informed opinions and voices to enter into scholarly discourse, which is an essential skill for undergraduate students to learn.

Writing specifically about the children's literature on the Holocaust, Elizabeth Baer explains the required balancing act in practice when she states that creating literature of atrocity for children "calls upon us to make judicious choices in sharing the horrors of the Shoah ... it calls for a consciousness on our part of the crucial need to confront the evil, to contextualize it, to warn children, and to provide them with a framework for consciousness, for making moral choices and taking personal responsibility."[23] While emphasizing the need to assist children with seeing the implications between what they are reading and their own personal lives and formation as global citizens, I ask students to consider Baer's call to "confront the evil." In class, we discuss the use of the word "evil" to describe the Holocaust. We will never fully understand the Holocaust, so authors of children's literature about the Holocaust or other genocides should not attempt to explain them simply. The use of the word evil implies a force that is beyond human; this abstraction negates the emphasis that authors or teachers should place on moral choices and personal responsibility when writing, reading, or teaching children's literature of atrocity. In his address at the "Understanding Atrocities" conference, James Waller explained that we protect ourselves by making the perpetrators into something incredibly different from us—evil—and he continued to delineate the processes that occur when "ordinary" people choose to commit acts of genocide.[24] Evil is human, and genocide depends on humans being willing to murder one another. Students must understand and be prepared to analyze how texts for young readers portray the inhumanity of war and the human aspect of violent perpetration.

In my experience teaching human rights, students are most engaged when they feel confident that they can meaningfully contribute to the course. Even though the course attracts students from political science, history, education, English, and international studies, I have found that most students know more about the Holocaust than they do about other wars and genocides, so one way I have been able to build their confidence and create a comfortable learning environment is to begin the course with the Holocaust. First, students read excerpts from several Holocaust memoirs, including Heda Kovaly's *Under a Cruel Star*, Mira Hamermesh's *River of Angry Dogs*, and Ruth Kluger's *Still Alive*, each from the Jewish child's perspective, and *A Child of Hitler* by Alfons Heck, from a Nazi child's perspective. While these are not intended for child audiences, they do provide insight into the lived experiences of actual children during the Holocaust. This also provides a framework for talking about tropes within children's literature of atrocity that include the effects of trauma and the role of memory in formulating testimony. This gives a frame of reference for the authenticity of fictional texts with child protagonists, which becomes increasingly important as the class progresses with a focus on historical accuracy. While there is a plethora of books written for young people that address aspects of the Holocaust, I assign *Once* and *Then* by Australian author Morris Gleitzman because they best exemplify most of the strategies discussed in the articles assigned.

Adrienne Kertzer claims that "children's books about the Holocaust seem to function primarily to explain what adult texts often claim is ultimately inexplicable."[25] Because of this, Kertzer is critical of books that try to offer simple explanations of the Holocaust, specifically, but of war and genocide in general, too. Some children's literature about war and genocide is sophisticated, and books that are most worthy of inclusion in curricula, such as *Breaking Stalin's Nose* by Eugene Yelchin and *A Million Shades of Gray* by Cynthia Kadohata, are those that do not attempt to offer simple explanations for complex issues. There are several guidelines that scholars have offered to authors who choose to write literature of atrocity for young people. These guidelines can be used as evaluation criteria when analyzing children's literature of atrocity. In class, we interrogate these guidelines and then use them to create an evaluative framework. To interrogate the guidelines, I allow students to choose an article from a list then answer questions about the main points of the article. The student must summarize the article for the class, and identify what the writer is saying and what it means. Then the student must enter into the academic conversation by explaining how the article converses with other articles we have read and our class discussions. Thirdly, the student must offer extensions or challenges to the argument presented in the article to input their own voice into the conversation.

Lawrence Langer argues that authors of children's literature about the Holocaust should "create a framework for responding, rather than meaning."[26] By this, he means that authors can raise questions in the readers' minds about the events without "using—and perhaps abusing—its grim details." Langer also warns against creating books about the Holocaust designed to entertain or delight children. Although delight is usually a top priority for authors, when it applies to literature of atrocity, it is important that readers not lose focus on the underlying moral lessons in the narrative and that they are repeatedly reminded that while the story they are reading may be fictional, the victims of war and genocide are not. These concerns merit true consideration and are important in setting up a framework of limitations within which authors of children's literature of atrocity should work. Writing specifically about Holocaust literature, Lydia Williams specifies these limitations in her article "We're All in the Dumps with Bakhtin: Humor and the Holocaust":

> The Holocaust should be represented, in its totality, as a unique event in history. Representations of the Holocaust should be as accurate and faithful as possible. No changes, even for artistic reasons, are acceptable. The Holocaust should be treated as a solemn, even sacred, event, with a seriousness admitting no response that might obscure its enormity or dishonor its dead. All writing about the Holocaust should adopt an ethical position that fosters resistance. And we must not forget.[27]

Students are asked to conceptualize what they should look for in children's literature of atrocity to determine if it is "good" or "appropriate" for educating and socializing young readers. Williams argues that "Holocaust stories immediately break some of the generally accepted norms of children's fiction. They introduce the child to a world in which parents are not in control, where evil is truly present and where survival does not depend on one's wits, but upon luck."[28] Because of this, students must reconsider their ideas about what is or is not "appropriate" material to include in children's books. Students reconsider their conceptions of children's literature and begin to understand how to analyze books written for young audiences according to authorial strategies used to depict graphic violence, provide a framework for understanding, and provide space for readers to explore their own ideas about discrimination, morality, and personal responsibility.

Gleitzman's texts are a good example of books that provide a frame of reference for young readers. He has a fantastic ability to write about tough subjects—war, death, cults, AIDS, bullying—for young people with honesty and without overwhelming them with a sense of impending doom or anxiety. Here I model analysis and point out how to pay attention to details, word choices, allusions, and the authorial strategies used to create distance between the reader and the events described. For example, the protagonist in *Once* and *Then* is nine-year-old Felix. Left in an orphanage, Felix isn't sure where his parents, Jewish booksellers, have gone, but when the Nazis come to the orphanage and burn books, he decides that he has to escape to let his parents know that the Nazis hate books and they must save the bookstore. Not until seventy pages in does Felix admit: "Maybe it's not our books the Nazis hate. Maybe it's us."[29] These kinds of revelations of the more gruesome aspects of the Holocaust are gradually introduced to Felix and therefore to the child reader. As Felix continues his journey, he also encounters good people who assist him. This integration of decent human beings in the midst of war and genocide is another technique used to avoid horrifying young readers. However, such tales of heroics must be integrated carefully to avoid negating the reality that more than six million Jews were systematically murdered during the Holocaust and more than eleven million people in total perished. For instance, Barney and Genia rescue children in *Once*, but neither of them survives Nazi persecution despite their righteous acts. When writing about tough subjects, Gleitzman also creates a relatable protagonist with whom readers can sympathize, but the constant reminders that this boy lives in Poland in the 1940s and has been abandoned by his parents during a time of war makes his situation less threatening to contemporary young readers in Australia, the United States, the United Kingdom, or Canada.

From reading responses, article summaries, and class discussions, students from the previous three years have compiled the following list of criteria against which they evaluate the books assigned in the course.

Authors should be historically accurate

This does not mean that they cannot omit specific details that may be too graphic; however, it does require that they not purposefully distort history or provide inaccurate details. One way that authors often provide accurate historical details without overwhelming readers is through the use of paratext. For instance, at the beginning of her picture book *Terrible Things: An Allegory of the Holocaust*, Eve Bunting provides the following author's note:

> In Europe, during World War II, many people looked the other way while terrible things happened. They pretended not to know their neighbors were being taken away and locked in concentration camps. They pretended not to hear their cries for help. The Nazis killed millions of Jews and others in the Holocaust. If

everyone had stood together at the first sign of evil would this have happened? Standing up for what you know is right is not always easy. Especially if the one you face is bigger and stronger than you. It is easier to look the other way. But if you do, terrible things can happen.[30]

The paratext in this book is important because the "Terrible Things" are not clearly defined or recognizable, and those targeted for persecution by Nazis are portrayed as forest animals. Baer argues that the book "makes no overt reference to the Holocaust and provides no context for understanding."[31] While I agree with Baer that "it would fall to the adult reader to provide context," the book uses paratext to situate the narrative and makes an overt reference to the Holocaust in the title. Yet, Baer's article reminds students that literature of atrocity for young children is best shared with a knowledgeable adult who can answer questions such books may raise in young readers' minds. My students and I tend to agree that this book is highly effective in achieving its intended purpose, which is to introduce young people to the Holocaust, to encourage discussion, and to highlight that standing by when bad things happen often results in lasting negative effects. In this instance, standing by leads to the loss of friends, neighbours, and family. Even though the story has animal characters to make it less threatening and perhaps more appealing to young children, the title and the paratext ensure that readers make the connection between the story and the actual event. Because the "Terrible Things" are portrayed as large grey masses without faces or a distinct shape, this book provides an opportunity for educators (or other adults) to apply the lesson about standing by to threats children may face in their daily lives, such as bullying or discrimination. The trope of emphasizing personal responsibility and the importance of individual choices is represented in this book.

Authors should strive for emotional honesty as well as historical accuracy

In *Then*, another work that demonstrates the value of paratext, Gleitzman explains that he read a lot of books about people who "lived and struggled and loved and died and, just a few of them, survived," but he goes on to say that he "also read about the generosity and bravery of the people who risked everything to shelter others … and by doing so sometimes saved them."[32] In the novel, Felix's Polish rescuer and his best friend, Zelda, are hanged in the town square, and Felix must find the courage and strength to rebuild his life after the devastation of losing those he loved most. While some may criticize Gleitzman for "killing off" two of the main characters who readers have been positioned to care about most, this allows the reader to experience the feelings of sadness and anger just as Felix does, and it allows readers the space to humanize the stories of the Holocaust. Reading fiction in a safe space acts as a means to make the Holocaust more, rather than less, real. The important criteria for children's literature of atrocity here is that authors must be honest about emotionally difficult materials. To omit that people lost those closest to them would be an injustice to the victims of war and genocide. As Lydia Kokkala writes, "Devices intended to spare the child can ultimately result in an evasion of the truth," and she concludes that "any device which limits the amount of truthfulness depicted would be acceptably responsible, but, that any device which distorts the truth is unethical."[33]

Felix is also an avid storyteller, and when times get scary, such as when he is locked into a cattle car heading for Auschwitz, he creates his own stories to distance himself from the violence around him, thus distancing the child reader as well. While the reader is aware something terrible may be about to happen, they do not have to confront graphic violence head on. This being said, young readers aren't completely shielded from violence either. The book is about the Holocaust, and the author embraces the need to be as historically accurate as possible. When scavenging for food, Felix finds a baby, still in its highchair, that has been shot in the face. He meets a small group of children with whom he hides in the sewers, and one of the children is shot while running from Nazis. When he's hiding with a Polish woman who claims he is her nephew, a German boy bullies him and nearly jerks his pants down to reveal his circumcision, but, in what quickly becomes a moment of comic relief for a lot of child readers, he defecates to deter the bullies and gets away.

Comic relief is also provided by Felix's sassy sidekick Zelda, whose parents were Nazis killed by the Polish resistance. Zelda is six, and she repeatedly chimes in with "Don't you know anything?" and we see the events as a child might—with a limited understanding of the magnitude of the danger around her, but a clear understanding of its constant presence. Through the development of Zelda's friendship with Felix, and Felix's cheery conversations with a boy from the Hitler Youth with whom he shares a favourite author, child readers are encouraged to consider how these children could grow into adults who hate each other enough to kill each other. They see that Nazis and Jews are not natural enemies, that Nazis were real humans, and that even when we belong to different groups, we may still have a lot in common. Vahan, the protagonist, echoes this sentiment in Adam Bagdasarian's *Forgotten Fire* when he thinks, "I had thought servants were born servants and that they were different from me. Now I knew that they were no different at all."[34] While seemingly simple in their language and plot structure, these texts provide a starting point for discussing the more complex aspects of genocide and of children's literature. The main point is that hatred of the Other is learned; therefore, it can be unlearned and combated with lessons that encourage respect for and acceptance of the Other.

Authors should resist simple explanations

To encourage child readers to continue thinking about the important themes raised in the books, authors often give their stories an ambiguous ending. Such endings are popular in more radical or subversive children's literature, such as Lois Lowry's *The Giver*, a dystopian novel about a young boy choosing to flee from his safe community after realizing that the utopia depends on killing some people for no reason. Three books that we read for this course that have particularly ambiguous, thought-provoking endings are *The Butter Battle Book* by Dr. Seuss, *Enemy: A Book about Peace* by Davide Cali and Serge Bloch, and *The Rabbits* by John Marsden and Shaun Tan. In *The Butter Battle Book*, the Yooks and the Zooks engage in a race to build the most destructive weapon to wipe out their enemy because they do not butter their bread on the same side. As Tanya Jeffcoat explains, "Each group assumes the other is somehow inferior for having made a different cultural choice. … Once people decide that their way is the best way and that those who don't agree are somehow essentially inferior, it becomes all too easy to justify discrimination and persecution."[35] The means by which perpetrators dehumanize potential victims becomes a major focus of analysis and discussion for the course. However, the ending of *The Butter Battle Book* portrays a face off on top of the wall between an old Zook and an old Yook. Both hold identical weapons, "the Bitsy Big-Boy Boomeroo," designed to blow the enemy to "small smithereens." As they eye each other and hold out their weapons, the texts reads, "Who's going to drop it? Will you … ? Or will he … ?"[36] Again the focus is on individual choice and personal responsibility emphasized by the use of the word "you," the question marks, and the ellipses to draw the reader in and more fully engage them in the tension of being faced with making this choice. The question really is: Reader, what would you do? We are encouraged by the text to think about the consequences of personal actions, and the absurdness of the texts, such as fighting over which side of the bread you butter, encourages readers to consider what might actually be a justifiable reason to engage in war given the destruction and devastation it causes.

Authors should resist closure and provoke thought

In *The Enemy: A Book about Peace*, the only characters are two soldiers sitting in their individual holes. One of the soldiers is the focalizing character, and readers get a firsthand account of his inner thought processes as he sits in a trench. He is hungry and tired and wants to go home and be with his family. Yet, he continues the war because he has been given a manual and a gun, and the manual informs him that the enemy is "a wild beast. … The enemy is not a human being."[37] While the soldier struggles with trying to find a way to end the war, his actions are mirrored by those of the other soldier, so readers can safely assume the other soldier's emotions also mirror those of the narrator. When the narrator makes his way to the other soldier's hole, he finds it empty and also discovers the enemy's manual and family photos. The narrator states, "I didn't expect him to have a family" and recognizes that he himself is portrayed as the "enemy" in the other soldier's manual. This picture book highlights how the "enemy" is constructed by those who benefit most from conflict, such as politicians and weapons manufacturers, in ways that fully seek to dehumanize the people who actually end up fighting the wars. Then it encourages readers to acknowledge the actual human toll of conflict by what I call "re-humanizing" the enemy. The family photos are real black-and-white photographs, so when juxtaposed to the simple scratch drawings on every other page, the reader is forced to connect the fictional story with real victims of real wars. On the last page, the narrator throws a peace request via a message in a bottle to the "enemy" who is now in the narrator's hole. As he does, the "enemy" again mirrors his action, and the book ends with these hopeful messages of peace in the air. Upon turning the page, though, readers see a full-page spread of soldiers lined up; two spots are empty, representing the fact that the two characters in the book are no longer there. Students in my class interpret this in several different ways. Some say it means the soldiers are dead. Others say it portrays them as deserters, while still others say it represents the personal choice and complicity required to carry out war and genocide. If all of the soldiers on the page chose to not fight, there would not be a war. While all of these are supportable interpretations, they demonstrate that the ambiguous ending is a key strategy authors use to force readers to think more about the issues associated with war and genocide long after the book is closed.

Authors should inspire hope

This, however, does not mean that the book must have a happy ending. For instance, at the end of the picture book *Rose Blanche*, by Roberto Innocenti and Christophe Gallaz, the young protagonist is shot and killed by Russian soldiers on their way to liberate the concentration camps. Child readers do not witness her death; the text simply states, "There was a shot," and when they turn the page, Rose Blanche, who has been present on every spread, is no longer there. While this may sadden readers, the last spread is the natural landscape in spring. Whereas the prior spreads were mostly grey, dark reds, and browns, this spread shows green grass, flowers of all colours blooming, and the regeneration of the natural landscape. This regeneration is symbolic of the fact that even though people die during war, after the war, life continues and can be good. On the last page, in the same position where Rose Blanche last stood, there is a red poppy.[38]

Other criteria students have compiled include emphasizing how things happened, not just the outcome—focusing on what led to the event, not just the event itself; promoting understanding without offering conclusive resolutions; recognizing and adhering to the limits of representation of genocide through the use of silence, allusion, and shadows; and distancing young readers from the horrors through strategies such as using child focalizers who have a limited understanding of what is unfolding around them and allowing readers to gradually learn as the character does.

Students also acknowledge that there are certain things authors of children's literature of atrocity should not do. For instance, authors should not romanticize or glorify conflict; generalize too much or rely on stereotypes; or try to offer simple answers to complex questions simply to ease child readers' minds. Interestingly, most of my students agree that while graphic violence for its own sake should be excluded from children's literature of atrocity, child readers should be a bit shocked by the texts so that they are more likely to continue thinking about it after reading and to do something to try to prevent such atrocities in the future.

Other books we read include *My Hiroshima*, *So Far from the Sea*, *Yertle the Turtle*, *Breaking Stalin's Nose*, *Persepolis*, *Maus I*, *Deogratias*, *A Million Shades of Gray*, *The Bosnia List*, *Fallen Angels*, *A Long Walk to Water*, and *Forgotten Fire*. To provide context I give some details on each war or conflict and use resources not necessarily intended for child audiences. These include excerpts from *Bury My Heart at Wounded Knee*, *Schindler's List*, *In the Land of Blood and Honey*, *The Killing Fields*, *Hotel Rwanda*, and *War Witch*. Another important aspect of the course is that I have students read a popular work of fiction that is not as clearly about war and genocide as most texts for the class. This is important because it helps students see how conflict is ingrained in our society as something that is inevitable and that children are exposed to concepts associated with war and genocide from early ages with little context. The texts used so far are *The Hunger Games* by Suzanne Collins and *Ender's Game* by Orson Scott Card. The film versions were released during the semester in which the class read them, and students were more engaged with the texts given the surrounding hype. In 2014, the class read Suzanne Collins's newly published picture book *A Year in the Jungle*, about her personal struggles being a six-year-old whose dad fought in the Vietnam War and returned with post-traumatic stress disorder.

To assess student learning and provide opportunities for students to develop their reading, writing, research, group work, and presentation skills, I assign reading responses for each academic article required for the course. Most students are juniors or seniors, so I review for them how to read academic texts closely as researchers. This involves multiple readings, looking for key ideas, identifying claims and evidence, determining their own opinions in response, justifying those opinions, and articulating their responses. In this way, students become more prepared for further research in the humanities or social sciences, and potentially for graduate school. A common weakness among students is their inability to form their own responses to the readings, or to interject their own voices into the ongoing academic dialogue related to the topics we study. These reading responses give each student two chances per semester to practice. After the first, formative feedback is provided so student responses are more developed the second time. This is designed according to the "seven principles of good feedback practice," which state that formative feedback should "help clarify what good performance is … provide opportunities to close the gap between current and desired performance … and provide information to teachers that can be used to help shape the teaching."[39]

Another assignment is a small group project where I allow students to choose from a list I provide a book that they would like to analyze and present to the class based on the framework we have established. Students are given a loosely detailed assignment sheet so that they have a lot of choice in determining how they prefer to demonstrate their learning. For instance, the minimum requirements are that they provide background information and statistics related to the conflict represented in the book and that they thoroughly summarize and offer an analysis of the book. Groups have addressed these requirements in various ways, including standard class presentations using Prezi or PowerPoint, making a video, and constructing a website. The group members evaluate one another, every student evaluates each group according to a provided rubric, and each student completes a reflective writing on what they learned from the project about the topic, themselves, and working as a group. While initially, most students cringe at group work, particularly on a campus that is made up mostly of commuters, I attempt to motivate them by explaining that knowledge construction occurs in dialogue with others, and that learning is communal; that students need the professional skills of being able to manage their time, to work with others whose opinions, visions, and working styles may differ from their own, and to produce something meaningful with other people. All of this contributes to the emphasis placed on working together to improve society as a whole. Students also have to complete a literary analysis research essay to demonstrate their ability to analyze children's literature of atrocity with close consideration of the criteria established during the course.

War is not inevitable, and if people see it is as such, it removes any personal responsibility we have to try to prevent it. As a professor, I want my students to leave the course empowered to make the world a more peaceful place. This is one reason each class completes a Promoting Peace Project. Students have to work together to organize a campus- or community-wide event that promotes a more peaceful society. This idea was inspired by the US Holocaust Memorial Museum's "From Memory to Action" exhibition. This exhibit exists, in part, to get people to think about what they can do to prevent atrocities. For this project, the entire class works together to organize an event aimed at promoting peace on our campus, in our community, or around the globe. They begin with a budget of zero and have four months to complete the project. Grades are derived from peer evaluations, my observations, each person's willingness to cooperate and collaborate, the overall evaluation of the event, and bi-weekly blogs by each student throughout the process detailing how the project unfolds and what they contribute. Students also complete a reflection on the project and explain how it relates to what they have learned in class and about the whole group-work process. The first year of the course, students organized a bone-making event for the national art installation, One Million Bones. Students on UNC Charlotte's campus created more than 600 bones that were then shipped to the National Mall for an installation designed to "create a powerful visual petition against ongoing genocide and mass atrocities."[40] In fall 2013, students organized a peace rock painting event on campus and created a peace garden behind Atkins Library. When people passed by, students asked them to write on a whiteboard what peace means to them and then took their picture and posted it to the event's Facebook and Instagram pages. The peace garden full of painted rocks is still on campus. In fall 2015, the class organized "Pinwheels for Peace" through the organizations Students Rebuild. Their goal was to have people make at least 300 pinwheels, and for each pinwheel the Bezos Foundation donated $2 to children's education programs for Syrian refugees. The class surpassed their goal, making 581 pinwheels and raising over $1,100. At all events, students had children's books on display and talked to their fellow students about what they were learning in class while the students made a bone, folded a pinwheel, or painted a rock. People are usually surprised to learn that there is so much children's literature about war and genocide, and it serves to remind them of the millions of children affected by conflict every day.

Ultimately, my goal as a professor is to do what I can to educate my students and empower them to do what they can, where they are, with what they have. The War and Genocide in Children's Literature course allows students to gain a deeper awareness and appreciation of children's literature in general because it challenges any misconceptions that children's literature is unsophisticated, apolitical, or unworthy of academic study. In addition, they develop the necessary skills for evaluating books for young audiences that tackle tough issues, and they gain the ability to decide how to best present conflict to young audiences and to talk to children about atrocities, such as the events of 9/11, and the ongoing genocide in South Sudan. Mostly, I aim to remind students of our common humanity, to teach them that every human life is valuable, that genocide and war are preventable, and that we all have a personal responsibility to take action to prevent it. One of the students in my course in 2013 summed it up best in the personal mantra she was asked to devise after reading Linda Sue Park's novel *A Long Walk to Water*. She wrote, "The probability that what you do will not make a positive difference does not negate your responsibility to try."

NOTES

1   "Children Targeted in the Genocide," Human Rights Watch, http://www.hrw.org/reports/2003/rwanda0403/rwanda0403-03.htm (accessed 10 January 2013).

2   Mavis Reimer, "Making Princesses, Re-making a Little Princess," in *Voices of the Other: Children's Literature in the Postcolonial Context*, ed. Rod McGillis (New York: Routledge, 2012), 112.

3   Zohar Shavit, *A Past Without Shadow: Constructing the Past in German Books for Children* (New York: Routledge, 2005), 294.

4   Lawrence Langer, *The Holocaust and Literary Imagination* (New Haven, CT: Yale University Press, 1975).

5   Kimberley Reynolds, *Radical Children's Literature: Future Visions and Aesthetic Transformations in Juvenile Fiction* (New York: Palgrave Macmillan, 2010), 10.

6   This course was developed after attending the Silberman Seminar for Faculty Development at the US Holocaust Memorial Museum. I am indebted to the generosity of that institution, to the instructors, and to my fellow participants.

7   Peter Hollindale, "Ideology and the Children's Book," in *Literature for Children: Contemporary Criticism,* ed. Peter Hunt (London: Routledge, 1992), 27.

8   Ibid., 32.

9   The main readings that inform the framework for the course are Doris Bergen's *War and Genocide: A Concise History of the Holocaust* (London: Rowman & Littlefield,

2003), Steven K. Baum's *The Psychology of Genocide: Perpetrators, Bystanders, and Rescuers* (Cambridge: Cambridge University Press, 2008), Adam Jones's *Genocide: A Comprehensive Introduction* (New York: Routledge, 2010), Christopher R. Browning's *Ordinary Men* (New York: Harper Collins, 2013), and Cathy Caruth's *Unclaimed Experience: Trauma, Narrative, and History* (Baltimore, MD: John Hopkins Press, 2010).

10 Susan Honeyman, *Elusive Childhood: Impossible Representations in Modern Fiction* (Columbus: Ohio State University Press, 2005), 2.

11 Michele Kelemen, "2014 A Year of 'Unspeakable Brutality' for Children in Conflict Zones," National Public Radio, 8 December 2014.

12 Honeyman, *Elusive Childhood*, 2.

13 John Stephens, *Language and Ideology in Children's Fiction* (London: Longman, 1992), 3.

14 Perry Nodelman, *The Pleasures of Children's Literature* (New York: Longman, 1992), 20.

15 Julianne Chiaet, "Novel Finding: Reading Literary Fiction Improves Empathy," *Scientific American*, 4 October 4 2013.

16 Lindsay Myers, "What Do We Tell the Children? War in the Works of Roberto Innocenti," *Bookbird: A Journal of International Children's Literature* 47, no. 4 (October 2009): 46.

17 Katherine Patterson, *The Day of the Pelican* (Boston: Clarion Books, 2009), 50.

18 Ibid., 90.

19 Lydia Williams, "We Are All in the Dumps with Bakhtin: Humor and the Holocaust," in *Children's Literature and the Fin de Siecle*, ed. Roderick McGillis (Westport, CT: Praeger, 2002), 130.

20 Ruth Gilbert, "Grasping the Unimaginable: Recent Holocaust Novels for Children by Morris Gleitzman and John Boyne," *Children's Literature in Education* 41, no. 4 (2010): 355.

21 Honeyman, *Elusive Childhood*, 145.

22 Sarah Jordan, "Educating without Overwhelming: Authorial Strategies in Children's Holocaust Literature," *Children's Literature in Education* 35, no. 3 (2004): 200.

23 Elizabeth R. Baer, "A New Algorithm in Evil: Children's Literature in a post-Holocaust World," *The Lion and the Unicorn* 24, no. 3 (Sept 2000): 391.

24 James Waller, "The Dead End of Demonization," paper presented at "Understanding Atrocities: Remembering, Representing, and Teaching Genocide," Mount Royal University, Calgary AB, 19–21 February 2014.

25 Adrienne Kertzer, " 'Do You Know What "Auschwitz" Means?' Children's Literature and the Holocaust," *The Lion and the Unicorn* 23, no. 2 (1999): 240.

26 Langer, *The Holocaust and the Literary Imagination*, 12.

27 Lydia Williams, "We Are All in the Dumps," 129.

28 Ibid., 130.

29 Morris Gleitzman, *Once* and *Then* (Victoria, AU: Penguin, 2005).

30 Eve Bunting, *Terrible Things: An Allegory of the Holocaust*, illus. Stephen Gammell (Philadelphia, PA: The Jewish Publication Society, 1980).

31 Baer, "Children's Literature in a Post-Holocaust World," 387.

32 Gleitzman, *Then*, 339.

33 Lydia Kokkola, "Holocaust Narratives and the Ethics of Truthfulness," *Bookbird: A Journal of International Children's Literature* 45, no. 4 (2007): 9.

34 Adam Bagdasarian, *Forgotten Fire* (New York: Random House, 2000).

35 Tanya Jeffcoat, "From There to Here, from Here to There, Diversity is Everywhere," in *Dr. Seuss and Philosophy*, ed. Jacob M. Held (New York: Rowman & Littlefield, 2011), 94.

36 Dr. Seuss, *The Butter Battle Book* (New York: Random House, 1984).

37 Davide Cali and Serge Bloch, *The Enemy: A Book about Peace* (New York: Schwartz & Wade, 2009).

38 Christophe Gallaz and Roberto Innocenti, *Rose Blanche* (Mankato, MN: Creative Paperbacks, 1985).

39 Charles Juwah, et al., "Enhancing student learning through effective formative feedback," 2.

40 http://studentsrebuild.org/find-challenge/one-million-bones-challenge/why-challenge (accessed 23 September 2015).

9

Thinking About Nazi Atrocities Without Thinking About Nazi Atrocities: Limited Thinking as Legacy in Schlink's *The Reader*

Lorraine Markotic

I love the old questions. Ah the old questions, the old answers, there's nothing like them![1]

—Samuel Beckett, *Endgame*

Only one who recognizes the new as the same will serve that which would be different.
[Nur wer das Neueste als Gleiches erkennt, dient dem, was verschieden wäre.][2]

—Theodor Adorno, *Reflexionen zur Klassentheorie*

Introduction

The extent to which Nazi genocidal murderers thought about and reflected upon what they did has been a question and a concern at least since Hannah Arendt's *Eichmann in Jerusalem: A Report on the Banality of Evil* portrayed Eichmann as a fairly mindless, even if overzealous, bureaucrat.[3]

Bettina Stangneth's more recent response to Arendt, *Eichmann Before Jerusalem*, shows that Eichmann was actually an ardent and active believer in National Socialist ideas.[4] Eichmann's on-trial presentation of himself as someone who simply obeyed orders, as merely a "cog in the machine," was a calculated pose, Stangneth argues. In fact, Eichmann seems to have read and dismissed the philosophies of Kant and Nietzsche for being too internationally oriented—in other words, for having universal principles.[5] Christopher R. Browning also denies that Eichmann was a mere cog in the machine but shows that the Nazi murder apparatus did have many such cogs, many ordinary Germans, who were willing to kill Jews, believing that they should co-operatively "do their part," and who allowed this belief to override their moral and physical qualms.[6]

It is interesting, therefore, that Bernhard Schlink's *The Reader*, a novel concerned with the Shoah, an influential book that was translated into almost forty languages, actively discourages thinking. As well as constitutively proscribing certain questions, it has a narrator who—though presented as thoughtful and reflective—does not think much or, if he does think, only thinks about certain things and only in a limited way. Of course, *The Reader* is a work of fiction; but this work of fiction is one of the most widely read Holocaust novels in the world. It is regarded as an important pedagogical tool: the book has been used to teach A-level and university students in Britain, to teach German courses in the United States, and to teach advanced high school (*Gymnasium*) students in Germany. To what extent the Nazi perpetrators—whether Eichmann or the "ordinary Germans" who pulled triggers—did or did not *think* is clearly an important issue. Hence, an internationally successful work about the Shoah that manifests limited thinking on the part of its first-person narrator and which itself intrinsically inhibits questioning—while at the same time representing the protagonist and the novel itself as reflective—clearly calls for further examination. Although *The Reader* does not directly aid us in understanding atrocities, it unwittingly teaches us to be suspicious and distrustful of our thinking precisely when we think about, represent, and remember genocide.

Context and Limited Thinking

The reception of *The Reader* was, in the astonished words of Ursula Mahlendorf, "nothing short of amazing."[7] The novel was welcomed enthusiastically, both in Germany and abroad, in the *Frankfurter Allgemeine Zeitung, Die Zeit, Der Spiegel, Le Monde*, the *Observer*, and the *New York Times Book Review*, among others. Acclaim for the book emphasized its exploration of the imbrications of evil, especially the fact that it presents a perpetrator, Hanna Schmitz, who seems not simply evil, but someone with whom one might empathize—even while one condemns her actions. The main problem, the obvious problem, however, is that *The Reader* presents us with a Nazi perpetrator whose actions stem from her unusual situation: her illiteracy. In other words, not only does the novel seem to explain Hanna's behaviour; at some level, it seems to *excuse* it. Cogent critics of the book, among them Cynthia Ozcik, Ian Samsom, and William Donahue, were quick to point out that *The Reader* makes too easy the slide between empathizing with Hannah's motives and excusing Hannah's atrocities.[8] Here I am less interested in Hanna,[9] however, than I am in Michael Berg, *Der Vorleser* (the person who reads aloud), the narrator to whom the German-language title refers (something lost in the English-language translation, *The Reader*, which could eventually refer to Hanna as well). Michael does think, but only in a very limited way, and the book does seem to encourage reflection, but ultimately does not do so.

The Reader is a work of what Germans call *Vergangenheitsbewältigung*, the process of coming to terms with, or mastering the past. The novel ostensibly explores the relationship between the generation that lived during the Nazi regime and the postwar generation, and the insistence of the latter upon *Aufarbeitung* (reappraisal; working-through) of the National Socialist past. In my view, however, *The Reader* fails to confront National Socialism in any genuine way because of the restricted manner in which the narrator thinks. Of course, one cannot think about everything. But since Michael, the narrator, claims to be concerned with confronting Nazi atrocities and with understanding those who lived and acted during the Nazi regime, there are certain things about which one would expect him to think, certain things that plainly should occur to him. For *The Reader* is filled with the narrator's reflections, ruminations, associations, thoughts chasing down other thoughts, musings on motives, ponderings about decisions and actions, and the relationship between the two. Michael repeatedly questions, but there are certain questions he does not ask, certain things about which he does not think.

Precisely in his thoughtlessness, Michael resembles the way the Nazi generation behaved both during and after the National Socialist reign—despite Michael's preoccupation with the rift between the two generations. Again, one cannot prescribe how someone should think—certainly not a character in a novel—but one can measure such thinking against the way that thinking is presented, either by them, or in the case of fictional beings, by the literary work. Michael's thinking is limited in ways that undercut his alleged concerns. He can, of course, simply be regarded as an unreliable narrator. Certainly, Michael's view is skewed.[10] But here I focus on Michael not as an unreliable narrator, which he definitely is, but on Michael as an "unthinking" narrator, a narrator whose thinking is restricted, and whose thinking excludes as well as misinterprets. I address what Michael's reflections clearly omit. Michael is, in fact, exceedingly introspective, and draws us in with his ponderings and deliberations. But just because a character has thoughts running through his head, thoughts he pursues and returns to and revaluates, does not mean he is doing that much thinking. Just because a character notes that there are no easy answers, does not mean he is considering complexities. And even though a character poses question after question, this does not mean he is questioning; neither does it mean that there are not many more questions that he does not ask even though he may console us with his questioning, something I return to at the end of this chapter.[11]

As a young man, Michael and his generation actively protest and seek to break the taboo-like silence that, during the postwar years, cordoned off the period of National Socialism. Unsurprisingly, he and his generation regard themselves as distinct from their parents, the generation that refuses to talk about the Nazi period and which, for the most part, repudiates it.[12] But the older Michael, who narrates events, himself tends to repress, deny, and simply ignore critical questions and conspicuous concerns. The novel purports to be, and has been regarded as being, both an *Auseinandersetzung*, an attempt to come to terms with the past, and an exploration of the intergenerational conflict in Germany. Unfortunately, it is neither. *The Reader* does not explore the Nazi genocide in more than a shallow and self-centred manner, and it refuses to think about the ways in which the postwar generation assimilated aspects of Nazi "thinking"—including its limited nature.

Continuity

The Reader presents us with an account written by Michael Berg as a middle-aged man who relates his earlier encounters with Hanna Schmitz. During the 1950s, as a young boy of fifteen, Michael has a relationship with Hanna, who is thirty-six. He seems to fall in love with her; he visits her frequently, sometimes reads aloud to her, and they have a lot of sex (an aspect highlighted in the movie). Then Hanna suddenly disappears, leaving Michael bereft and distraught. In the second part of the book, Michael graduates from high school and goes on to study law. As a law student in the 1960s, he and some classmates are sent to observe the trial of a number of former concentration camp guards. Michael suddenly sees Hanna again. He learns that before their relationship she had been a guard at Auschwitz. Hanna is on trial for having participated in the selections at the camp and for letting several hundred Jewish prisoners burn to death. The women were on a death march and were locked in a church for the night. A bomb hit the church, and the church caught fire, but the guards did not open the locked doors and all the women, except for one mother and daughter, burned to death. Hanna is accused of having written the report that provides evidence of the guards' guilt and of being their leader. At this point, well over halfway through the novel, something suddenly hits Michael, something of which there were hints all along: Hanna is illiterate and she is deeply ashamed of her illiteracy. She could not have written the report, but she is too ashamed to admit this. Michael wrestles with whether or not to reveal Hanna's illiteracy to the judge, but ultimately does not, and part 2 ends with Hanna sentenced to life imprisonment.

As Michael recalls his student days, he depicts the feelings of condemnation his generation felt towards the generation that experienced the Nazi period. Indeed, the novel as a whole explores this intergenerational conflict, which played a significant role in German society in the 1960s. Hanna clearly represents, and Michael regards her as representing, Germany's perpetrator generation; his having been seduced by Hanna represents the postwar generation's convoluted relationship with the previous one. The novel and Michael's narrative seek to bridge the gap between the two generations. But seeking to bridge a gap is, indubitably, a way of asserting that two things are separate and distinct. Although Michael relates that his generation objected that after the war "so many old Nazis had made careers in the courts, the administration, and the universities,"[13] he does not consider that such a persistent Nazi presence might have had an influence on him. As a man in his fifties looking back critically on the tension between the two generations, one might expect it to occur to Michael that certain attitudes, orientations, or assumptions from the Nazi period *could have been passed on to him*. A dozen years of brutal, fascistic rule—during which various atrocities were acceptable—are not going to disappear without leaving a trace. Even when Germany began to lose the war, the Nazi regime was not overthrown by the Germans; it was defeated by the Allied forces. Michael himself—not just his parent's generation—manifests a certain amount of *continuity* between aspects of the Nazi period and the time that came afterwards. It is somewhat peculiar, therefore, that Michael, a middle-aged man reflecting back on his earlier self and on the postwar period, refuses to think about any continuity between the outlook and behaviour of the Nazi generation and that of his own.

Michael seems oddly unaware that his thinking sometimes remains within the parameters of the Nazi generation. In my view, his limited thinking illustrates his limited capacity, and perhaps the limited capacity of many of his generation, for *Aufarbeitung*, for a reappraisal or working-through of the past—although this is exactly their goal. Especially during the trial of Hanna and the other guards, aspects of Michael's reflections disconcertingly resemble the thinking of the Nazi generation. The way in which Michael thinks through and formulates what happens at the trial is telling. Salient for him is the predicament in which he finds himself. He agonizes over whether he has the right to reveal Hanna's illiteracy to the court, for Hanna is deeply, deeply ashamed of not being able to read and write, and she is determined to conceal her inability. Michael's reflections, however—his deliberations with himself, his discussions of his moral dilemma with his friends and eventually his father—are extremely narrow. Michael seeks advice, but he seems to want to conceal the fact that he is talking about Hanna's situation, so he provides examples of dilemmas he considers analogous.[14] In the manner of certain forms of analytic philosophy, Michael's reflections disregard the complexity of the situation, filter out its many dimensions, and reduce it to a moral quandary: whether or not one has the right to go against a person's wishes and reveal something about this person in order to help her or him.

> Imagine someone is racing intentionally towards his own destruction and you can save him—do you go ahead and save him? Imagine there's an operation, and the patient is a drug user and the drugs are incompatible with the anesthetic, but the patient is ashamed of being an addict and does not want to tell the anesthesiologist—do you talk to the anesthesiologist? Imagine a trial and a defendant who will be convicted if he doesn't admit to being left-handed—do you tell the judge what's going on? Imagine he's gay, and could not have committed the crime because he's gay, but is ashamed of being gay. It isn't a question of whether the defendant should be ashamed of being left-handed or gay—just imagine that he is. (137)

Michael does not want his friends to latch onto the examples, but to grasp the quandary of whether one should reveal the truth about someone if it will benefit this person or whether one should respect the person's right to self-determination even when s/he is not acting in their own best interest. Michael does not seem to know what to do and is trying to figure it out. But his examples eliminate the victims—as if, like the Nazi generation after the war, he cannot face or refuses to think about them.[15] In Michael's first example, the addict's life is threatened because he is so ashamed that he does not want to tell an anesthesiologist of his drug consumption even though the drugs may be incompatible with the anesthetic; but while this addict may have broken the law through drug use, s/he has not harmed anyone else. Michael's second example involves a defendant who will be convicted because he does not want to admit being left-handed or gay, but who has *not* committed a crime. Of course, Hanna has not written the report; but she *has* committed a crime and she has certainly harmed others. There is therefore something inappropriate, if not a little obscene, about making an analogy between a drug user or an innocent left-handed or gay defendant, and someone who participated in the Nazi genocide.

In the end, Michael does go to speak with the judge, but then finds himself unable to disclose Hanna's illiteracy. Moreover, in his self-deliberations preceding this visit, he concludes that Hanna would not have wanted him "to barter her self-image for a few years in prison" (137), as if he concurs that "exposure as an illiterate" (137) would damage someone's self-image more than designation as leader of a group of murderous concentration camp guards. It is rather disconcerting that Michael is not incensed either at Hanna, or at his society, that she feels less shame in falsely admitting to being the leader of guards responsible for hundreds of women burning alive—for most of the women did not suffocate but literally burned to death—than to admitting not to have learned to read and write.

Shame is a compelling, motivating force for Hanna; furthermore, Michael repeatedly recounts that his generation felt overcome with shame at what their parents' generation had done. It is striking , therefore, that in his narration Michael does not attend more to the experience of shame. In fact, *The Reader* opens with a description of Michael being ill when he was fifteen and his shame at this illness. Although the young Michael clearly belongs to the postwar generation, his particular feelings of shame suggest a continuity between the Nazi and postwar period. In the second paragraph of the novel, we read: "I was ashamed of being so weak. I was even more ashamed when I threw up" (2).[16] Without a doubt, the Nazis had little tolerance for weakness and would have thought it should make one feel ashamed. Michael is a teenager and it is easy to feel embarrassed at that age, but Michael does not say that he felt embarrassed—he says that he felt ashamed.[17] It seems odd to feel *shame* at being weak and vomiting. Even more odd is that the narrator, the older Michael recalling the event four decades later, does not reflect on the feeling he had then: on his shame at being "weak," a "weakness" that the opening sentence explains is hepatitis. Clearly, there is a certain continuity between the two generations insofar as the postwar generation understands and experiences events through inflections of the Nazi period.

Indifference

The court trial is a central aspect of *The Reader*. But Michael's thinking during the trial has further, disturbing elements. In his reduction of Hanna's illiteracy to a dilemma about self-determination, in his preoccupation with the question of whether he should or should not reveal Hanna's secret to the court, Michael loses sight of any broader concerns. Michael does not think much about justice in relation to the perpetrators, obligation towards the victims, or social responsibility. First, the other guards who accuse Hanna of writing the report receive lighter sentences than she does because Hanna is considered their leader—even though one of them wrote the report. It never seems to disturb Michael, however, that if he keeps Hanna's illiteracy to himself, the other guards (including the one who actually wrote the report) will have succeeded in lying and laying the blame for what they did on someone else. Michael relates that during the 1960s, he and his generation felt ashamed that "former" Nazis simply continued to occupy their positions in the newly created German Federal Republic. The fact that "so many old Nazis had made careers in the courts, the administration, and the universities ... all this filled us with shame, even when we could point at the guilty parties" (168). Michael and his generation saw the trial of the camp guards as an inculpation of the previous generation, the generation that desired to disregard the Nazi past: "The generation that had been served by the guards and enforcers, or had done nothing to stop them, or had not banished them from its midst as it could have done after 1945, was in the dock, and we explored it, subjected it to trial by daylight, and condemned it to shame" ["und wir verurteilten sie in einem Verfahren der Aufarbeitung und Aufklärung zu Scham"] (90/87). In relation to his father, Michael says that he had

> lost his job as lecturer in philosophy for scheduling a lecture on Spinoza, and had got himself and us through the war as an editor for a house that published hiking maps and books. How did I decide that he too was under sentence of shame? But I did. We all condemned our parents to shame, even if the only charge we could bring was that after 1945 they had tolerated the perpetrators in their midst. (90)

Looking back, Michael obviously thinks it unfair of him to have placed his father under a sentence of shame, and unfair of his generation to have condemned the previous generation merely for having "tolerated the perpetrators in their midst." But while Michael's father and his generation may have *tolerated* perpetrators in their midst, Michael himself makes it possible for Nazi perpetrators to *reside* in their midst. His decision to keep silent about Hanna's illiteracy allows the other Nazi guards, including the one who actually wrote the report, to return to civilian life more quickly.

Yet Michael himself never seems to feel any shame—either at the time or looking back—that his own action allows perpetrators to elude justice and return to society. The thought does not cross his mind.

Second, and more disconcerting perhaps, Michael does not feel any responsibility to the victims, either to the several hundred[18] women who died in the burning church or to the mother and daughter who survived. The daughter herself comes to the court to testify, but as William Donahue points out, Michael does not consider the right of the mother and daughter to the truth:

> In focusing on the dilemma between Hanna's happiness versus her alienable dignity and freedom as a human subject, [Michael] Berg, Schlink, and the critics (at least those who champion the novel's innovative morality) apparently lose sight of those who have at least as compelling a claim to the truth that might have been brought to light by Berg's timely intervention in the judicial process: the surviving victims. ... Though his action could conceivably have advanced the cause of those with the most immediate and palpable interest in learning the truth, the mother and daughter whose lives are spared by pure chance, these people, it is worth noticing, do not once enter into Michael's ethical calculations.[19]

And "calculations" is the correct word here, although "ethical" probably is not.

During their affair, a few months before Hanna disappears, Michael begins to feel that he is betraying Hanna, and to feel guilt at his betrayal. Michael does not acknowledge Hanna to his friends or in front of them, as if he were ashamed of her. When Hanna suddenly leaves town, he assumes it is because of such an act of betrayal on his part. Later on, he realizes that she actually left because she was about to be promoted and would have had to take a written test. He recalls and reflects that

> I had been sure that I had driven her away because I had betrayed and denied her, when in fact she had simply been running away from being found out by the streetcar company. However, the fact that I had not driven her away did not change the fact that I had betrayed her. So I was still guilty. And if I was not guilty because

one cannot be guilty of having betrayed a criminal, then I was guilty of having loved a criminal. (133)

Michael's reasoning about betrayal and guilt seems rather shaky, and he seems somewhat fixated (even looking back) on his betrayal of, and guilt in relation to, Hanna.[20] What is most noteworthy, however, is that he does not experience any guilt at all for betraying the mother and daughter survivors who leave the trial with an incorrect version of what happened to them.

At one point in the novel, Michael hitches a ride from a man who tells him that the murder of the Jews took place not because the perpetrators felt hate, or even because they were following orders, but rather because they were utterly indifferent to what happened to their victims. This man, who turns out to have been an officer who executed Jews in Russia, tells Michael that it was just a matter of getting the day's work done:

An executioner is not under orders. He's doing his work, he doesn't hate the people he executes, he's not taking revenge on them, he's not killing them because they're in his way or threatening him or attacking him. They're a matter of such indifference to him that he can kill them as easily as not. (150)

The mother and daughter survivors may not be a matter of complete indifference to Michael, but he is not especially concerned with them. Even at the end of the novel, when Michael goes in person to visit the surviving daughter and tell her about Hanna, he does not feel any shame or remorse that she did not learn the truth at the trial—a truth he could have revealed.[21]

Third, just as Michael does not seem to feel any obligation towards the individual survivors and their right to know what happened, so he does not seem to feel any broader social responsibility for working through the Nazi past. Ironically, he and his generation claim to be preoccupied exactly with this: "Reappraisal! Reappraisal of the past. We students in the seminar saw ourselves as the avant-garde of the reappraisal" (89, translation modified).[22] Michael further recounts that he and his fellow students sought to tear "open the windows and let in the air, the wind that finally whirled away the dust that society had permitted to settle over the horror of the past" and to make "sure people could breathe and see" (89). The students struggled to expose the atrocities of the Nazi period, which too many people wanted to deny or forget. Yet as Michael himself notes, if Hanna is clearly understood to have been someone who was in charge as the church burned, this tended to absolve the people in the village who also did not open the doors: "the existence of a leader exonerated the villagers; having failed to achieve rescue in the face of a fiercely led opposing force looked better than having failed to do anything when confronted by a group of confused women" (135). The daughter who testifies at the trial writes a book about her experiences in the camps, about the forced march, and about being locked in the burning church.[23] The daughter's book appears in German, which would result in the incident of the burning women becoming widely known in Germany. Had Michael felt any serious commitment to *Aufarbeitung*, he would at least have considered the broader social consequences of the circulation of an incorrect version of this notorious event. To the contrary, Michael refuses to think about how he is contributing to the myth of ordinary Germans' lack of responsibility for Nazi atrocities, how he is shutting the windows, keeping in the air, preventing the dust from whirling, permitting it to settle over the horrors of the past, rather than making sure people could breathe and see.

Let me be clear here: I am not suggesting that Michael should unhesitatingly have revealed Hanna's illiteracy to the presiding judge (German trials generally do not involve juries). Rather, I am pointing to the deleterious manner in which Michael thinks—or rather does not think—about the people and the events connected with the trial. To summarize: first, Michael does not think about the fact that his silence means that perpetrators get away with lies and receive reduced sentences. Second, he does not consider the surviving victims' right to know what happened to them. And, finally, he does not feel any concern that an atrocity in a German village is publically misrepresented. What is striking is not just that Michael's thinking is so limited during the trial, but that four decades later—looking back on his youthful self—Michael does not re-evaluate the thoughts he had at the time other than to express his feeling that it was unfair of his generation to have condemned their parents to shame: "How did I decide that he [Michael's father] too was under sentence of shame? But I did. We all condemned our parents to shame" (90).

The older Michael is critical of his generation's attitudes and activities, a self-critique that is not only limited, but also injudicious. Michael notes that his generation manifested a troubling eagerness:

> When I think about it now, I think that our eagerness to assimilate the horrors and our desire to make everyone else aware of them was in fact repulsive. The more horrible the events about which we read and heard, the more certain we became of our responsibility to enlighten and accuse. Even when the facts took our breath away, we held them up triumphantly. Look at this! (91)

Although the zealousness of Michael's generation may have been questionable, seeking to expose Nazi atrocities should hardly be regretted. In the early 1960s, many Germans remained unaware of the extent of the network of concentration and extermination camps that had existed in Europe under the Nazi regime; moreover, what had been perpetrated in the camps was rarely, if ever, discussed. The name Auschwitz was almost unknown.[24] So while the eagerness of Michael's generation may have been repulsive, exposing the atrocities was important. Even the feeling of triumph is understandable in the face of the systemic repression and denial that existed in postwar Germany for almost two decades. Furthermore, Nazi war criminals, both within and outside Germany, were not being pursued and had readily resumed or rebuilt their lives. The younger generation's eagerness definitely deserves to be questioned, but Michael's sense of "responsibility to enlighten and accuse" hardly deserves to be dismissed as "repulsive" (91).

Self-Absorption

As noted, during the trial Michael's thoughts are focused on his own perceived predicament regarding Hanna's right to self-determination. At an earlier point in the novel, however, the older Michael's train of thought regarding his time with Hanna is so self-centred it is almost implausible. In this instance of reflection, the older Michael wonders why it makes him so sad to think back to the time when he was with Hanna, although it was not a sad time for him, but one during which he was extremely happy. He poses the following questions:

Why does it make me so sad when I think back to that time? Is it yearning for past happiness—for I was happy in the weeks that followed, in which I really did work like a lunatic and passed the class, and we made love as if nothing else in the world mattered. Is it the knowledge of what came later, and that what came out afterwards had been there all along?

Why? Why does what was beautiful suddenly shatter in hindsight because it concealed dark truths? Why does the memory of years of happy marriage turn to gall when our partner is revealed to have had a lover all those years? Because such a situation makes it impossible to be happy? But we were happy! Sometimes the memory of happiness cannot stay true because it ended unhappily. Because happiness is only real if it lasts forever? Because things always end painfully if they contained pain, conscious or unconscious, all along? But what is unconscious, unrecognized pain? (35–36)

Now, the first time one reads the novel, when one does not yet know of Hanna's past, Michael's line of questioning might seem apposite.[25] But when one re-reads the novel (or if one already knows the story) Michael's questioning, and the analogies he constructs, are once again extremely disconcerting. For it makes complete sense that he would feel sad thinking back to his time with Hanna, even if he had felt happy at the time, because Hanna is now associated with horror and atrocity. In other words, one would assume that Michael's "beautiful" past is shattered because of the hideous images now linked to Hanna. (Had the movie included even a short scene of the women inside the church screaming and burning, and desperately banging on the door while the guards outside did not open them, I'm fairly sure it would have been a different movie.[26] In its downplaying of the atrocities, the movie is true to the book.)

And there is another related reason for Michael to feel sad thinking back: he must now realize that although *he* had been happy, Hanna could not have been that happy: she would have been living in an unabated state of anxiety because of her illiteracy. Indeed, later on in the novel, Michael reads about illiteracy and realizes that Hanna's inability to read and write must have rendered her constantly insecure and afraid. He states: "I knew about the helplessness in everyday activities, finding one's way or finding an address or choosing a meal in a restaurant, about how illiterates anxiously stick to prescribed patterns and familiar routines, about how much energy it takes to conceal one's inability to read and write, energy lost to actual living" (186).

But Michael does not believe he feels sad when he thinks back to his time with Hanna either because he now realizes that he had been in love with a mass murderer or because he now realizes how exhaustingly anxious Hanna must have been. Rather, Michael makes a different set of associations. Thinking back, he recalls the teenager he was then: "My arms and legs were too long, not for the suits, which my mother had let down for me, but for my own movements. My glasses were a cheap over-the-counter pair and my hair a tangled mop, no matter what I did" (36). In other words, Michael was gawky, had non-prescription glasses, and experienced perpetual bad hair days. At that time, however, he felt youthful optimism and ebullience:

> But there was so much energy in me, such belief that one day I'd be handsome and clever and superior and admired, such anticipation when I met new people and new situations. Is that what makes me feel sad? The eagerness and belief that filled me then and exacted a pledge from life that life could never fulfil? (36)

This could, indeed, be why Michael feels sad. But other people in his situation might feel sad because they cannot rid themselves of an image of women screaming as they burned alive, or because they now realize that Hanna's days must have been depleted from concealing her illiteracy. For reasons of plot, of course, Michael's early reflections can reveal neither that Hanna is a mass murderer nor that she is illiterate. But this does not make it any less disconcerting that the older Michael concludes that he feels sad *not* because of the fact that when he recollects his time with his lover he is forced to think about the atrocities she committed but simply because, probably like many older people, he no longer experiences the youthful exuberance he did then.

Near the end of the novel, Michael makes his self-preoccupation explicit. He goes to see Hanna in prison very shortly before her release and finally speaks with her about what she did. What he wonders is whether she thought of the atrocities *when she was with him*. She responds that only the dead can call her to account; she says they come to her, especially at night, and she is unable to chase them away as she was able to do before the trial. Michael's response, as he thinks about what Hanna has said, is to wonder where this leaves the living. But by "the living," he does not mean those who may have survived Hanna's selections at Auschwitz, or the mother and daughter who survived the burning church. The daughter was only an adolescent, and it is difficult to imagine (and Michael certainly does not try to do so) how she copes with memories of both the burning women and the fact that she had to spend the rest of the night and a full day hiding amongst several hundred charred corpses. These are not "the living" about whom Michael thinks:

> I accused her [Hanna], and found it both shabby and too easy, the way she had wriggled out of her guilt. Allowing no one but the dead to demand an accounting, reducing guilt and atonement to insomnia and bad feelings—where did that leave the living? But what I meant was not the living, it was me. Did I not have my own accounting to demand of her? What about me? (199–200)

Whereas Hanna does think about the surviving daughter, and leaves her her money,[27] thoughts of the actual survivors do not cross Michael's mind. Michael's focus on his own well-being to the exclusion of others is troublingly similar to the self-preoccupation of the perpetrator generation.

Michael is an upper-middle-class person who—until Hanna's situation finally hits him—has probably never thought about illiteracy (which is probably why it takes so long for it to occur to him that Hanna is illiterate). Hanna's wish to conceal her illiteracy is what led her to abandon her streetcar job, and Michael. Earlier, it had led her to leave her job at Siemens and join the SS; and subsequently it leads her to "admit"—falsely—to writing the report and being the leader of the SS guards. Hanna has a lifelong influence on Michael. After she disappears, he feels numb and never quite seems to recover. The fact that Michael's later marriage ends in divorce is attributed to his earlier relationship with Hanna. Yet never once, in all his ponderings, musings, and reflections, does Michael wonder *why* Hanna is illiterate. His lack of curiosity in this regard is stunning, especially given Hanna's unflagging influence on his life. Michael knows little about Hanna other than that she grew up in Siebenburgen (a German community in Romania) and came to Berlin when she was sixteen. Were there no schools, or not enough, in Siebenburgen? Was her family too poor to allow her to go to school? Why does she so love being read to aloud and why does she insist that Michael concentrate on his studies? Is she simply in awe of the readerly and writerly world from which she is excluded? Or did she want to go to school and was not allowed to attend? Were only boys considered worth educating? The questions would seem to go on and on. But for Michael they never begin! Never, in all his reflections, does it occur to him to wonder why Hanna is illiterate. When Michael recounts the trial, his reflections on his dilemma regarding Hanna's right to self-determination seem to exclude a concern for other people, including the victims. But by the end of the novel, we realize that Michael is not even interested in Hanna—certainly not in the Hanna before she met him.

At the end of World War Two, Germany literally lay in ruins. Many non-Jewish families had lost at least one person, and the food shortage was dire. Most Germans focused on survival and concentrated on rebuilding and trying to leave the past behind. Michael's extreme self-centredness and his lack of interest in others, including even Hanna, resembles the perpetrators, but it also resembles the self-preoccupation and the refusal to think about the past that characterized the perpetrator generation after the war.

The Reader's Aporia and Structure

Michael is, at the very least, a flawed and morally confused character, and some readers might be tempted to conclude that Michael's self-centred focus on his own "victimization," and lack of concern for victims of the Shoah, illustrates the limits of the postwar generation and its inability to face up to the past. But there is more to the novel. *The Reader* itself discourages us from thinking, and it structurally constructs Michael as a victim. As Sansom notes, Hanna's illiteracy is the novel's central conceit.[28] But it is also the novel's aporia. The novel cannot reveal the reason for Hanna's illiteracy without unravelling (just as showing the burning, screaming women would unravel the film). On the one hand, if Hanna did not learn to read and write because she was mentally challenged, or because she was told she was, then the third part of the book, in which after a few years she teaches herself to read by means of books on tape, would be implausible, if not impossible; for Hanna's accomplishment is nothing short of astounding, even if someone in prison might have a lot of time on their hands. On the other hand, if Hanna did not learn to read and write because she was not allowed to learn, then her deep shame is preposterous. For Hanna is not simply ashamed; she feels deep, overwhelming, unshakable shame—shame that overrides any shame at being regarded the leader of a group of Nazi guards responsible for a massacre. To reiterate: Hanna must believe herself at least somewhat intelligent in order to have set about learning to read *all by herself*; this means that she must have been, to some extent at least, prevented from learning. But if she was *prevented* from learning to read and write, then the fact that her shame at being illiterate overrides her shame about the atrocities she committed becomes odious—and the empathy we might otherwise have for her is undermined. In other words, the novel cannot work if we learn why Hanna is illiterate: had she been incapable of learning, the novel would be rendered implausible; had she been prevented from learning, this would undermine the novel's ability to present a somewhat sympathetic perpetrator.

Not only, then, is Michael's thinking severely limited (as well as narcissistic), but the novel itself constitutively proscribes the question of the reason for Hanna's illiteracy. Schlink has created a protagonist whose thinking is limited and whose questioning is circumscribed, but he has also written a novel that precludes any attempt to ask or even wonder about the very situation—Hanna's illiteracy—that impels the narrative. Throughout this chapter, I have focussed on analyzing Michael and not conflating this first-person narrator with the author. But here the fact that the novel intrinsically rules out the question of the origin of Hanna's illiteracy—and her extreme shame—needs to be pointed out. This aporia is constitutional, and I have not seen it discussed in the secondary literature. It is exceedingly significant that the novel itself inherently precludes thinking outside its frame, just as did the Nazis during the war and just as the perpetrator generation sought to do after the war.

In addition to structurally excluding certain questions, the novel (and not just Michael's self-understanding) positions Michael as a victim. As the war ended, Germans suffered under the massive Allied bombings, and after the war they suffered from hunger and cold in the bombed-out buildings. Many felt that they had been carried along by the National Socialists, that they had had little chance to oppose the course of destruction, and little knowledge of the extent of the evil committed by the regime. They saw themselves as victims of the Nazi *Verbrecher* (criminals). Michael, too, is a victim. When he first meets Hanna, he is underage. Hanna seems to be the one who takes control of their relationship and who consistently has the upper hand. Michael is devastated when Hanna disappears without saying a word, and even after a few years have passed, he writes: "I know that even if I had said goodbye to my memory of Hanna, I had not overcome it" (86). After Michael becomes an adult and marries, he is still unable to shake Hanna's influence:

> I could never stop comparing the way it was with Gertrud [his wife] and the way it had been with Hanna; again and again, Gertrud and I would hold each other, and I would feel something was wrong, that she was wrong, that she moved wrong and felt wrong, smelled wrong and tasted wrong. I thought I would get over it. I hoped it would go away. I wanted to be free of Hanna. But I never got over the feeling that something was wrong. (171)

Michael gets divorced, and subsequently admits to himself that in order to have a relationship with a woman, she "had to move and feel a bit like Hanna, smell and taste a bit like her for things to be good between us" (172). The relationship Hanna had with Michael when he was fifteen is not something he seems able to shake.[29] The book makes clear that Michael was and will always be a victim of Hanna.[30] Insofar as *The Reader* positions Michael as victim, and insofar as Michael barely regards himself as an agent, this parallels the way in which many people amongst the Nazi generation positioned themselves after the war: as bamboozled victims of the National Socialist regime.[31]

Finally, not only does the structure of the novel position Michael as victim—the book's style reinforces this as well. A chance encounter brings Michael (as an adolescent) together with Hanna, and a strange coincidence leads him to re-encounter her at the trial.[32] As he narrates, Michael depicts himself as someone caught up in events, subject to the many things that happen to him. The first paragraph of the book's very short concluding chapter ends with the following sentence: "Whatever I had done or not done, whatever she had done or not to me—it was the path my life had taken" (214). The novel presents Michael as swept up into his relationship with Hanna, forced to confront the fact that earlier she had committed atrocities, and unable ever to leave her influence behind. Noteworthy is that the *way* the story is told resembles the *way* the Nazi generation spoke about what had "happened" to them under the National Socialists, how they were inadvertently "carried along," subject to the events that "befell" them.

The Novel's Success and Style

Since its initial success and celebration, *The Reader* has been incisively and convincingly criticized in many ways. But the fact that it was so widely acclaimed is worth thinking about. It seems to me that much of the book's allure lies in its style. As Michael looks back and relates the events of his past, he reflects on how he felt, on his presumptuousness, his arrogance, his uncertainly, his episodes of guilt, his distance from those around him, and his helplessness. Michael does not just recount events, he reflects upon them (though in a specious way, I have argued), and these reflections seem genuine. Michael's presentation of incidents, experiences, and memories does not purport to be unambiguous. We are not told what to think; in fact, we do not have to think much, since Michael seems to be doing a lot of thinking for us. He seems to be pondering, to be wondering about things, to worry that he is retroactively reconstructing what occurred, and to put forth ideas and then retract them. Michael's contemplations and questions carry us along, and it is not unpleasant to be carried along. He explores possibility after possibility, his thoughts now taking this direction, now that—for the most part without presuming he is on the right track:

> I knew none of this then—if indeed I know any of it now and am not just making patterns in the air [mir nicht nur zusammenreime]. (14/18)

> Everything was easy; nothing weighed heavily. Perhaps that is why my bundle of memories is so small. Or do I keep it small? I wonder if my memory of happiness is even true. (86)

I thought that if the right time gets missed, if one has refused or been refused something for too long, it's too late, even if it is finally tackled with energy and received with joy. Or is there no such thing as "too late"? Is there only "late," and is "late" always better than "never"? I don't know. (187)

Subtly, the novel encourages us to content ourselves with Michael's inconclusive and ongoing reflections.

Sansom attributes the success of *The Reader* to the fact that the critics "have been mesmerised and soothed by Michael's hypnotic quibbling and querying."[33] I would agree. While lauded for the moral complexity it allegedly exhibits, *The Reader* actually lulls and sedates. Michael ponders and muses, pursuing a train of thought here, another one there. He pokes his head into all kinds of nooks and crannies. But ultimately, he does not stir up too much dust.[34] His thinking never goes too far or too deep. Michael's tale may be unsettling, but the way he tells it is quite comforting.[35] He does not just recount his being swept along; his telling sweeps us—the readers—along as well. The novel is written in such a way that we, as readers, have to shake ourselves out of our stupor to notice not only the disturbingly self-involved nature of Michael's questions, but also the narrowly restricted way in which he frames problems and issues, and the exceedingly obvious questions he declines to ask—and how well this all seems to work.

I fear that part of the success of *The Reader* may lie in the fact that it is a conciliatory work. Michael wants to reconcile himself with the past, with the Nazi generation and with Hanna, the representative of this generation. The novel insists on the complexities of the Nazi period, and seeks to reconcile us to the past precisely by complicating it. As noted, many commentators have strongly criticized Schlink's anomalous Hanna character as representative of Nazi perpetrators. Hanna is not typical. First, she is illiterate. Second, at her trial, although Hanna seeks to conceal her illiteracy, she actually tries to tell the truth, to answer the judge's questions honestly, and to reflect upon what she has done. Most former concentration camp guards, including the other characters in the novel who are on trial with Hanna, downplay their responsibility and lie when they can get away with it. Moreover, as soon as Hanna becomes literate, she begins to read about the concentration camps. Hanna is a victim of her illiteracy, of the other guards, and to some extent of the obtuse judge who sentences her. Michael is a victim of Hanna and of the events that befall him. All in all, *The Reader* is a novel about victims. Whereas many young postwar Germans found themselves in the uncomfortable position of wondering whether their parents or grandparents had committed atrocities during the era of National Socialism, this is not the case with Michael. Under the Nazis, his father planned to teach the work of Spinoza, a Jewish philosopher, and consequently lost his job. His father, too, was a victim. Perpetrators, other than Hanna, only appear in the novel as very minor, unnamed characters. *The Reader* seeks to reconcile us to the past and, concurrently, to present itself as an unorthodox work insofar as it challenges Manichean representations of this past and caricatured representations of Nazi perpetrators. The day before Hanna is about to be released from prison, she commits suicide, presumably out of a feeling of guilt. The novel concludes with Michael visiting her grave. The final sentence of *The Reader* is: "It was the first and only time I stood there [at Hanna's grave]." Ultimately, *The Reader* is not a novel that seeks to understand atrocities, but a work that wants to recount a genocidal past, bury it, and move on.

Conclusion

Decades after the war, Germans of the Nazi generation were often accused of not having wanted to know about what was happening in the camps. Michael belongs to the postwar generation, and he clearly does want to know about the camps; he even tries to learn more about them by twice going to see a camp (Struthof). But there is much Michael does not want to know, many things about which he does not seem to want to think. One of these is the influence of the previous generation on his own, even though *The Reader* is concerned precisely with intergenerational relations. And generations tend to hand things down: one generation passes things on to the next, either explicitly or implicitly. This is not rocket science, as the saying goes. Michael, then, seems particularly thoughtless to me insofar as he does not wonder what the prior generation might have passed on to him and his contemporaries. Michael feels he was deeply in love with Hanna, and he never gets over her. One would presume it would occur to him to wonder what he might have picked up, consciously or unconsciously, from her and from her generation. One would expect Michael to wonder what ideas, attitudes, or orientations he might have assimilated. But Michael chooses not to think about this, as he chooses not to think about so many other things. It is difficult to avoid wondering if what Michael *did* pick up from the prior generation is precisely the inability or refusal to reflect.

Neither Michael nor Hanna are, in my view, especially empathetic characters. But perhaps *The Reader* can most charitably be interpreted as being about empathy and about how someone who has committed the most horrible atrocities might be someone with whom one might empathize in some way. One can conjecture that Schlink, and those who applaud the book, feel that lack of empathy was a defining characteristic of the Nazis, and that encouraging empathy and compassion is a good antidote. Specifically, the novel seems to want to address a dilemma experienced by many young Germans of the postwar generation: the fact that one might care deeply about someone whom one subsequently learns has been guilty of things one does not want to contemplate. But not wanting to contemplate is exactly the problem. If *The Reader*'s central message is that we should not judge, or should not judge too quickly or harshly, the novel also encourages us not to think, and not to think too deeply or arduously—certainly not about the past and our relation to it. And this does not at all bode well for the future.

The Reader teaches us little about the Shoah, I have argued, and even less about those who lived under, permitted, or participated in the atrocities of the Nazi regime. What the novel does teach us is the importance of thinking about how we think about atrocities. Few countries, if any, have a history that does not involve some form of genocide, be it a genocide of peoples or cultures. If we are trying to understand atrocities from our past, it is critical that we think about the fact that our ideas—or aspects of our ideas, even in partial or fractional form—may stem from this past and continue into our present. We may have assimilated certain attitudes, orientations, or assumptions from the time of the atrocities. It is absolutely crucial that we think about this. We need to consider how our thinking and our representations might—in whatever small ways—resemble the thinking of those who enacted or made possible the atrocities. We need to reflect upon the ways in which our thinking might be limited and restricted. We need to ask questions about what questions we might not be asking. It is not enough to reflect upon and analyze atrocities and instances of genocide. It is imperative that we think about the continuity between our own lack or limited thought and the thinking of that time period. What *The Reader* (unthinkingly) teaches us is that remembering and representing genocide are hardly enough; we need to think about the ways in which we think about our genocidal past.

NOTES

1   Samuel Beckett, *Endgame* (New York: Grove, 1958), 38.

2   Theodor W. Adorno, *Reflexionen zur Klassentheorie. GS 8, Soziologische Schriften I* (Frankfurt: Suhrkamp, 2003), 376.

3   Hannah Arendt, *Eichmann in Jerusalem: A Report on the Banality of Evil* (London: Penguin, 1967).

4   See also Donna Mounsef's critique of Arendt's presentation of Eichmann's "thought-lessness" at the beginning of her chapter in this volume. Mounsef draws on Zizek's appropriation of Lacan to argue that there is always an element of *jouissance* in inflicting suffering, including bureaucratically imposed suffering and humiliation.

5   Bettina Stangneth, *Eichmann Before Jerusalem: The Unexamined Life of a Mass Murder-er*, trans. Ruth Martin (New York: Knopf, 2014), 283ff. Stangneth concludes the section as follows: "It is temptingly easy to dismiss his [Eichmann's] ramblings; like all dogma, his is ultimately just bad philosophy. But it is a disturbing fact: for Eichmann the logic of these terrible constructs provided stability and inner fortitude. To unbalance one of the most effective mass murderers in history, the ability to think in itself was not enough" (293).

6   Christopher Browning, *Ordinary Men: Reserve Police Battalion 101 and the Final Solution in Poland* (New York: HarperCollins, 1993).

7   See Ursula R. Mahlendorf, "Trauma Narrated, Read and (Mis)understood: Bernhard Schlink's 'The Reader': '…irrevocably complicit in their crimes,' " *Monatshefte* 95, no. 3 (2003): 458–481; quote from 459. The appeal of the novel is something I return to at the end of this article.

8   See Cynthia Ozick, "The Rights of History and the Rights of Imagination," *Commentary*, 1 March 1999, 22–27; Ian Sansom, "Doubts about the Reader," *Salmagundi* 124/125 (1999): 3–16; William Collins Donahue, "Illusions of Subtlety: Bernhard Schlink's *Der Vorleser* and The Moral Limits of Holocaust Fiction," *German Life and Letters* 54, no. 1 (2001): 60–81. Sansom recoils: "If the first part of the book was slightly queasy-making, the second part is hugely disturbing" (See "Doubts," 9). Katharina Hall points out, however, that no matter how critical academics are of the book, the demands of "readabili-ty" and conventions of the romance novel shape the general readership's interpretation of the work, just as conventions of hard-boiled detective novels shape interpretations of Schlink's earlier *Selbs Justiz* (written with Walter Popp), which also deals with the Nazi past. Hall draws on Iser's and especially Eco's reception theories. See Katharina Hall, "The Author, the Novel, the Reader and the Perils of 'Neue Lesbarkeit': A Comparative Analysis of Bernhard Schlink's *Selbs Justiz* and *Der Vorleser*," *German Life and Letters* 49, no. 3 (July 2006): 446–467.

9   An exceedingly problematic character, Hanna has been discussed and criticized by many commentators, especially Jane Allison, Bill Niven, and William Collins Donahue. See Allison, "The Third Victim in Bernhard Schlink's *Der Vorleser*," *The Germanic*

Review: Literature, Culture, Theory 81, no. 2 (2006): 163–178; Niven, "Bernhard Schlink's 'Der Vorleser' and the Problem of Shame," *The Modern Language Review* 98, no. 2 (2003): 318–396; Donahue, *Holocaust as Fiction: Bernhard Schlink's "Nazi" Novels and Their Films* (New York: Palgrave, 2010). Donahue states in his introduction that the very fraught figure from *The Reader*, Hanna Schmitz, makes an appearance in almost every chapter of his study (18).

10   Mahlendorf ("Trauma Narrated") thoroughly and convincingly shows the many ways in which Michael's perspective is unreliable. Niven ("Shame"), Helmut Schmitz, and Daniel Reynolds also emphasize Michael as an unreliable narrator, especially regarding Hanna. See Schmitz "Malen Nach Zahlen? Bernhard Schlinks *Der Vorleser* und die Unfähigkeit zu Trauern," *German Life and Letters* 55, no. 3 (July 2002): 296–311 and *On Their Own Terms: The Legacy of National Socialism in Post-1990 German Fiction* (Birmingham: University of Birmingham Press, 2004); and Reynolds "Bernhard Schlink's *Der Vorleser*," *Seminar* 39, no. 3 (2003): 238–256.

11   Schmitz argues that "the novel is structured by a chain of questions that for the most part remain unanswered, because Schlink's protagonist is not capable of directing them to the sole person who would be able to answer them" [Der Roman ist strukturiert von einer Kette von Fragen, die in ihrer Mehrzahl unbeantwortet bleiben, weil Schlinks Protagonist sie nicht an die Person zu richten vermag, die allein sie beantworten könnte] ("Malen Nach Zahlen?," 4). I agree, but I also think that Michael neglects to ask certain questions, questions that should be ineluctable to someone concerned with the relationship between his own and the Nazi generation.

12   Mahlendorf, Niven, and Schmitz all commend the novel for showing how the Nazi generation's behaviour harmed the postwar generation, especially in terms of the latter generation's limited ability to emphasize with suffering. Mahlendorf demonstrates that the way in which the postwar generation was subject to the power abuses and silence of the perpetrator generation led to a traumatization entailing emotional denial and an inability to empathize with the victims. She is rightly concerned with the resulting "blunting of sensitivity" (See "Trauma Narrated," 477). Niven regards the novel as demonstrating the postwar generation's "emotional dependency" on the previous generation (See "Shame," 389). Schmitz considers the novel to portray Michael's inability to emphasize with the victims of the Nazis. He sees Michael as an almost archetypal instance of what the psychoanalysts Alexander and Margarete Mitscherlich depict as an "inability to mourn" in postwar German society. Michael may have difficulty empathizing and difficulty mourning, but he also has difficulty thinking. Schmitz refers to "Michael's troubled and reflective mind" (*On Their Own Terms*, 71), but although Michael's mind is indeed troubled, in my view it is not sufficiently reflective. Michael's lack of, or limited, reflection may of course be connected with his emotional state, but this limited thinking needs to be noted.

13   Bernhard Schlink, *The Reader*, trans. Carol Brown Janeway (New York: Vintage, 1997), 168 (hereafter cited in text) / *Der Vorleser* (Zurich: Diogenes, 1995).

14   It is unclear to me why Michael has to use any analogy with his father. He could simply tell his father that he has learned that the defendant is illiterate (without mentioning their earlier sexual relationship), and discuss the situation and whether he should reveal this information to the judge. The father, with whom the children have to make appointments, is completely unlikely to be inquisitive about Michael's personal life.

15   Although, in the early 1960s, someone might have been ashamed to be gay, and in Germany to be left-handed, the older Michael, looking back decades later, should

question such oppressive norms, especially since this lack of tolerance echoes that of the Nazi period.

16   As Martin Swales states: "the key junctures in the story-line have all to do with shame" and the narration begins with Michael's shame about his illness (11). See "Sex, Shame, and Guilt: Reflections on Bernhard Schlink's *Der Vorleser* (*The Reader*) and J. M. Coetzee's *Disgrace.*" *Journal of European Studies* 33, no. 1 (March 2003): 7–22.

17   Swales makes the important distinction between shame and guilt ("Shame," 10). I would also want to distinguish shame and embarrassment.

18   Michael never clarifies and does not seem interested in how many women died – whether it was two hundred, three hundred or five hundred. It is unlikely that any court would accuse defendants of being responsible for deaths, but leave the number vague. (The film, if I recall, refers to three hundred.) Michael becomes a lawyer (as was Schlink), so what can be the purpose of the imprecise and implausible "several hundred" (mehrere hundert) other than to suggest that it does not really matter to Michael or postwar Germans how many Jews died.

19   Donahue, "Illusions of Subtlety," 79.

20   The final chapter of the book makes clear that it is feelings of guilt in relation to Hanna that are most significant for him. The final chapter begins: "All this happened ten years ago. In the first few years after Hanna's death, I was tormented by the old questions of whether I had denied and betrayed her" (214).

21   Allison shows the quite numerous ways in which the novel positions Hanna in order to favourably and sympathetically contrast Hanna with her surviving Jewish victim. Sheridan focuses on how Hanna's poverty, in the novel and especially the film, is contrasted with the surviving daughter's wealth in a way that garners sympathy for Hanna and draws on certain anti-Semitic stereotypes.

22   Janeway's English translation is: "Exploration! Exploring the past! We students in the camps seminar considered ourselves radical explorers." The original German is: "Aufarbeitung! Aufarbeitung der Vergangenheit! Wir Studenten des Seminars sahen uns als Avantgarde der Aufarbeitung" (87).

23   Here I would conjecture that Schlink was influenced by Ruth Klüger's autobiographical *Weiter Leben: Eine Jugend* (Munich: dtv, 1994). Klüger's book contains no account of a burning church but Michael's description of the tone of the book that was written by the daughter (who like Klüger was pubescent at Auschwitz) and Schlink having his mother and daughter characters survive because the mother did the "right thing for the wrong reasons" (122) seems to have been drawn from Klüger's *Weiter Leben*. Ruth Sheridan points out that the daughter's statement in the film ("Nothing good comes out of the camps") "appears to be lifted straight from the pages of Ruth Klüger's memoir." See Sheridan, "Sympathy with the Perpetrators: Examining the Appropriation of Schlink's 'Der Vorleser' in the Film 'The Reader'," *The Australian Journal of Jewish Studies* 27 (2013): 131.

24   This lack of awareness of Auschwitz, and the extent of the torture and exterminations that took place there, is presented in the film *Labyrinth of Lies* (German: *Im Labyrinth des Schweigens*—literally "In the Labyrinth of Silence") that fictionally portrays the difficulties and opposition state prosecutors experienced in their quest to bring Auschwitz workers to trial in the early 1960s. *Labyrinth of Lies*, directed by Giulio Ricciarelli (Universal 2014; Sony Home Video, 2016), DVD.

25 As Sansom notes: "Michael's orgies of questioning do become tiresome, and many of his questions are simply trite, or simply self-absorbed, or obvious, irrelevant, or uninteresting (Why does what was beautiful suddenly shatter ...)" ("Doubts," 12–13).

26 The striking images from the movie are the steamy sex scenes at the beginning with an exceedingly attractive Hanna (Kate Winslet); as a result, the most shocking scene for the audience is when the middle-aged Michael re-encounters Hanna and sees an old woman.

27 As Ann Parry notes, Hanna's gesture reveals that "even at this late stage" (i.e., after Hanna has read accounts written by Holocaust survivors) Hanna somehow "thought that a gift could be a trade-off that would somehow mitigate that 'zero moment' that occurred when she and those with her refused to release the Jewish women from the burning church and save their lives." See Ann Parry, "The caesura of the Holocaust in Martin Amis's *Time's Arrow* and Bernhard Schlink's *The Reader*," *Journal of European Studies* 29, no. 3 (Sept 1999): 261.

28 Sansom states: "The book's really big and important confusion is the central conceit of Hanna's illiteracy, which is presumably supposed to represent but which in fact exaggerates and caricatures her lack of moral intelligence. Because it is something that can be taught and easily remedied, it both diminishes the seriousness of Hanna's failings and holds out the promise of improvement and perfectibility" ("Doubts,"14).

29 Joseph Metz makes a thorough and convincing argument for the many ways in which fascism is coded as feminine throughout the novel and how that femininity is destructive: "the hapless male protagonist is duped and undone by Hanna and her sexuality, before which he is helpless and to which he systematically loses his moral subjecthood." See Metz, " 'Truth is a Woman': Post-Holocaust Narrative, Postmodernism, and the Gender of Fascism in Bernhard Schlink's *Der Vorleser*," *German Quarterly* 77, no. 3 (Summer 2004): 305. Schmitz—less critically—also regards Michael as an injured party. He states that Michael says he has made peace with his and Hanna's story, but that "this peace does not consist of a closure in which the past is 'aufgehoben' (sublated) in the Hegelian sense, rather it consists of an acceptance of the failed life which is still determined by the injuries of youth." See Schmitz, *On Their Own Terms*, 77.

30 When Michael, as an older man, meets up with the surviving daughter in New York, the daughter refers to Hanna's "brutality" ("Was that woman ever brutal," 211—my translation [Was ist diese Frau brutal gewesen, 202]). In *Holocaust as Fiction*, Donahue points out:

> What she means, we soon discover, is not Hanna's treatment of the inmates trapped in the burning church, or her behaviour as camp guard, or even what she did (or failed to do) on the death march, as one might expect; rather, the survivor is referring to the sexual and emotional abuse that the young [Michael] Berg endured during the mismatched love affair. ... This validation of Berg as victim, bestowed at this privileged moment in the novel by the sole Jewish survivor, may finally explain why Hanna's war crimes have never been clearly delineated: they would have distracted from her victimization of Berg." (129)

Donahue further points out that the surviving daughter asks Michael whether he thought Hanna realized what she had done to him: "In the novel as well as in the film, this amounts to a conferral of victim status from an unimpeachable source." See Donahue, *Holocaust as Fiction*, 180.

31   Although he makes a quite different argument, John E. Mackinnon argues that *The Reader* involves a "studied effort to erode the distinctions between guilty and innocent, between perpetrators and victims" (16), ending his article—appropriately I feel—with the word "insidious." See Mackinnon, "Crime, Compassion, and the Reader," *Philosophy and Literature* 27 (2003): 1–20; quote from 16. See also Omar Bartov's "Germany as Victim," *New German Critique* 80, Special Issue on the Holocaust (Spring–Summer 2000): 29–40. Richard Crownshaw, to the contrary, argues that Schlink attempts to intervene critically in the binary thinking that marked German memory of perpetrators and victims in both the 1960s and 1990s. See Crownshaw, "Reading the Perpetrator: Bernhard Schlink's *Der Vorleser (The Reader)* and *Die Heimkehr (Homecoming)*," in *The Afterlife of Holocaust Memory in Contemporary Literature and Culture* (London: Palgrave McMillan, 2010), 145–181.

32   As Carola Jensen recently reminded me, a novel that centres around former Nazis on trial in a German court distracts from the fact that the vast majority of Nazis were never even tried. Not only were many able to emigrate shortly after the war, but others simply remained in Germany without legal consequences. In 2014, the German justice system finally sought (for the most part, unsuccessfully) to prosecute still living former SS guards from Auschwitz, all of whom were eighty-eight or older and generally unfit to stand trial. In other words, almost seventy years after the end of war, there seemed to be a concerted attempt to "catch up," visibly to make up for all the trials that never took place. An article in *Der Spiegel* by Klaus Wiegrefe, "The Auschwitz Files: Why the Last SS Guards Will Go Unpunished," quotes the historian Andreas Eichmüller: "of the 6,500 members of the SS who served in Auschwitz and survived the war, only 29 were convicted in West Germany and reunified Germany, while about 20 were convicted in East Germany." See Wiegrefe, "The Auschwitz Files: Why the Last SS Guards Will Go Unpunished," *Der Spiegel*, 28 August 2014, 1.

Cynthia Ozick protests that "the plot of Schlink's narrative turns not on the literacy that was overwhelmingly typical of Germany, but rather on an anomalous case of illiteracy, which the novel itself recognizes as freakish" (See Ozick, "The Rights of History vs Imagination" 26–27). Ozick objects to this violation of the "right of history" by the alleged "right of the imagination." Although students who now learn about the Shoah through *The Reader* will likely realize that illiteracy was atypical, or presume it is a metaphor in the novel, they might not know just how extremely rare were trials (not to mention convictions) of former Nazis in postwar Germany. Hence, the "right of history" that is violated by the "right of imagination" in the novel might be less the "freakish" case of illiteracy that it portrays than the overall impression it leaves: that in the 1960s former Nazis were finally legally pursued in Germany. Such an impression could easily have been corrected by Michael, who is a lawyer and works as a legal researcher. During the trial, Michael does reflect on the question of what the second generation should do with the knowledge of the horrors of the extermination of the Jews, and he mentions the lack of convictions (102), but this fact is not emphasized, and the courtroom drama is centre stage in the novel (and movie). Moreover, the plot of Schlink's novel turns not on the denial of culpability that was overwhelmingly typical of perpetrators, but rather on an anomalous case of a Nazi perpetrator who, with the one exception, seeks to speak the truth during her trial.

In his book, *Ordinary Men*, Christopher Browning states that Reserve Police Battalion 101 "participated in the direct shooting deaths of at least 38,000 Jews" (142) and that overall, for this "battalion of less than 500 men, the ultimate body count was at 83,000 Jews" (142). Browning concludes his chapter "Aftermath" with the following paragraph: "The interrogations of 210 men from Reserve Police Battalion 101 remain in the archives of the Office of the State Prosecutor in Hamburg. They constitute the prime source for this study. It is hoped that they will serve history better than they have served justice" (146). The last chapter of Wendy Lower's book, *Hitler's Furies: German Women in the Nazi Killing Fields*, is titled "What Happened to Them?" Here Lower recounts that very few of the women who contributed to, or directly participated in, the genocide in the east were prosecuted, and "even fewer were judged and convicted" (196). The final two sentences of the chapter are: "What happened to them? The short answer is that most got away with murder" (197). See Wendy Lower *Hitler's Furies: German Women in the Nazi Killing Fields* (London: Chatto & Windus, 2013).

Of course, one of Schlink's points seems to be that courts and legal proceedings are not to be equated with justice. But in *The Reader* the court is presented as actively interested in pursuing justice for the victims, which is misleading if not dishonest. See Lower's *Hitler's Furies*, 167ff.

33   Sansom, "Doubts," 14.

34   Schmitz writes: "Schlink's book and its version of *Vergangenheitsbewältigung* without closure, peace without appeasement, is a further indication of a gradual shift towards an ownership of the heritage of National Socialism that is aware of its inherent problems and ruptures" (See Schmitz, *On Their Own Terms*, 78). My argument has been that the novel *seems* to eschew closure and appeasement, but actually serves to appease by closing itself off from all too many considerations. It excludes ownership (assuming that there could be such a thing) of the heritage of National Socialism by not thinking about what might have been inherited. Hall notes that while both *The Reader* and *Selbs Justiz* (Schlink's earlier co-written mystery) "challenge their readers to consider genuinely difficult questions about guilt and moral accountability in relation to the Holocaust, they also close these questions down." See Hall, "The Author, the Novel, the Reader," 449.

35   In choosing which books to read aloud to Hanna, Michael states: "I do not ever re-member asking myself whether I should go beyond Kafka, Frisch, Johnson, Bachmann, and Lenz, and read experimental literature, literature in which I do not recognize the story or like any of the characters" (183). One's first response might be: What Kafka did Michael read wherein he recognized the story and liked the characters? One's second response might be to realize that this is probably the kind of account Michael himself is seeking to write: one in which we recognize the story and like the characters. But a recognizable story with likeable characters does not seem especially appropriate to the Shoah, even if one's focus is the relationship of the postwar generation to the war generation.

10

Atrocity, Banality, and *Jouissance* in Performance

Donia Mounsef

The Banality of Evil in Performance

In *Eichmann in Jerusalem: A Report on the Banality of Evil*, Hannah Arendt argued that atrocities are committed by ordinary people who are victims of neither perversion nor monstrosity. For Arendt, reporting on Otto Adolf Eichmann's trial from Jerusalem in 1961, evil is the result of two systems: the first is a system that commits atrocities by merely diverting the attention of its participants onto bureaucratic concerns; the second is a system that fails to accomplish its goals by disconnecting its participants from the principles of the institutions they are serving. Eichmann, according to Arendt, "was not stupid. It was sheer thoughtlessness … that predisposed him to become one of the greatest criminals of that period. And if this is 'banal' and even funny, if with the best will in the world one cannot extract any diabolical or demonic profundity from Eichmann, that is still far from calling it commonplace."[1] This, in essence, is "the banality of evil"—that atrocities can be committed by ordinary people who are "neither demonic nor monstrous." In a lecture Arendt gave ten years after the Eichmann trial, she asserted that large-scale evil deeds—"which could not be traced to any particularity of wickedness, pathology, or ideological conviction in the doer"—were perhaps the result of extraordinary shallowness.[2]

It would have been more "comforting indeed to believe that Eichmann was a monster" writes Arendt.[3] But the problem with evildoers like Eichmann is precisely

> that so many were like him, and that the many were neither perverted nor sadistic, that they were, and still are terribly and terrifyingly normal. From the viewpoint of our legal institutions and of our moral standards of judgment, this normality was much more terrifying than all the atrocities put together, for it implied ... that this new type of criminal, who is in actual fact *hostis generis humani*, commits his crimes under circumstances that make it well-nigh impossible for him to know or to feel that he is doing wrong.[4]

What became evident in the Eichmann trial is that the perpetrator followed ordinances and rules within the confines of the law, demonstrating that there is a certain blind obedience governing the actions of people like Eichmann, who follow bureaucratic rules to the teeth but fail to reflect on the content of such arbitrary rules.

Arendt's position on Eichmann is frequently criticized for failing to account for the evil that is committed with full knowledge and intent, or as a blatant disregard for ethics. Most critical positions on Arendt's rendering of the Eichmann trial argue that she trivialized the man's fanatical and radical anti-Semitism by ascertaining that evil has no roots, that it is never "radical, that it is only extreme, and that it possesses neither depth nor any demonic dimension. It can overgrow and lay waste the whole world precisely because it spreads like a fungus on the surface. ... That is its 'banality.' Only the good has depth and can be radical."[5] For Arendt, it is unequivocally "sheer thoughtlessness—something by no means identical with stupidity—that predisposed [Eichmann] to become one of the greatest criminals of that period."[6]

Other critics, such as Slavoj Žižek in *The Plague of Fantasies*, have pointed out different blind spots in Arendt's position: that *jouissance* makes clear the inadequacy of the "banality of evil." From the French, *jouissance* is contrasted with pleasure as a form of transgressive enjoyment combined with a sense of loss. Using Lacan's notion of the master's enjoyment in inflicting pain that structures the relationship of domination, Žižek contends that, beyond its banality, evil is a function of an "imaginary screen" that maintains distance with the victim and the horror inflicted. The "imaginary screen" is the self-delusion, the story that glosses over the real motivation for becoming an agent of atrocity. For example, the Nazi guards hide behind an imaginary screen by telling themselves that they are "civilized Germans" who are doing a "necessary job" and following orders thoroughly while drawing secret enjoyment or sadistic *jouissance* from the bureaucratic violence they are committing. In other words, political subjects are allowed "inherent transgressions" sanctioned by the system to produce this secret *jouissance*. For Žižek, in order to understand the way executioners carry out atrocities without the slightest indignation, we have to supplement the purely *symbolic* bureaucratic logic involved in the notion of the "banality of evil" with these two other components: the *imaginary* screen of satisfactions and myths "which enable the subjects to maintain a distance towards (and thus to 'neutralize') the horrors they are involved in and the knowledge they have about them," and "the *real* of the perverse (sadistic) *jouissance* in what they were doing (torturing, killing, dismembering bodies)."[7] This very neutralization of the crime, according to Žižek, is precisely what makes it "ambiguous in its libidinal impact," and thus morbidly enjoyable since

on the one hand, it enabled (some of) the participants to neutralize the horror and take it as "just another job"; on the other, the basic lesson of the perverse ritual ... was in itself a source of an additional *jouissance* (does it not provide an additional kick if one performs the killing as a complicated administrative-criminal operation? Is it not more satisfying to torture prisoners as part of some orderly procedure—say, the meaningless "morning exercises" which served only to torment them—didn't it give another "kick" to the guards' satisfaction when they were inflicting pain on their victims not only by directly beating them up but in the guise of an activity officially destined to maintain their health?). ... One cannot claim that [the Nazi guards] were grey, dispassionate bureaucrats blindly following orders in accordance with the German authoritarian tradition of unconditional obedience: numerous testimonies bear witness to the *excess of enjoyment* of "unnecessary" supplementary inflicting of pain or humiliation. ... One cannot claim that the executioners were a bunch of crazy

fanatics oblivious of even the most elementary moral norms. ...
One cannot claim that they were terrorized into submission, since
any refusal to execute an order would be severely punished: before
doing any "dirty work," members of the police unit were regularly
asked if they were able to do it, and those who refused were excused without punishment.[8]

It is this very "libidinal impact" that makes representations of atrocities
highly problematic, as artistic, creative, and fictional works often risk
trivializing, aestheticizing, or sensationalizing the atrocity they represent.
Adrienne Rich underlined this same contradiction by arguing in favour
of art as a necessary critique of totalizing systems in "Legislators of the
World," an article she wrote for the *Guardian* in 2006:

Poetry has been charged with "aestheticizing," thus being complicit in the violent realities of power. ... If to "aestheticize" is to glide
across brutality and cruelty, treat them merely as dramatic occa-
sions for the artist rather than structures of power to be described
and dismantled—much hangs on that word "merely". ... We can
also define the "aesthetic," not as a privileged and sequestered rendering of human suffering, but as news of an awareness, a resistance, which totalizing systems want to quell: art reaching into us
for what's still passionate, still unintimidated, still unquenched.[9]

There is an undeniable disjunction between art, politics, violence, and
jouissance that reframes the binary distinction between "ethicism" (the
notion that art is guided by ethical concerns) and aestheticism (the notion that art and ethics belong to autonomous spheres). If perpetrators
of atrocities can hide behind an "imaginary screen," so can audiences of
atrocity conceal themselves behind the safety of the fourth wall. Can art
represent atrocity without being complicit in the structures of power that
it purports to critique?

After tracing a brief history of violence in performance, this chapter
will interrogate the way recent theatrical representations have challenged
binary configurations of good and evil, and problematized simplistic regimes of "us" and "them," giving shape to Arendt's view that evil is as ordinary as it is banal all the while embodying Žižek's "libidinal impact"

of such representations. Three examples of recent artistic representations of atrocities will be examined: a play by Canadian playwright Judith Thompson, *Palace of the End* (2007), and multimedia performances by the Iraqi-American performance artist Wafaa Bilal, *Shoot an Iraqi* (2007), and *... and Counting* (2010). These plays and performances question the representation of violence and the violence of representation by arguing that performance does not construct the real violence or reconstruct it for the audience—on the contrary, it estranges it, not unlike Brechtian alienation, revealing an exchange that is both realist and anti-realist, artistic representation and reproduction of actuality, spectacle and mimesis.

Spectacular Atrocity

How can theatre and performance, in their intimate and contained settings, speak about atrocities, and other acts committed on a large scale, with a complex set of actors, victims, and perpetrators? Unlike representations of other major historical traumas, atrocities and genocide are not simply reproduced, nor are they reproducible on stage for a variety of reasons. Theatre has, for the most part, subscribed to a certain sense of decorum (propriety, or what the French call *bienséance*) when it comes to representing extreme violence. The rule of good taste, as it has been known, governs what is allowed on stage and what shall remain off stage. In general, extreme violence was not depicted in front of an audience for a good part of theatre history even though violated bodies found their way into ancient Greek theatre, but they had to be moved off stage using the *ekkyklema*, or the wheeled platform, to conceal their provocative horror. Nevertheless, ancient Romans introduced blood spectacles and gladiator fights depicting the live slaughter of humans for the entertainment of the elite. Similarly, medieval drama and passion plays showed martyrdom, sacrifice, and morbid mutilations as part of the action. Even Shakespeare's theatre did not avoid some gory stage violence. Except in seventeenth-century neoclassical France, the rule of good taste did not categorically prohibit the showing of extreme violence, which became the hallmark of the modern theatre. Whereas the early twentieth century showed a moderate amount of violence on stage—acting mostly as a contemplation of its consequences in the theatre of Bertolt Brecht or Samuel Beckett, for example—the theatre of the late twentieth century and early twenty-first century, influenced by television and media, exploited a more graphic depiction of violence.

What became known in the 1990s as "in-yer-face" theatre (as per Aleks Sierz's term) was part of a long tradition of theatre of provocation, which is most broadly defined as a theatre that aims at shocking, provoking, and offending an audience. Like other forms of provocation theatre, what in Britain became known as the New Brutalist movement[10] dominated the London scene of the 1990s with daringly graphic representation of violence as part and parcel of the theatrical avant-garde. New Brutalists such as Sarah Kane, Anthony Neilson, Naomi Wallace, David Eldridge, Martin McDonagh, and Mark Ravenhill pushed the limits of what is acceptable on stage, multiplying physical and verbal violence, mutilated bodies, horrific tortures, and gory scenes, and frequently offending their audiences with an extremely gruesome and unapologetic cruelty. Sarah Kane's *Blasted* (1995), which coincided with the aftermath of the Rwandan genocide, is often considered the quintessence of the New Brutalist movement. These violent and offensive acts changed the way we experience or "consume" staged violence. They aimed not at creating new scenes of gore, as nothing could shock an audience accustomed to filmic and mediatized violence, but at breaking the codes of how we see and experience that brutality.

Despite the ubiquitous rule of good taste, from Aeschylus to McDonagh, the theatre has a long tradition of terrifying acts of physical aggression, murder, dismemberment, even cannibalism. The difference is that in the late twentieth century, instead of following the classical rule of *bienséance*, playwrights represented the violence with either extreme realism or extreme stylization combined with an autobiographical impulse. For example, one cannot dissociate Sarah Kane's *Psychosis 4.48* from the playwright's relationship to self-harm, and the severe depression that lead to her suicide in 1999. Nevertheless, as violent and as horrifically real as the New Brutalist aesthetic was, there is a distancing effect at play—not in the Brechtian sense of distance for critical awareness—but in the sense of a numbing distance.

If stages in the 1990s were littered with corpses, rape, murder, blood, and bones it was perhaps a way to express ideological disillusionment after the collapse of the Soviet Union, the fall of the Berlin Wall, and the end of the binary opposition between the Eastern and the Western Blocs, while the international will to stop mass atrocities (from Rwanda to Somalia to

Kosovo to Bosnia) was being challenged. With the end of the Cold War and the disappearance of a clearly defined ideological Other, theatre turned violently inward, where the body became the site of a real and imagined violence packaged in realist, surrealist, or farcical overtones.

Yet, as in any representation of symbolic violence, the audience will always demand more, making the need for excess at best tedious and at worst ethically problematic. What would the logical evolution from extreme "represented" violence be if not "presented" violence or the unacceptable terrain of snuff, where "actors" (not characters) are actually tortured and subjected to extreme violence? Is there a danger of rendering an audience immune to such violence to the point that it may identify not with the victim but with the perpetrator? How do we control, if that is even possible, the slippery slope of representation and identification with atrocity in live performance? I am not sure if these questions are on the minds of most playwrights when they are writing extremely violent and gory scenes, but they are likely on the minds of audience members leaving the theatre who may feel guilty, angry, or simply offended for having willingly or unwillingly, consensually or non-consensually, participated in brutally orgiastic violence.

And yet, the mass dissemination and representation of atrocities continued past 9/11 and into the War on Terror with the return to spectacular violence exposed in the massive distribution of the images of the American prison scandal at Abu Ghraib.[11] Beyond their political or military significance, the Abu Ghraib photographs performed a certain colonial nostalgia for a fetishistic representation or desire to subjugate otherness through the *mise en scène* of a soft-core pornographic performance meant to endow the director/soldier/voyeur with a "screen" of superiority over the dangerous "subhuman" Other. Spectacular atrocities such as the Abu Ghraib prison scandal (and the continued fallout of torture scandals revealed in massive cable leaks) or the highly stylized ISIS beheading videos put an end to Michel Foucault's "age of sobriety" in punishment and brought back to the forefront questions of the representation and representability of violence on a large scale. It is perhaps because atrocities in the global era have morphed into messy crises made even messier by what Michael Mann called "the dark side of democracy," and because democratic ideals convert *demos* into *ethnos*, we are witnessing the rise of "organic nationalism" that only helps promote the cleansing of minorities. Consequently, representations of these atrocities have become problematic: no longer is it important to stage these events as a reminder of our struggle to "remain human," as Christian Biet argued when he wrote that representations of the Holocaust were necessary "to lead the audience to a humanistic and universal understanding of the difficulty every human must face in the struggle to remain human."[12] But beyond that need to remain human, violent history is un-representable because it destroys the very foundation of language we need to represent it. In effect, it may only be possible to represent history in an artistic rendering. As Shoshana Felman and Dori Laub pointed out in *Testimony: Crises in Witnessing*, "art alone can live up to the task of contemporary thinking and of meeting the incredible demands of suffering, of politics and of contemporary consciousness, and yet escape the subtly omnipresent and the almost unavoidable cultural betrayal both of history and of the victims."[13]

"Between the Spectacular and the Embodied"

In their book, *Violence Performed*, Patrick Anderson and Jisha Menon suggest that "violence acquires its immense significance in a delicate pivot between the spectacular and the embodied."[14] This delicate pivot is what brings the public to convene around scenes of mass atrocity, as Mark Seltzer observed in his classic study of trauma and wound culture. According to Seltzer, the pathological public sphere functions as a form of "convening of the public around scenes of violence," with a "fascination with torn and opened bodies and torn and opened persons, the collective gathering around shock, trauma and the wound."[15] As fascinated as we are by torn bodies, we continue to grapple with their representability in art and the paradox of the impossibility of witnessing. Felman and Laub observed judiciously that a witness is required "when historical accuracy is in doubt and when both the truth and its supporting elements of evidence are called into question."[16] Conversely, writing on Arendt's Eichmann, Felman warns of the danger of dramatizing the struggle between law and pathology, and the surfacing of a "juridical unconscious" during trials that attempt to give a voice to victims of trauma. She maintains that a pattern "emerges in which the trial, while it tries to put an end to trauma, inadvertently performs an acting out of it. Unknowingly, the trial thus repeats the trauma, reenacts its structures."[17] There is, however, a contradictory process at play in representing atrocities: the compulsion to speak and make the trauma visible and the pressure to remain silent in the face of one's inability to articulate a truthful representation of the experience. As Felman observed brilliantly: "testimony does not simply tell *about* the impossibility of telling: it dramatizes it—*enacts it*—through its own lapse into coma and its own collapse into silence."[18] Theatre is the site of this problematic dramatization between the experience, the understanding, the re-enactment, and the recollection.

The Spectacular

In Judith Thompson's 2007 play, *Palace of the End,* the first of a three-part monologue titled "My Pyramids" is told from the perspective of the female soldier, Lynndie England, who appeared in many of the Abu Ghraib photographs gleefully committing acts of atrocity and torture, and later becoming the scapegoat for the entire debacle. An earlier incarnation of the play, from 2005, showcased a single monologue entitled "My Pyramids," and was then expanded into three monologues with the addition of "Harrowdown Hill" and "Instruments of Yearning." The three-part play was first produced in Toronto at the Canadian Stage in 2007. "My Pyramids" gives us a different and more human side to Lynndie England, who appears pregnant and in good health after her return from a tour of duty in Iraq that ended with the infamous scandal. The monologue begins with Lynndie (referred to as "Soldier") "googling" herself to find out, much to her naïve surprise, that her name produces six hundred thousand hits. The media frenzy around Lynndie's actions at Abu Ghraib sheds light on the way the public response often works to assign blame without any complex analysis of ethical or political responsibility. Lynndie's naïveté makes her lament the fact that she will never be a hero like Jessica Lynch:

> SOLDIER. I mighta had a TV movie made about me, too. She is truly a hero she is, and hey, did you know she's from West Virginia too? Yeah, she's a country girl, like me, and us country girls kick butt! *Nobody* messes with a country girl, oh no, let go! Can you imagine how scared she felt? Everybody in her company killed except her? Prisoner of the most brutal people on earth? Yeah. I reckon Jessica Lynch is America's sweetheart. I am America's secret that got shouted out to the world.[19]

If it is possible to scapegoat this young naïve woman from West Virginia it is because she is, compared to the other female hero, an anti-hero, an "anti-Jessica Lynch," as Melissa Brittain proposed in her chapter "Benevolent Invaders, Heroic Victims and Depraved Villains," in *(En)Gendering the War on Terror*.[20] Lynndie expects that the public will demonize her and condemn her for her despicable actions—all those "liberals, PEACE PINHEADS. Pink cotton candy cowards afraid of being at war."[21] This is perhaps the playwright's attempt at implicating her audience in an active dialogue with the banality of evil veiled in naïve patriotism or nationalistic rhetoric. When Lynndie is done with her racist, orientalist tirade we are left with a crash through the "looking glass of culture," as she imagines herself standing in—metonymically—for what makes America powerful and vulnerable: "I said you don't MESS with the eagle you don't MESS with the eagle, dude or the eagle tear your eyes out and that's what I did I tore 'em out and I flew, man, for just that night I flew through Abu G. my wingspan like a football field. And I soared through the air. 'Til I crashed back. Through the looking glass."[22]

Brittain further observes that when the Abu Ghraib prison scandal erupted we saw many photographs of male perpetrators and their male and female victims. When the pictures became public and the story turned into a scandal, "we began seeing fewer and fewer photographs of male soldiers torturing Iraqi men, and began seeing and hearing more and more about the photographs that depicted Lynndie England sexually humiliating Iraqi male prisoners."[23] The images of white female perpetrators served a different purpose, according to Brittain:

> The images of Arab men being broken, subdued, shamed and disciplined by a white woman allow for the realization of the "American dream" of the total demasculation and humiliation of Arab men, while white masculinity remains outside the category of "depravity," and the white male establishment, both military and governmental avoids blame. The pleasure a deeply racist society experiences when viewing images of a white woman grinning at the sexual humiliation of Arab men diverts attention away from the larger question of who is ultimately responsible for the abuses, and on to a discussion of one "sexually deviant" woman.[24]

This is because, according to Brittain, focusing on England was an effective way to manage yet another crisis in US authority: "In the fantasy world of US benevolence, England is the 'anti-Jessica Lynch,' the 'whore' in the conventional virgin/whore dichotomy. The fetishization of England as a 'phallic female' turned the scandal into a cautionary tale of what happens when women get too much power, while sparing white masculinity the bad press."[25] Similarly, in contrast to the elemental evil portrayed by Lynndie, the "media mobilized Lynch's working-class status through reference to her humble ambitions and 'down-home' tastes, replacing the middle-class femininity of colonial narratives with an image of working-class white femininity worth protecting."[26] Thompson's play works against the ideological manipulations of England versus Lynch by offering a vision of the female soldier as yet another pawn in a hyper-military, hyper-masculine system that turns atrocity into spectacle.

In an earlier interview with playwright Ann Holloway, Judith Thompson discusses the same issue of dehumanizing the soldier in "My Pyramids." The portrayal in "My Pyramids" of Lynndie's childish amusement at her torture of Iraqi prisoners as well as her tendency to downplay her personal responsibility for the abuse of these prisoners is highlighted in the interview.[27] Thompson reminds Holloway that at Abu Ghraib, Lynndie went as far as to perform certain torture "skits"—such as walking the soldiers on leashes—for the entertainment of other, mostly male, soldiers.[28] Thompson sees in Lynndie more than just elemental evil, and points to her lack of education and sophistication and her pathetic susceptibility to the flattery of any kind of sexual attention from male soldiers. In a sense Thompson gives credence to Arendt's view that thoughtlessness and delusion are at the roots of evil when she remarks in the interview that "self-delusion is funny, and the way she talks is funny. And I do think that unfortunately there is an element of class condescension—that we are laughing, I guess, at her lack of education."[29]

In the play, the thoughtlessness with which Lynndie proceeds is evident in her complete ignorance of her obligation as a jailer and of her prisoner-subjects. She starts by viewing Iraqis not as men, but as a "bunch of terrorists" who all look and act the same: "these are not men, they are terrorists. ... Actually, it's the first thing that came to my mind when I walked into that prison and seen all them men that look exactly alike. I know what might be fun: HUMAN PYRAMID WITH NIKKID CAPTIVE MEN."[30]

Following these racist musings, Lynndie recalls an incident where as a child she tormented a young girl in West Virginia: "Lee Ann Wibby is an American, she was very VERY different from the APES AT ABU GH-RAIB. They was monsters in the shape of human beings."[31] What makes Lee Ann Wibby different from the Iraqi "apes"? Is it because the victim is an American girl who is by definition innocent? Or is it because in torturing and dehumanizing Arab men who are "animals" and "monsters" she feels more useful in this system of instrumentalized power without responsibility? As an agent of this unquestionable neo-colonial system, Lynndie rules over "evil RAKEES" who must be subdued and moulded into an ideological entity that carries its guilt by simply being the *Other* in the colonial binary.

Nick Stevenson observed that the American war machine must often construct otherness as evil at the outset of war in order to justify abuse and domination. He writes that leading up to the first Gulf War in 1991, media and television stories were constructed to focus on "the personalised evil of Saddam Hussein, the promotion of inadequately verified horror stories of Iraqi atrocities, racist projections of uncivilised Arabs and the marginalisation of alternate perspectives."[32] The media hallucination (or the "ecstasy of communication" as Jean Baudrillard would call it) makes it possible to hide behind our self-deluded view of our neo-colonial mission and helps us avoid any ethical and historical responsibility. Even though no one in the West believes that the war was about exporting democracy to Iraq or ridding it of its evil dictator, it became absolutely necessary for the media to represent the "savage," uncivilized Other in need of help, while in effect bringing out layers and layers of violence, exploitation, and abuse. "My Pyramids" is a piece about our ethical porosity and inability to look at the Other as equal, which the play's second monologue addresses in different ways.

In "Harrowdown Hill" we are presented with the perspective of Dr. David Kelly, the British weapons inspector who was found dead in mysterious circumstances in 2003—an apparent suicide—two days after he appeared in front of a British government inquiry and denied claims that Iraq had weapons of mass destruction. The title references the wooded area near his home where Kelly's body was found. In the play, we meet him in the last few hours before his death, and we hear a monologue that is more dialogic and less self-centred than Lynndie's "Pyramids," in which he addresses the audience and invites us into the scene of his death. Kelly predicts the public response to his impending death: "almost nobody will believe it. There will be rock songs, art installations by angry Germans, television movies and the Internet will roil with talk of the murder of David Kelly by men in black, that's how I'll be remembered. The mousey scientist who set off a storm. Another casualty of the War in Iraq."[33] Kelly is capable of discerning the constructed division between a neo-colonial self, and a cultural Other by demonstrating a capacity to apprehend the humanity of Iraqis. In his hazy rant, he recounts his close friendship with Jalal—the bookshop owner in Baghdad—who was killed along with his family by American soldiers, who also raped his young daughter.[34] Jalal, having noticed that some US soldiers were watching his daughter with "evil in their eyes," had appealed to Kelly for help. Kelly was unable to help his Iraqi friend and his daughter while reassuring him that the soldiers are "carefully monitored by their commanding officers, and they would never dare approach her."[35]

Kelly's monologue is a reminder of what happens when we stand idly by and do nothing to stop the atrocities committed in our name. Susan Sontag argued in *Regarding the Pain of Others* that the pain of others is what interpolates us in pictures of atrocity, but if we are left unable to do anything about what we are witnessing, and if we are unable to learn something from what we are seeing, then we succumb to our voyeuristic tendencies. Dr. Kelly's final testament is a reminder that doing nothing is damning in itself because it strips us of our conscience and makes us complicit in the very acts that we purport to condemn:

[DAVID] You see, this might be the only way I can have an impact, the only way I can make up for what I did not do. …

I'm beginning to think that it's the greatest sin of our time.

Knowing, and pretending that we don't know, so that we won't be inconvenienced in any way. Do you understand what I am saying?

I knew. All the things I knew. And I did nothing.[36]

Like Lynndie, Kelly must walk "through the looking glass" in his final scene, revealing the truth about his guilt-ridden self. After he shouts his need to tell the truth, his breathing becomes laborious, he lies down, thanks the audience for witnessing his dying moments, has an imaginary conversation with his daughter, to whom he sings a song from "Winnie the Pooh," and then prepares to let go: "But I, David Kelly, I am *here*, and I promise, I will always be here."[37] David Kelly's ghostliness transforms the stage into a thanatological site where the living become memorials to unrecoverable loss.

Foreshadowing the spectral appearance of its protagonist, the third monologue begins where the second left off: "One of my earliest memories is drawing with my own blood" says Nehrjas Al Saffarh of "Instruments of Yearning."[38] The final monologue is recited by the ghost of an Iraqi woman, tortured along with her children by the Saddam regime. We soon find out that she was killed in a US bombing during the first Gulf War. She was subjected to all sorts of brutality by the Saddam regime for refusing to reveal the whereabouts of her husband, the leader of the Iraqi Communist Party. The monologue is titled "Instruments of Yearning" after the nickname given to Saddam's secret police. Nehrjas (which means daffodil in Arabic) is a gentle, loving mother whose poetic recounting brings the audience close to the stage. She even comments on the cultural divide that separated her from us: "Wait. I can see you are pulling away from me when I say 'Communist.' But this is not the Communist Party of Stalin, or Mao or Pol Pot, or post-war Europe, far far from it. All the kind and thinking and peace loving people in Iraq at that time were members of the Communist Party."[39] Some critics have dismissed the first two monologues, perhaps because of the unease with which we have to face a Western subjectivity responsible for either perpetrating or justifying atrocities. Sam Thielman writes in the online magazine *Variety*: "If 'Palace of the End' was nothing but this third section, it would be an excellent play with a lot to say about an underexplored period in history. As it is, it's a painfully mediocre retread of everything everyone thinks about Iraq. But, with a triumphant finale."[40]

Nevertheless, "Instruments of Yearning" is the most graphic of the three monologues in terms of its depiction of atrocities, and yet it remains the most poetic. As we listen to Nehrjas recount the death of her sons and her torture at the hands of Saddam's secret police, we also listen to her recite beautiful Arabic poetry and describe in poetic terms the mythical significance of the palm tree, which seems surreal when contrasted with her horrendous accounts:

> NEHRJAS. Like an American horror movie. Now, the castle has three stories. The highest floor is where they would take you to talk. … Then if you didn't wish to talk, they would send you down to main floor. It was what we call Torture Lite.
>
> Beatings. Broken bones. Nails removed. … And if you still didn't talk, you were sent to the basement. There were bodies everywhere. Bodies of people you knew. Once you have smelled the smell of death, of mass murder and suffering, nothing smells sweet again, not ever again.[41]

The Nehrjas of "Instruments of Yearning" is everything we refuse to see or relate to in Iraq: she is a woman, she is gentle, she recites poetry, and she is strong in the face of unspeakable suffering. To the death, she will not betray her political convictions, even when her son is tortured and killed on the roof of the prison.[42] While we witness Lynndie's vibrant health and obvious pregnancy in the beginning, and are called to witness as Dr. Kelly's dying moments are consumed by guilt, we are invited to listen to Nehrjas's posthumous testimony as a tribute to what remains human in all of us in the face of unimaginable atrocity. If the soldier, Lynndie, needs to defend her innocence and irresponsibility, and Dr. Kelly pleads for forgiveness for his inaction, then Nehrjas wants us to open our eyes in the hope that we better understand what happens on the other side of our war machine. By performing three different first-person accounts, these three testimonies imply that it is up to the spectator to move from irresponsibility, guilt, and complacency to action, empathy, and understanding. The triptych of *Palace of the End* references the tension between atrocity and representation, and poses a fundamental question as old as the Oresteia, as Marvin Carlson observed in *The Haunted Stage*: "How does one break out of an ongoing cycle of almost unimaginable cruelty and revenge?"[43]

The Embodied

Wafaa Bilal, an Iraqi-American performance artist, proposes a different perspective on the problems of responsibility, atrocity, and representation. By showing and enacting the atrocity, performance art offers an ontological approach to the epistemological tension between telling and showing. While texts narrate the horror, sometimes metaphorically, performance art locates us face to face with the suffering body and the difficult embodiment of otherness as "a people" not just "people." As Adam Muller argued in chapter 3 of this collection, "the signal casualty of genocide is *a people*, not *people*, and thus a highly morally and politically charged form of (and capacity for) belonging."[44]

Bilal's performance piece and interactive installation, *Shoot an Iraqi* (2007; also known as *Domestic Tension*), was based on the artist's experience of living for one month in a Chicago gallery with an internet-controlled paintball gun aimed at him at all times that allowed people all over the world to shoot him. Bilal explains that the idea came from a newspaper article he read about a young American soldier who goes to work every day in Colorado to execute orders of firing remotely controlled missiles and drones at Iraqis. After the first twelve days in the gallery, Bilal was shot at over forty thousand times. By the end of the performance, over sixty thousand people from over a hundred and thirty countries had fired the internet paintball gun at him, while some hackers tampered with the gun to make it fire automatically instead of a single shot per person.

Shoot an Iraqi does not expose the banality of evil; on the contrary, it performs the banality of *jouissance* associated with the enjoyment of perpetrating a remote violence with no tangible consequences. It shows that our complacency is the result of being desensitized to the suffering of others. Not unlike the ethical complexities revealed in the Milgram Yale experiment and the Zimbardo Stanford experiment,[45] where people's critical resistance is easily compromised by authoritarian regimes, Bilal's gallery experiment reveals how easy it is for ordinary people to inflict extreme violence and gleefully become agents of the most unimaginable atrocity. Bilal foresees that his approach may be controversial; he argues that this "sensational approach to the war is meant to engage people who may not be willing to engage in political dialogue through conventional means. DOMESTIC TENSION [depicts] the suffering of war not through human displays of dramatic emotion, but rather through engaging people in the sort of playful interactive video game with which they are familiar."[46]

Bilal's experiment points to Žižek's critique of Arendt: that there is an avoidable enjoyment or *jouissance* associated with inflicting pain that underpins the relationship of domination. The internet gun is a function of an "*imaginary* screen" that maintains distance from the victim and "the *real* of the perverse and sadistic *jouissance*" discussed above. Bilal critiques this perversity further in his other performance project ... *and Counting*. In this 2010 live tattooing session set up at the gallery of the Elizabeth Foundation for the Arts in New York, Bilal had 105,000 dots representing the official Iraqi death count, and 5,000 dots representing American deaths, tattooed on his back. Green ink was used to represent Iraqi deaths, and was visible only under ultraviolet light, while red ink was used for the American deaths. Bilal explains that the dots also embody the death of his brother Haji, who was "killed by a missile at a checkpoint in their hometown of Kufa, Iraq in 2004. Wafaa Bilal feels the pain of both American and Iraqi families who've lost loved ones in the war, but the deaths of Iraqis like his brother are largely invisible to the American public."[47] In addition to the tattooing, during the performance different people from different backgrounds were invited to read the long list of names of Iraqis and Americans killed in the war.

Turning his body into a living gravestone, Bilal uses primitive forms of engraving to slow down the frenzied violence of modern regimes, who through a click of a button can annihilate a whole people. There is a secular *mythopoiesis* (the creation of myth) at play in this performance as the sharing of the tattoo session encodes the body with the here and now, transforming the distancing and telematic structures of remote violence into embodied experiences—a shared modern Eucharist, elevated to the level of mythology devoid of mystical connotations. Bilal shows us how important it is to embody suffering and atrocity through a violation of textual boundaries producing permanent, fleshy documentary evidence which cannot be disputed. Bilal's tattooing displays atrocity by bringing the external experience inward in order to resist sensationalizing, trivializing, or aestheticizing it. Consequently, by becoming the corporeal site of suffering, Bilal's embodied testimonial points to the fact that representing atrocity is not only a story of trauma—it is also a story of survival and resistance.

Conclusion

Both Judith Thompson and Wafaa Bilal point out that what is real, what is plausible, what is provable, and what is reproducible, is not necessarily representable. When we are asked to witness the dying moments of David Kelly, or the painful live tattooing of the artist in order to make a statement on the embodied nature of atrocity, we assume that there is a general cultural context in which this shared knowledge is recognizable. Addressing the modalities of perception of the audience bearing witness to atrocities, this chapter argues in favour of considering the space of performance not as a site of construction of truth or a mirror to atrocity, but as a space of resistance where being present, listening, and reflecting becomes an ethical responsibility. While we are faced with the ethical density of atrocities, we have a responsibility as cultural critics and as artists to reflect on their historical, material, and existential conditions. In conclusion, we can only echo what Toni Morrison said when asked how she can write about slavery: "if they can survive it, I can write about it."

NOTES

1   Hannah Arendt, *Eichmann in Jerusalem: A Report on the Banality of Evil* (New York: Penguin, 1994), 287–288.

2   Hannah Arendt, "Thinking and Moral Considerations: A Lecture," *Social Research* 38, no. 3 (Fall 1971): 418.

3   Arendt, *Eichmann in Jerusalem*, 5.

4   Ibid., 276.

5   Ibid., 26.

6   Ibid., 27–28.

7   Slavoj Žižek, *The Plague of Fantasies* (London: Verso, 1997), 55.

8   Ibid., 55–56. Italics in original.

9   Adrienne Rich, "Legislators of the World," *Guardian* (London), 18 November 2006, http://www.theguardian.com/books/2006/nov/18/featuresreviews.guardianreview15 (accessed 20 January 2013).

10 The expression "New Brutalism" was coined by the British architects Alison and Peter Smithson to refer to the architectural style exhibiting a brutalist aesthetic (from "brutalism," derived from Le Corbusier's use of *béton brut*, or raw cement, in the 1950s).

11 The Abu Ghraib prison scandal erupted in 2004 when internet accounts and photographs of abuse and torture of Iraqi prisoners held by the US Army's 372nd Military Police Company were made public. The senior officer in Iraq at the time, Lieutenant General Ricardo Sanchez, ordered an investigation which Major General Antonio Taguba conducted, issuing a damning report that confirmed widespread prisoner

abuses at the hands of US Army personnel: waterboarding, humiliation, sodomy, attack with dogs, sleep deprivation, burning with phosphoric acid, etc. A media storm ensued with in-depth reporting by programs such as *60 minutes* (broadcast on 28 April 2004), and the *New Yorker* magazine (10 May 2004), accusing high-ranking officers of turning a blind eye to the violations.

12   Christian Biet, "Rwanda 94: Theater, Film, and Intervention," *Cardozo Law Review* 31, no. 4 (2010): 1046.

13   Shoshana Felman and Dori Laub, *Testimony: Crises of Witnessing in Literature, Psychoanalysis, and History* (New York: Routledge, 1991), 34.

14   Patrick Anderson and Jisha Menon, eds., *Violence Performed: Local Roots and Global Routes of Conflict* (New York: Palgrave, 2008), 5.

15   Mark Seltzer, "Wound Culture: Trauma in the Pathological Public Sphere," *October* 80 (1997): 3.

16   Felman and Laub, *Testimony*, 6.

17   Shoshana Felman, *The Juridical Unconscious: Trials and Traumas in the Twentieth Century* (Cambridge, MA: Harvard University Press, 2002), 5.

18   Ibid., 161. Italics in original.

19   Judith Thompson, *Palace of the End* (Toronto: Playwrights Canada Press, 2007), 10.

20   Melissa Brittain, "Benevolent Invaders, Heroic Victims and Depraved Villains" *(En) Gendering the War on Terror*, ed. Krista Hunt and Kim Rygiel Eds (Hampshire: Ashgate, 2006), 86.

21   Thompson, *Palace of the End*, 7.

22   Ibid., 18–19.

23   Brittain, "Benevolent Invaders," 89.

24   Ibid.

25   Ibid., 89–90.

26   Ibid., 88.

27   Quoted in Ann Holloway, "Hedda & Lynndie & Jabber & Ciel: An Interview with Judith Thompson," in *The Masks of Judith Thompson*, ed. Ric Knowles (Toronto: Playwrights Canada Press, 2006), 143.

28   Ibid., 141.

29   Ibid.

30   Thompson, *Palace of the End*, 12.

31   Ibid., 14.

32   Nick Stevenson, *Understanding Media Cultures: Social Theory and Mass Communication* (London: Sage Publications, 1995), 188.

33   Thompson, *Palace of the End*, 23.

34   Ibid., 25–26.

35   Ibid., 28.

36   Ibid., 24.

37   Ibid., 30.

38 Ibid., 32.

39 Ibid., 38.

40 Sam Thielman, "Palace of the End," *Variety*, 23 June 2008, http://variety.com/2008/
    legit/reviews/palace-of-the-end-1200508877/ (accessed 1 February 2014).

41 Thompson, *Palace of the End*, 41.

42 Ibid., 44.

43 Marvin Carlson, *The Haunted Stage: The Theatre as Memory Machine* (Ann Arbor, MI:
    University of Michigan Press, 2002), 47.

44 See Adam Muller's contribution to this volume, "Troubling History, Troubling Law:
    The Question of Indigenous Genocide in Canada."

45 The Milgram shock experiment was conducted at Yale University in 1961 shortly after
    the beginning of the Eichmann trial. The experiment was devised by social psychol-
    ogist Stanley Milgram to measure the willingness of participants to follow orders
    even if those orders contravened their ethical and moral imperatives. The experiment
    measured how much pain an ordinary citizen would inflict on another through a fake
    electric shock just because he was ordered to do so. By the end of the experiment, 26 of
    the 40 participants (65 percent) would have inflicted the highest voltage, enough to kill
    their subject. The Zimbardo experiment, also known as the Stanford prison experiment,
    was conducted by a team of researchers in 1971 headed by psychology professor Philip
    Zimbardo and funded by the US Office of Naval Research. The experiment, which was
    interrupted after six days, examined the behavior of 24 participants randomly assigned
    the role of prisoner or guard. The guards were instructed to inflict psychological torture
    and mild abuse on the prisoners, a role that many assumed willingly, demonstrating
    that abusive behaviour by average individuals without sadistic or authoritarian tenden-
    cies develops by virtue of being in an oppressive setting.

46 Wafaa Bilal, *Shoot an Iraqi. Domestic Tension*, 2007, artist's website: http://wafaabilal.
    com/html/domesticTension.html (accessed 1 May 2012).

47 Wafaa Bilal, . . . *And Counting*, 2010, artist's website: http://wafaabilal.com/html/and-
    Counting.php (accessed 1 May 2012).

Contributors

AMARNATH AMARASINGAM is a Social Science and Humanities Research Council of Canada Postdoctoral Fellow in the Resilience Research Centre at Dalhousie University in Halifax, Nova Scotia.

ANDREW R. BASSO is a PhD candidate in the Department of Political Science at the University of Calgary in Calgary, Alberta.

KRISTIN BURNETT is an associate professor in the Department of Indigenous Learning at Lakehead University in Thunder Bay, Ontario.

LORI CHAMBERS is a professor in the Department of Women's Studies at Lakehead University in Thunder Bay, Ontario.

LAURA BETH COHEN is a PhD candidate in the Division of Global Affairs at Rutgers University in Newark, New Jersey.

TRAVIS HAY is a PhD candidate in the Department of History at York University in Toronto, Ontario.

STEVEN LEONARD JACOBS holds the Aaron Aronov Endowed Chair of Judaic Studies and is an associate professor of religious studies in the Department of Religious Studies at the University of Alabama in Tuscaloosa, Alabama.

LORRAINE MARKOTIC is an associate professor in the Department of Philosophy at the University of Calgary in Calgary, Alberta.

SARAH MINSLOW is an adjunct lecturer in the Department of English and the Department of Global, International and Area Studies at the University of North Carolina in Charlotte, North Carolina.

DONIA MOUNSEF is an associate professor in the Department of Drama at the University of Alberta in Edmonton, Alberta.

ADAM MULLER is an associate professor in the Department of English, Film, and Theatre at the University of Manitoba in Winnipeg, Manitoba.

SCOTT W. MURRAY is an associate professor of history in the Department of Humanities at Mount Royal University in Calgary, Alberta.

CHRISTOPHER POWELL is an associate professor in the Department of Sociology at Ryerson University in Toronto, Ontario.

RAFFI SARKISSIAN is the founder and chair of the Sara Corning Centre for Genocide Education, an instructor at Centennial College, and vice principal at A.R.S. Armenian Private School in Toronto, Ontario.

Index

ethnocentricity, 71. *See also* cultural genocide; settler colonialism
ethnosphere, 21–23
Europa, Europa, 10
extermination camps, 235
Extraordinary Chambers in the Courts of Cambodia, 54

F

Fallace, Thomas, 108
Federal Party (in Ceylon), 29–30
Federation of Turkish Canadian Associations (FTCA), xiii, 116,
Fein, Helen, 6, 25, 176
Felman, Shoshana, 11, 260–61
First Nations, 9, 142n.29, 145–47, 151–54, 155–56, 161, 163n.9. *See also* Aboriginal Peoples; Indigenous Peoples
First World War, 118, 172, 175, 176, 177, 179, 180
Fort Albany, 145, 151, 161
Foucault, Michel, 96, 259
Foundation for Human Rights, 37
Friedlander, Saul, 104n.30

G

Gacaca courts (Rwanda), 183, 185–88
gender, 9, 147–8, 156–60, 160–61, 261–64. *See also* misogyny; patriarchy; sexual violence
General Framework Agreement on Peace (Dayton Peace Agreement), 49, 53, 74n.18
genocide: of African American peoples, chapter 5; Armenian, *see* Armenian genocide; Bosnian, *see* Bosnia; bystanders to, 20–21, 61, 112, 117, 185, 204; Cambodian, *see* Cambodian genocide; comparative studies of, 4, 9, 107, 136, 169–70, 175–76, 180–81, 190–91; complicity in, 4, 100, 108, 132, 215; cultural, *see* cultural genocide; definitions and definitional debates, 4–6, 8, 9–10, 20–23, 23–26, 85–90, 92–93, 102n.7, 104n.29, 131, 135–36, 149–51, 202; Holocaust, *see* Holocaust; intent, 6, 7–8, 23, 54, 85,

86–88, 92–96, 96–101 104n.29 and 30, 131–33; of Indigenous peoples, *see* settler colonialism as genocide; prevention of, 1–3, 53, 85, 113, 120–21, 133–34, 138, 205–6, 216, 218–19; Rwandan, *see* Rwandan genocide; in Sri Lanka, *see* Sri Lanka. *See also* atrocity and genocide
Genocide Awareness Month, 116
genocide denial, 8–10, 16n.31, 60–63, 107–8, 110, 118–20; of Armenian genocide, 8, 9–10, 16n.31. chapter 4; of Bosnian genocide, 60–61, 63, 69, 70–72; of genocide against African American peoples, 134–38; of the Holocaust, 108, 139n 4, 235, 247n.12; of some victim groups' claims to genocide, 8–10, 120–21, 135–36, 181–90, 190–91; of settler colonialism as genocide, 9, 100–102, 146–47, 149–51
Genocide Studies and Prevention (GSP), 2–3
Genocide Studies International (GSI), 3
"genocidal society", 23, 39–40, 120
"genocidal priming", 40
German Federal Republic, 231
Gil Gil, Alicia, 95
Gladstone, William, 5–6, 14n.17
Gleitzman, Morris, 206, 208, 209–10, 211–12
Goldhagen, Daniel, 94
Great Fire of Smyrna, 179
Greco-Turkish War, 179–80
Greenwalt, Alexandar, 95
Gunn Allen, Paula, 9, 146
Gunter, Lorne, 147, 155–56, 163n.9

H

Habyarimana, Juvénal, 181
Hayner, Priscilla, 7, 73
Heimat, 10
Herero (Namibia), 91, 133, 138
Hilberg, Raul, 92
Himmler, Heinrich, 93
Hinton, Alexander, 3, 6–7, 40, 66, 180
Hindu peoples, 26, 33, 29
Historikerstreit ("historians' quarrel"), 10

Hitler, Adolf, 93, 94, 98, 119, 157, 203, 207, 213, 250–51n.32
Holocaust (Shoah), 3, 9–13, 16n.31, 17n.39, 20, 87–88, 92, 101, 104n. 30, 136, 137, 139n.4, 199, 206–13, 218, 251n.35, 260, chapter 9; denial of, *see* genocide denial; Holocaust education, 107–9, 112–15, 120–21, 126, 180; exceptionalism/uniqueness of, 1–5, 92–93, 150–51.
Holocaust and Genocide Studies, 1–2
Honeyman, Susan, 202–206
Hovanissian, Richard, 114–15
Hoffman, Tessa, 9–10
Horne, Gerald, 134
Howard-Hassmann, Rhoda, 137–38
Hudson, Graham, 97, 102
Hussein, Saddam, 264, 266–67
Hutu, 10, 120–21, 169, 181–190, 191; Hutu Power Movement, 184–85

I

identity-difference, 21–22, 23–26, 27, 28–31
Idle No More, 160
"imagined communities" (Benedict Anderson), 22, 62, 66
"imaginary screen" (Slavoj Žižek), 254–56, 269
India, 26, 30–32
Indian Land Treaties in Canada, 151, 161
Indian Residential Schools (IRS), xiii, 7–8, 83–84, 86, 97, 99–101, 102n.5, 150–51, 163n.21,
Indigenous peoples, 1, 7–10, 15.n28, 26, 40, 42–3n.9, 57, 142n.29, 184, chapters 3 and 6. *See also* Aboriginal peoples; First Nations; Native American Indian; settler colonialism as genocide
"intent to destroy", *see* genocide; intent.
interdisciplinarity, 1–2, 83–84
International Commission on Missing Persons (ICMP), xiii, 59, 77n.58
International Military Tribunal at Nuremberg, 54, 73n.14
inyenzi (Hutu extremist slur for Tutsi), 182, 184

International Association of Genocide Scholars (IAGS), xiii, 2–3, 83–84, 87, 102n.3, 113
International Court of Justice, xiii, 51, 133–34
International Criminal Tribunals, xiii, 53, 54, 58–59; for the former Yugoslavia Bosnia, 49–51, 73n.15, 80n.88 and 89; for Rwanda, 54, 183; for
International Crisis Group, 35
International Institute for Genocide and Human Rights Studies (IIGHRS), 2
International Network of Genocide Scholars (INOGS), xiii, 3
Iran, 3, 121
Iraq War, 260–67, 268–69, 270, 270n.11
Islamic State (also ISIS, ISIL, Daesh), xiii, 6, 14n.19, 259
Ittihat ve Terakki Cemiyeti, *see* Committee of Union and Progress
Iyamuremye, Augustine, 188

J

Jäckel, Eberhard, 104n.30
Jim Crow, 134, 137
Jones, Adam, 40
Journal of Genocide Research (*JGR*), 2–3
justice, 54–58, 58–60, 70–71, 120–21, 156, 169, 186–87, 250–51n.32; restorative, 55; retrospective, 55; transitional, 6–7, 49–51, 54–57, 63, 66–67, 70–71, 182–83

K

Kafka, Franz, 67–68, 251n.35
Kagame, Paul, 181–82, 185–90, 190–91
Karadžić, Radovan, 52, 58
Kashechewan, 145, 161
Katz, Stephen, 92
Kelly, David, 264–67
Kemalists, 170, 174–80
Kiernan, Ben, 3, 6
Kosovo, 73, 204–5, 259
Krstić, Radislav, 53, 58, 73n.15,

L

Langer, Lawrence, 11–12, 208–9,
LaRocque, Emma, 9, 148
Lemkin, Raphael, 7–9, 15–16n.29, 31, and
    33, 21–23, 42–43n.9, 85, 87–90, 90–
    92, 92–93, 101–2, 103n.18, 104n.29,
    125–28, 132–33, 139n.4, 140n.5–7
    and 10, 142n.29
Lemkin on Genocide, 132–33, 139n.4
Levant, Ezra, 158–60
Lessons Learnt and Reconciliation Com-
    mission (LLRC - Sri Lanka), xiii, 6–7
Levene, Mark, 6
Levi, Primo, 12
Lewy, Guenter, 110–11
Liberation Tigers of Tamil Eelam (LTTE or
    Tamil Tigers), xiii, 26, 30, 31, 33–34,
    37–38
Lower, Wendy, 250–51n.32

M

MacDonald, David, 97, 102
Mahlendorf, Ursula R., 225, 247n.10 and 12
Mahavamsa, 28
Martin, Charles H., 139n.1
McCarthy, Justin, 110–11
McDonnell, Michael A., 90–92
McParland, Kelly, 156, 164n.23
Meierhenrich, Jens, 2–3
Mein Kampf, 93, 98
Menon, Jisha, 11–12, 260
misogyny, 158–160. *See also* genocide; pa-
    triarchy; sexual violence; women
Missing Persons Institute of Bosnia and
    Herzegovina (MPI), 77n.58,
Mladić, Ratko, 52–53, 58, 69, 71, 81–82n.110
Moghalu, Kingsley Chiedu, 54–55
Morgenthau, Henry (American Ambassa-
    dor), 179
Moses, Dirk, 3–4, 90–92
Moyn, Samuel, 88
Mothers of Srebrenica, 52, 59, 68–69, 73n.6,
    77n.56 and 62, 81n.102
Mount Royal University, xi, 1, 150
Muslim peoples, 14n.19, 26, 29, 32–33, 49,
    64, 171–74, 175, 178

N

National Association for the Advancement
    of Colored People (NAACP), xiv,
    128–29, 139n.1
National Socialist German Workers Party
    (Nazi Party), 157, 224–27, 240–42,
    251n.34
nationalism, 22, 259–60, 262; Bulgarian,
    5; Sinhalese, 6, 27–29, 38, 40–41;
    Turkish, 115, 174, 179
Native American Indian peoples, 113,
    128–29, 138, 205
Nettelfield, Lara, 69
Niven, Bill, 246–7n.9, 247n.10 and 12
Northern Provincial Council (NPC - Sri
    Lanka), 34–35
Nyamwasa, Faustin Kayumba, 188

O

Occupy Wall Street movement, 160
Orić, Naser, 80n.89
Orientalism (Orientalist), 28–29, 262
Otherness (the Other), 22, 25, 107–8,
    114–15, 148, 160, 203–4, 213, 258,
    259, 264, 268
Ottoman Empire, 5, 112, 117, 119, chapter 7
Ottoman genocides: Armenian victims,
    9–10, 116, 138, 174; Assyrian
    victims, 9–10, 116, 169–71, 174–76,
    177–80, 191; Greek victims, 9–10,
    116, 169, 170–71, 174–81, 190–91;
    Kurdish victims, 175. *See also* Arme-
    nian genocide
Outcome Governing System (OGS), 97–99

P

patriarchy: and settler colonialism in Cana-
    da, 9, 145–47, 156–61
Patterson, William L. 8–9, chapter 5
perpetrators, 24–26, 44n.28, 57, 61–63, 119–
    20, 175–76, 184–85, 185–88, 207,
    231–34, 247n.12, 250n.31, 253–57
Podrinje, 52, 59, 68
Pontic Greeks (victims in Ottoman geno-
    cide), *see* Ottoman genocides
proto–genocide, 6–7, 19–20, 26–47